THE CHILDREN ACT
A Social Care Guide

Second Edition

Other SCA Co-publications

Residential Care: An International Reader
Meir Gottesman

Quality Counts:
Achieving Quality in Social Care Services
Des Kelly and Bridget Warr (Editors)

Social Care: Rivers of Pain, Bridges of Hope
Leonard Davies

Yesterday's Answers:
Development and Decline of Schools for Young Offenders
Jim Hyland

Insights into Inspection:
The Regulation of Social Care
Roger Clough

Keyworking in Social Care:
A Structured Approach to Provision
Ian Mallinson

Care Management and the New Social Work:
A Critical Analysis
Michael Sheppard

The Abuse of Care
Roger Clough

Forthcoming

Coping with Violence
Vaughan Bowie

Social Care: An Introductory Reader
Des Kelly and Chris Payne

Managing Change in Social Care
Des Kelly and John Harris

A Whiting & Birch/SCA Education Co-Publication

The Children Act

A Social Care Guide

Covering the Act, Associated Regulations, Department of Health Guidance, and Significant Legal Precedents

Second Edition

IAN MALLINSON

Whiting & Birch Ltd
London
MCMXCVI

Published by Whiting & Birch Ltd,
PO Box 872, Forest Hill, London SE23 3HL. United Kingdom.

London 1996

British Library Cataloguing in Publication Data
A CIP catalogue record is available on request from the British Library

ISBN 1 871177 81 2 (cased)
ISBN 1 871177 82 0 (paperback)

Printed in England

Outline Contents

A more detailed list of contents is given at the beginning of each chapter

PREFACE

The 1989 Children Act and associated Regulations form a comprehensive framework of public and private law relating to the care of children in England and Wales. The law provides a structure for decision-making and legal intervention relating to the care of children in the context of the family, in relation to local authority assistance to families and in relation to intervention for the protection of the child. In the provision of a child care service, a balance is struck between family autonomy and the protection of children.

The framework dictates how (depending upon the extent of their involvement) families, courts, local authorities and voluntary organisations will work together to determine and meet the child's welfare needs. It defines, for example, the local authorities' duties and powers in the provision of a child care service to parents and to children (in the context of parental responsibility and the rights and obligations of parents and others in relation to decision making). It gives mechanisms to resolve differences of opinion between parents and between others involved in the care of children. The requirements and machinery involved in planning for the child's future (where public and private services are involved) are also laid down; as are the means to ensure standards of quality child care in public services and in private spheres.

Substantial shifts in social work and legal practice were represented in this framework when it was implemented in 1991. For example the rights of Black children and their families were recognised for the first time in child care law. The main thrust of the Act towards preventive services (as opposed to statutory intervention) is very apparent throughout. The clearly defined nature of parental responsibility, and the resulting obligations and responsibilities placed upon those holding it, had major implications for parental rights and obligations, and for social work practice.

A new approach to services for children with disabilities was also provided through an integrated child care services within a common legislative base.

The Act is based upon a belief that children are best looked after within a family with both parents playing a full part and without resort to legal proceedings. Local authorities have a duty to encourage the upbringing of children in need by their families provided this is consistent with the welfare of the child.

The juvenile justice system was left largely (although not entirely) unaffected by the Act. Criminal prosecutions continue in the youth court as an exclusively criminal court. The previous offence condition in care proceedings was abolished. This book does not cover criminal proceedings.

The book traverses the middle ground of child care law and practice. It has been written on the premise that a fairly definitive knowledge of the law is required by a person holding a social care role. It is not a practice manual (in the sense of debating possible differing courses of action) rather it makes a clear and comprehensive statement of what the law says in an easily understandable sequence for the management and implementation of social care practice.

The legal presentation and discussion are correct at the time of going to press. An opportunity has been taken in this second edition to update the guidance issued by Central Government and incorporate significant legal precedents that have occurred in the courts. In particular new guidance from the Department of Health on day care and on restraint in children's homes is ncw itemised and discussed.

Whilst every care has been taken to avoid error, no responsibility can be accepted for any inaccuracy in this publication.

The author would like to acknowledge the assistance of Joan Beck, Mark Evans, Lawrence Innis, Gerry Layton, Dudley Roach and Jill Williams in compiling this volume.

Ian Mallinson
Edinburgh
January 1995

HOW TO USE THIS BOOK

In this book the whole text of the Act, as it applies to England and Wales, and all the associated regulations/statutory instruments (with the exception of amendments to the Adoption Acts) are laid out or summarised in a readily assimilated format in this typeface. Regulations have the full force of the law and must be obeyed under all circumstances. They include permissions and restrictions on what must be done. The regulations, together with the Act, form a clear definitive statement of what the law says. Sections of the Act are indicated at the end of each statement of the law by the letter 'S' and subsections given e.g. <S6(1/2)>. The Schedules of the Act are also indicated. Where other legal documents are involved, these are quoted in full.

Significant legal precedents in the courts are also summarised and references made to the Times or Independent law reports and in some cases to the Family Court Reporter e.g. <Re H (Times 5/6/92)> . References to unreported cases are made as well. Precedents in the courts are binding interpretations of the law unless overturned by the same or a higher court.

Department of Health guidance is given in the following italic typeface and indented.

> *The guidance forms statements of what is good practice and may provide a basis for challenge as to interpretation of the law. General guidance in the form of circulars has been issued by the Secretary of State in accordance with section 7 (1) of the Local Authority Social Services Act 1970. Local authorities are required to act in accordance with such guidance. Although guidance is not in itself law in the sense that the Act and regulations are, it may be quoted or used in court proceedings as well as framing local authority policy and practice.*
>
> *References are given in this part of the text to paragraphs to be found in these volumes of guidance: Volume One "Court Orders"; Volume Two "Day care and Family support"; Volume Three "Family Placements"; Volume Four "Residential Care" ; Volume Five "Independent Schools"; Volume Six "Children with Disabilities"; Volume Seven "Guardians Ad Litem and Other Court Related Issues"; Volume Eight "Private Fostering and Miscellaneous"; and "Working together: a guide to arrangements*

for inter-agency co-operation for the protection of children from child abuse". All these volumes are published by HMSO, 1991. This book summarises the most relevant parts of these volumes. Where circulars have been issued separately these are individually itemised e.g. <Circular LAC(93)1>. Readers who desire a detailed and comprehensive discussion of good practice requirements under the Act are directed to refer directly to the documents involved.

Other comments by the author, are also given in order to provide an easily understandable view of the law. These additional notes are in a *sans serif* typeface like this. These are given to guide the reader but do not carry any "official" weight.

Throughout the text of the Act, the Regulations, and Department of Health guidance, the male gender is generally used. (The only exception to this, in the Act, is the gender of nannies which happens to be female.) Where legal and other documents are quoted, any gender specific language has had to be retained.

The 1978 Interpretation Act categorically states however, that except where the contrary intention appears, words denoting the masculine gender include the female (and vice versa). Similarly, the singular includes the plural. <S6>

1
COURT HEARINGS

The opening provisions of the Act set the requirements and principles for all proceedings under the act. The welfare principle (see below) is expounded through a checklist which governs the conduct of each case. The courts have considerable discretion in their decisions. The application of the welfare principle gives direction to that discretion.

Court orders are not made as free standing entities. In many situations more than one order will be made. Court hearings enable the settlement of disputes and the transfer of rights and responsibilities between the various parties in a child's life. The Act thus consists of a welding of public and private law into one coherent framework in which there are placed preventive services in a continuum with public intervention and the resolving of private disputes.

> *The Department of Health state that the Act creates a concurrent system of jurisdiction for a wide range of family proceedings in magistrates' family proceedings courts, county courts and the High Court. <Vol. 1 (1.13/1.14)>*

Family proceedings replaced domestic proceedings under the old legislation. The Family Proceedings Courts (Constitution) Rules 1991 (and for inner London and the City of London, The Family Proceedings Courts (Constitution) (Metropolitan Area) Rules 1991) govern the arrangements for family panels, including eligibility of magistrates, composition and chairmanship.

The allocation and transfer of proceedings between the High Court, the county courts and the magistrates' courts are governed by The Children (Allocation of Proceedings) Order 1991 and The Children (Allocation of Proceedings) (Appeals) Order 1991.

The Family Proceedings Rules 1991, as amended by the Family Proceedings (Amendment) Rules 1991, state how hearings in the High Court and the County Court will be conducted, including procedures, party status, timing, attendance, documentary evidence, use of expert witnesses, confidentiality of documents, evidence, documentation and notifications required. Similar arrangements are made in The Family Proceedings Court (Children Act 1989) Rules 1991 for proceedings in magistrates' courts.

The Welfare of the Child

In determining any question with respect to the upbringing of a child; or the administration of a child's property or the application of any income arising from it, the child's welfare shall be the court's paramount consideration. <S1(1)> Where more than one child may be involved the welfare of each is considered as a balancing exercise. One child's welfare may not take precedence over that of another. <Re H (Times 23/2/93)>

The consideration of the child's welfare is the basic tenet of the Act and is the essential principle that the court will uphold.

The court will not however simply decide what is the best interests of the child, rather they will decide upon the application of conditions that must be met if the welfare principle is to be satisfied.

In relation to care and supervision proceedings (see chapter 4) and section 8 orders (see chapter 2), conditions the court must uphold are clearly outlined.

In particular:

the ascertainable wishes and feelings of the child (in the light of his age and understanding);
his physical, emotional and educational needs;
the likely effect on him of any change in circumstances;
his age, sex , background and any relevant characteristics;
any harm suffered or at risk of suffering;
how capable each parent and any other relevant person is of meeting needs;
and the range of powers available to the court under the Act in the proceedings in question. <S1>

The above checklist is not placed in order of precedence all factors are pertinent. Thus the wishes and feelings of the child do not take priority if his/her welfare appears to to be dictated by other factors. <Re P (Times 11/5/92); Re J (Times 14/5/92)>

Whatever order is applied for in private proceedings, the court may consider any other private law order or ask for a local authority investigation to see whether the authority should apply for an order to protect the child. The full range of orders is available to the court in any local authority application.

In any proceedings in which any question with respect to the upbringing of the child arises, the court shall have regard to the general principle that any delay in determining the question is likely to prejudice the welfare of the child. <S1(2)>

This principle applies equally to all proceedings concerning the upbringing of children, whether public or private and whether brought under the Act or not.

Department of Health guidance indicates that progress of a case is to be controlled by the court (rather than by the parties concerned). This is because proceedings are generally harmful to children not only because of uncertainty for them but also because of the harm it does to the relationship between parents and their capacity to co-operate with one another in the future. <Vol. 1 (1.8)>

Where a court is considering whether or not to make one or more orders under the Act, it shall not make an order unless it considers that doing so would be better for the child than making no order at all. <S1(5)>

The Department of Health indicate that courts will have two aims.

Firstly to discourage unnecessary court orders being made (e.g. as a "standard package"). Thus, so as to reduce conflict and promote parental agreement and co-operation, orders will be restricted to cases where they resolve a particular problem.

Secondly to ensure that orders granted will only positively improve a child's welfare and not simply be made because the grounds are there. <Vol. 1 (1.12)>

Welfare Reports

The court may ask: a probation officer, or the local authority; to arrange to report to the court on such matters relating to the welfare of the child as are required.

Regulations may be made specifying matters which, unless the court orders otherwise, must be dealt with in any report. The report may be made in writing or orally; as the court requires.

It shall be the duty of the probation officer or the local authority to comply with any request for a report. <S7(1-3/5)>

The court may take account of any statement contained in the report (regardless of any law that would otherwise prevent it from doing so).

It will take account of any evidence given in respect of the matters referred to in the report in so far as it is relevant to the question under consideration. <S7(4)>

Guardians ad Litem

In proceedings concerning care or supervision orders (including interim orders and contact with the child), the protection of children, and other proceedings which may be specified by rules of court; the court shall appoint a guardian ad litem for the child concerned unless satisfied that it is not necessary to do so in order to safeguard his interests.

<S41(1/6)/ The Family Proceedings Rules 1991 (Rule 4.2)/ The Family Proceedings Courts (Children Act 1989) Rules 1991 (Rule 2)>

The guardian ad litem shall be appointed in accordance with rules of court; and be under a duty to safeguard the interests of the child. <S41(2)/ The Family Proceedings Rules 1991 (Rules 4.10/4.11)/ The Family Proceedings Courts (Children Act 1989) Rules 1991 (Rules 10/ 11)>

The appointment of a guardian ad litem and the associated reporting procedures are essential to the court's ability to make independent judgments in order to safeguard the welfare of the child.

In particular the guardian ad litem shall:

appoint (and instruct) a solicitor to represent the child unless such a solicitor has already been appointed;

give such advice to the child as is appropriate having regard to his understanding:

advise the court on whether the child is of sufficient understanding for any purpose including the child's refusal to submit to medical or psychiatric examination or other assessment that the court has the power to require, direct or order;

advise the court on the wishes of the child in respect of any matter relevant to the proceedings including his attendance at court;

advise the court on the appropriate forum and timing of the proceedings;

advise the court on the options available in respect of the child and the suitability of each including what order should be made;

advise the court on any other matter concerning which the court seeks his advice or concerning which he considers that the court should be informed;

and make such investigations as may be necessary to carry out his duties, in particular inspect records and obtain any necessary professional assistance. <The Family Proceedings Rules 1991 (Rule 4.11)/ The Family Proceedings Courts (Children Act 1989) Rules 1991 (Rule 11)>

Where the child is, or may be capable of conducting proceedings on their own behalf, the guardian should discuss any likely difficulties with the solicitor acting for the child. Where any conflicts of interest may be involved the guardian should either take out a summons for directions or bring a conflict of interest to the court's attention. <M (minors)(care proceedings: conflict of children's wishes: instruction of expert witnesses) 1994 1 FCR 866>

The Secretary of State may by regulations provide for the establishment of panels of persons from whom guardians ad litem must be selected. <S41(7-9)>.

Regulations have been made concerning panels of guardians ad litem and reporting officers, complaints boards and panel committees, appointments, termination of membership, administration, expenses, fees and allowances, monitoring, training, and complaints. <The Guardians ad Litem and Reporting Officers (Panels) Regulations 1991>

The Department of Health also draw attention to their "Guide for Guardians ad Litem in Public Law Proceedings" 1995. Panel managers and panel committee members should be familiar with the content of this documents.

Rules of court may make provision as to:

the assistance which may be required of the guardian ad litem by the court;

consideration to be given by the guardian ad litem whether to apply for variation or discharge of orders made in the proceedings;

and the participation of guardians ad litem in reviews (specified in the rules) conducted by the court. <S41(10) The Family Proceedings Rules 1991, The Family Proceedings Courts (Children Act) Rules 1991>

The court may take account of:

any statement (relevant to the question the court is considering) contained in the report made by the guardian ad litem;

and any evidence given in respect of such matters referred to in the report. <S41(11)>

The guardian ad litem has the right at all reasonable times to examine and take copies of:

any records of, or held by the local authority (or an authorised person i.e. NSPCC officer or person authorised by the Secretary of State) compiled in connection with the making or proposed making of any application under the act with respect to the child;

any other records compiled in connection with any functions of the social services department that relate to the child;

and any records of, or held by an authorised person which were compiled in connection with the activities of that person, so far as those records relate to that child.

Where a copy of a record is taken, it shall be admissible as evidence of any matter referred to in the guardian ad litem's report or evidence (regardless of any law which would otherwise prevent the record being used as evidence). <S42/ Courts and Legal Services Act 1990, Schedule 16(18)>

The independent view of the guardian ad litem is essential to safeguard the welfare of the child, particularly in disputed cases. An independent view may however be challenged by the parties to the proceedings.

Appointment of Solicitor

Where the child is not represented by a solicitor and no guardian ad litem has been appointed, the child has sufficient understanding to instruct a solicitor and wishes to do so, and it appears to the court to be in the child's best interests for him to be represented by a solicitor, the court may appoint a solicitor to represent him. Any solicitor thus appointed shall represent the child in accordance with rules of court.<S41(3-5)>

If there is any doubt about the ability of the child to issue rational instructions, due to emotional disturbance, expert opinion on the question may be sought from persons already involved in the case. <Re H (Times 5/6/92)>

Attendance of Children at Hearings

In any proceedings concerning an application for care and supervision (see chapter 4) or the protection of children (see chapter 5) subject to rules of court, the court may order the child concerned to attend when they are considering whether to make such an order. <S95(1/2)>

Where an order requiring the child's attendance at court has not been complied with, or the court has reasonable cause to believe that it will not be complied with, the court may make an order authorising a constable or other person (specified in the order) to:

take charge of the child and bring him to court;

and to enter and search any premises specified in the order if he has reasonable cause to believe that the child may be found on the premises.

The court may order any person (who is in a position to do so) to bring the child to the court.

Where the court has reason to believe that a person has information about the whereabouts of the child it may order him to disclose it to the court. <S95(3-6)>

Privacy for Children

Rules may make provision for a magistrates' court to sit in private in any proceedings relating to children. <S97(1/7)>

No person shall publish any material which is intended, or likely, to identify any child as being involved in any proceedings under the Act; or an address or school as being that of a child involved in proceedings.

The court or the Secretary of State may, if satisfied that the welfare of the child requires it, by order dispense with the requirements to such an extent as may be specified. <S97(2-6/8)>

Evidence

Where a child is called as a witness in any civil proceedings and does not understand the nature of an oath, the child's evidence may be heard by the court, if in its opinion:

he understands that it is his duty to speak the truth;

and he has sufficient understanding to justify his evidence being heard. <S96(1/2)>

Provision may be made (by order of the Lord Chancellor) for the admissibility of evidence (in specific classes of civil proceedings and in connection with the upbringing, maintenance or welfare of a child) which would otherwise be inadmissible under any rule of law relating to hearsay. <S96(3-6)>

In any proceedings for care and supervision, or for the protection of children, no person shall be excused from giving evidence or answering a question in the course of giving evidence, on the grounds that doing so might incriminate him or his spouse of an offence.

A statement or admission made in such proceedings shall not be admissible in evidence against the person or his spouse in proceedings for an offence other than perjury. <S98>

When expert witnesses are to be called the following practices should be observed:

The area of expertise must be defined, general orders for disclosure of papers should not be made;

Leave of the court should be sought early on;

Particular experts should be identified and instructed at the earliest opportunity. In cases of doubt the Guardian ad Litem should be asked to advise on the choice of expert;

All relevant information should be placed before the court who have a duty to enquire about the category of expert, the relevance of the evidence, and whether joint instruction with the Guardian ad Litem is appropriate.

Where a local authority wish to carry out an assessment the court should:

Identify the purpose of the assessment;

Specify the time in which the assessment is to be carried out

Consider what evidence is required to bring the case to conclusion. <Re G (Children's cases: Instruction of Experts) (1994) 2 FCR 106, as endorsed by the Children Act Advisory Committee>

Requirement for Leave of Court

On disposing of any application for any order under the Act the court may (whether or not it makes any order in response to the application) order that no application of a specified kind by any person named in the order may then be made without leave of the court. <S91(14)>

This addresses situations where applications may be made repeatedly with no prospect of success. The court may then act to prevent the hardship this may cause the other people involved, including the child.

Appeals

An appeal lies to the High Court against:

the making by a magistrates' court of any order under the Act;

or any refusal by a magistrates' court to make such an order. <S94(1)>

(This does not apply in the case of an interim order for periodical payments in respect of financial provision for children.) <S94(3)>

On appeal the High Court may make such orders as may be necessary to give effect to its determination of the appeal (including also such incidental or consequential orders as appear to be just).

Any order so made shall be treated as if it were an order from the magistrates' court from which the appeal was made. <S94(5/9)>

No appeal applies when a magistrates' court uses its powers to decline jurisdiction because it considers that the case can be more conveniently dealt with by another court. <S94(2)>

Department of Health guidance indicates that most public law applications will start in the magistrates' family proceedings court but may be transferred to a higher court if of exceptional complexity, importance or gravity; or there is a need to consolidate with other proceedings; or the case is urgent. (Subject to the overriding principle that delay is likely to prejudice the welfare of the child.) <Vol. 1 (1.15)>

Appeals against decisions in care or supervision proceedings heard in the County Court or High Court will continue to go to the Court of Appeal. <S77(1) County Courts Act 1984/ S16 Supreme Court Act 1981>

2
PRIVATE LAW

The concept of private law is generally taken to mean legislation which may not directly involve public authorities. (Although private law will have implications for the work of authorities.)

The Department of Health indicate that courts may use private law orders to safeguard the welfare of children as well as to resolve disputes between parents. <Vol. 2 (Annex A 1.37)>

A range of flexible orders is available for use in "family proceedings". Parental responsibility for a child is clarified and whether there are any restrictions on this. "Section 8 Orders" provide the means to resolve disputes between two or more persons holding parental responsibility, and decide how responsibilities may be affected by other parties.

Additional social work help may also be given (under family assistance orders) to assist persons in meeting their parental responsibility.

The range of orders replace those for custody, access and custodianship under previous legislation, and reduce the need for wardship.

The Department of Health state that section 8 orders focus on the child's interests, so as to resolve specific areas of dispute rather than allocating legal rights. They are designed to encourage both parents to maintain their involvement in the child's life. They will be made principally in private family proceedings but they can also be made in care proceedings. Indeed it is the availability of these orders in care proceedings which greatly increases the options open to the courts to make orders that best suit the needs of the child. <Vol. 1 (2.1)>

There is no right of action in private law for a child injured as a result of a local authority's alleged failure to comply with the duties imposed upon it by the Act. <X (Minors) v Bedfordshire CC (Times 24/11/93)>

SECTION 2: PARENTAL RESPONSIBILITY

As the cornerstone of private law relating to children the concept of parental responsibility replaces parental "rights" and "duties" and creates a clear distinction between parenthood and guardianship (which concerns the status of non-parents appointed to bring up the child on the death of his parents).

Definition

The rights, duties, powers, responsibilities and authority which by law a parent of a child has in relation to the child and his property. <S3(1)>

Parental responsibility is a concept of parenthood encompassing both the obligations and the corresponding rights of parents which flow from their responsibility. Parental responsibility is not affected by parental separation.

The term parental responsibility unifies the many references in legislation to parental rights, powers etc. It also more accurately reflects that the true nature of most parental rights is of limited powers to carry out parental duties. The effect of having parental responsibility is (subject to the limitations described) to empower a person to take most decisions in the child's life. It does not make them a parent or relative of the child in law.

Parents are expected to retain their responsibilities and to remain as closely involved as is consistent with their child's welfare, even if the child cannot live at home either temporarily or permanently. Where involved, it is the social worker's task to enable this.

The courts have come to regard parental responsibility as a collection of powers and duties which follow from being a parent and bringing up a child, rather than rights which may be enforced by law. The exercise of parental responsibility is left largely to the discretion of the adults involved. The Act places on a consistent basis rules about who acquires parental responsibility, when it may be exercised and what effect an order under the Act will have upon this.

Scope

Includes the rights, powers and duties which a guardian of the child's estate would have had prior to the implementation of the Act. (In particular the right of the guardian to receive or recover in his own name, property for the benefit of the child.) <S3(2)>

Does not affect:

any obligation which a person (with or without parental responsibility) may have in relation to the child (such as a statutory duty for maintenance);

or any rights which in the event of the child's death he (or any other person) may have in relation to the child's property. <S3(4)>

A person who does not have parental responsibility for a particular child, but has the care of the child, may (subject to the provisions of the Act) do what is reasonable in all the circumstances of the case for the purpose of safeguarding or promoting the child's welfare. <S3(5)>

When more than one person has parental responsibility for a child, each of them may act alone and without the other (or others) in meeting that responsibility.

Nothing in this part of the Act shall be taken to affect the operation of any enactment which requires the consent of more than one person in a matter affecting the child. <S2(7)>

If necessary one person with parental responsibility may ask a court to make a section 8 order which would require another person to inform him before a particular step is taken or not taken.

The fact that a person has parental responsibility for a child shall not entitle him to act in any way which would be incompatible with any order made with respect to the child. <S2(8)>

Parental responsibility may be granted by the court even when it does not allow contact with the child. <Re H (a minor) 1 Family Court Reporter 85, CA 1993>

Persons with Parental Responsibility

Where a child's father and mother were married to each other at the time of birth, they shall each have parental responsibility for the child.

The rule of law that a father is the natural guardian of his legitimate child is abolished. <S2(1/4)>

Where a child's mother and father were not married to each other at the time of his birth, the mother shall have parental responsibility for the child; the father shall not have parental responsibility for the child unless he acquires it in accordance with the provisions of the Act. <S2(2/3)>

A person who has parental responsibility for a child shall not cease to have it solely because some other person subsequently acquires it. <S2(5/6)>

A person who has parental responsibility for a child may not surrender or transfer any part of that responsibility to another but may arrange for some or all of it to be met by one or more persons acting on his behalf. That person may himself be a person who already has parental responsibility for the child concerned.

The making of such an arrangement shall not effect any liability of the person making it which may arise from any failure to meet any part of his parental responsibility for the child concerned. <S2(9-11)>

Department of Health guidance indicates that parents have the right to delegate responsibility of their child on a temporary basis, for example to a babysitter or for a school trip. It will still be the parent's duty to ensure that any arrangements made for the temporary care of the child are satisfactory. Otherwise, the parent may be guilty of a criminal offence of cruelty against the child under section 1 of the Children and Young Person's Act 1933. <Vol. 1 (2.10)>

Acquisition of Parental Responsibility by Father

Where a child's father and mother were not married to each other at the time of his birth: the court may, on the application of the father, order that he shall have parental responsibility for the child; or the father and mother may by an agreement ("a parental responsibility agreement") provide for the father to have parental responsibility for the child.

Such an agreement must be made and recorded in the form prescribed by the regulations made by the Lord Chancellor.

An agreement shall continue in force until the child is 18, unless it is brought to an end earlier. <S91(8)/S4(1-3)>

The Parental Responsibility Agreement Regulations 1991 prescribe the form and recording of agreements.

The Department of Health indicate that parental responsibility agreements are intended as a cheap method by which unmarried parents may share parental responsibility without going to court. <Vol. 2 (Annex A 1.7)>

A court order for parental responsibility or parental responsibility agreement may only be brought to an end by an order of the court made on application of:

any person who has parental responsibility;

or the child himself (with the leave of the court, if they are satisfied that he has sufficient understanding to make the proposed application).

In cases where a residence order has been made in favour of the father of the child who would not otherwise have had parental responsibility; an order to discharge parental responsibility will not be made whilst the residence order remains in force. <S4(3/4)/S12(1/4)>.

A father who is entitled to have the child live with him under a court order will always have parental responsibility for him.

Financial Relief

Section 15 and schedule 1 make provision for the financial relief of children by a parent.

Consent to Marriage

Unless a residence order or care order is in force with respect to the child, the consent of each parent who has parental responsibility for the child and each guardian (if any) is needed.

Where the child is subject to a residence order, only the consent of the person with whom he lives as a result of the order is required. (In most cases a residence order will cease to have effect when the child is 16 but only the consent of the person with whom the child was to live under the previous residence order would be required.) <Schedule 12 (5)>

SECTION 5: APPOINTMENT OF GUARDIANS

Definition

A person appointed as a child's guardian shall have parental responsibility (see above) for the child concerned. <S2(6)>

Department of Health guidance indicates that the Act clarifies the law, enables appointments to be made more simply and introduces a number of provisions which recognise that guardians are generally intended to take over the care of a child where they would not otherwise have a parent with parental responsibility. <Vol. 2 (Annex A 1.10)>

Guidance also indicates that the object is to provide someone to take parental responsibility for a child whose parents have died. All guardians will be non-parents (except in an exceptional case where an unmarried father is appointed guardian instead of being given parental responsibility under section 4). Once the appointment takes effect the guardian will have the same parental responsibility as a natural parent. Appointments are made by any parent with parental responsibility, or any guardian or by a court. Generally speaking a private appointment cannot take effect, nor can a court appointment be made, if the child has a surviving parent with parental responsibility for him. <Vol. 1 (2.13)>

Duration

An appointment shall continue in force until the child is 18, unless it is brought to an end earlier. <S91(7/8)>

Circumstances of Appointment

Appointments can only be made under the provisions of section 5:

where a child has no parent with parental responsibility for him;

or a residence order has been made in favour of a parent or guardian who has died while the order is in force (except where there is an order in favour of a surviving parent of the child);

the court may (on application) appoint an individual to be the child's guardian.

These powers may also be exercised in any family proceedings if the court considers that the order should be made. <S5(1/2/9)>

A parent who has parental responsibility for his child may appoint another individual to be the child's guardian in the event of his death. <S5(3)>

A guardian of a child may appoint another individual to take his place as the child's guardian in the event of his death. <S5(4)>

These appointments shall not have effect unless made in writing, is dated and is signed by the person making the appointment (or is signed under the direction of the person making the appointment, in his presence and in the presence of two witnesses who each attest the signature) or is made under the direction of the testator in accordance with section 9 of the Wills Act.

An appointment may be made by two or more persons acting jointly. <S2(5/10)>

Where on the death of any person making an appointment the child concerned has no parent with parental responsibility the appointment shall take effect on the death of that person.

In a case where immediately before the death of any person making an appointment, a residence order in his favour was in force with respect to the child (other than when there is one in favour of a surviving parent of the child) the appointment shall take effect on the death of that person (except where the child does not have a parent with parental responsibility when the appointment shall take effect when the child no longer has a parent who has parental responsibility). <S2(7-9)>

Subject to rules of court, no court shall exercise the High Court's inherent jurisdiction to appoint a guardian of the estate of any child. <S5(11/12)>

Revocation and Disclaimer

A person who is appointed by a parent or guardian in the event of death, may disclaim his appointment by an instrument in writing signed by him and made within a reasonable time of first knowing that the appointment has taken effect. This measure is subject to recording in the prescribed manner. <S6(5/6)>

Any appointment of a guardian may be brought to an end at any time by order of the court:

on the application of any person who has parental responsibility;
on the application of the child concerned;
or in any family proceedings, if the court considers that it should be brought to an end. <S6(7)>

Financial Relief

Section 15 and schedule 1 makes provision for the financial relief against parents by guardians.

SECTION 8: ORDERS

Definition

A *Contact Order* (concerning the form of contact the child is to have with other people);

a *Prohibited Steps Order* (to prohibit anything specified being done in relation to the child);
a *Residence Order* (determining with whom the child will live);
and a *Specific Issues Order* (settling any other particular matter concerning the child and their upbringing);
and any order varying or discharging such an order. <S8(1/2)>

The Department of Health state that these orders do not remove parental power and authority from one parent or confer sole power and authority on the other. Rather they simply settle particular matters which neither party may then upset. Parents will still be able to act as parents in ways that are not affected by the order. They allow the court to make whatever arrangements seem best in the particular case, dealing with practical questions rather than abstract rights. Wardship remains available to private individuals but these orders make the need to use it rarer. <Vol. 2 (Annex A 1.33)>

GENERAL ASPECTS APPLICABLE TO ALL SECTION 8 ORDERS

Effect

Additional directions concerning how the order may be carried into effect may be imposed.

Conditions may be specifically imposed and expressed that must be complied with by:
any person in whose favour the order is made;
any parent of the child concerned;
any person who has parental responsibility;
or person with whom the child is living.

These conditions may have effect for a specified period, or contain provisions that have effect for a specified period.

Any additional, supplemental or consequential provision may also be made as the court sees fit. <S11(7)>

Applications

The court can consider making an order at any time in family proceedings (even though it is not in a position to finally dispose of those proceedings).

An order can be made in these circumstances though no application has been made. Additionally applications can be made by specific categories of persons prescribed in the rules of court. <S10(1/7)/S11(3)>

Department of Health guidance indicates that section 8 orders can be made in most proceedings specifically relating to the care and upbringing of children; i.e. wardship proceedings, and *proceedings under the Act itself, including applications for care and supervision orders and adoption proceedings (but not emergency protection and child assessment proceedings or secure accommodation proceedings). Orders may also be made in certain proceedings concerned with disputes between adults but in which the interests of children may be important. These include divorce, nullity and judicial separation proceedings, maintenance proceedings in magistrate's courts and domestic violence or ouster proceedings in both magistrate's and the higher courts. <Vol. 1 (2.36)>*

In most cases application may be made by any genuinely interested party (except the local authority) without leave. This "open door policy" recognises the need for such persons to be able to ask the court to consider a specific question which has arisen about a child's welfare. The persons who may apply as of right for section 8 orders are detailed below under the particular order concerned.

In all other cases leave of the court is required. <S10(1/2)>

If the Local Authority believes a child to be at risk of significant harm application should be made for care or supervision (see chapter four) under public law provision (Part IV of the Act) rather than private law such as a Prohibited Steps Order. <Re P (Independent 7/4/93)>

Applications cannot be made by a person who (at any time during the last six months) has been a local authority foster parent, with respect to the child unless:

he has the consent of the local authority;
he is a relative of the child;
or the child has lived with him for at least three years proceeding the application for leave of the court to apply for a section 8 order. (This period need not be continuous but must have begun not more than five years before the making of the application.) <S9(3/4)>

In the case of variation and discharge, additional applications may be considered from those not otherwise entitled, so long as the order was originally made on their application. <S10(6)>

Where the person applying for leave of application is the child concerned, the court may only grant leave if it is satisfied that he has sufficient understanding to make the proposed application. <S10(8)>

In all other cases, the court will consider:

the applicant's connection with the child;
any risk of harm resulting from disruption to the child's life;
and where the child is being looked after by the local authority, the authority's plans for the child's future and the wishes and feelings of the child's parents. <S10(9)>

In all proceedings the court will draw up a timetable (based upon rules of court) with a view to determining the question without delay.

It will give such directions it considers appropriate for the purpose of ensuring, so far as is reasonably practicable, that the timetable is adhered to. <S11(1/2)

Duration

The order and its provisions may have effect for a specified period. <S11(7)>

No court shall make any section 8 order, other than one varying or discharging such an order, with respect to a child who has reached the age of 16 unless it is satisfied that the circumstances of the case are exceptional. <S9(7)>

No court shall make a section 8 order which will end after the child has reached the age of 16 unless it is satisfied that the circumstances of the case are exceptional.

Department of Health guidance gives an example of exceptional circumstances as being the case of a mentally handicapped child. <Vol. 1 (2.49)>

Such orders will absolutely cease to have effect on the age of 18.

Any order which would otherwise still be in force when the child reaches the age of 16 shall cease to have effect. <S9(6)/S91(10/11)>

The making of a care order will discharge a section 8 order. <S91(2)>

Department of Health guidance draws attention here to the clear distinction in the Act between children being provided with accommodation or other services by the local authority (see chapter 3) and children formally in the care of the local authority (see care orders in chapter 4). Parental responsibility is only acquired by the local authority when a care order is made. Private law powers should not be used to interfere with the local authority's exercise of its parental responsibility.

If an individual is unhappy with the arrangements for contact with a child in care they should apply under section 34 of the Act (see care order: contact with parents in chapter 4). Prohibited steps orders and specific issue orders are also not available to individuals as a means to challenge local authority decisions when a child is in care nor are they available to the local authority. The authority can, however, apply for leave of the court to make an application for a section 8 order, where a child is provided with accommodation or other services. The only section 8 order that can be made in respect of a child in care is a residence order, which has the effect of discharging the care order. <Vol. 1 (2.46-8)>

Requirements to Be Met by the Court

The child's welfare is of paramount consideration. In particular:
the ascertainable wishes and feelings of the child (in the light of his age and understanding);
his physical, emotional and educational needs;
the likely effect on him of any change in circumstances;
his age, sex , background and any relevant characteristics;
any harm suffered or at risk of suffering;
how capable each parent and any other relevant person is of meeting needs;
and whether the order is required at all. <S1>

The welfare of the child is the essential principle that the court will uphold. The court will not however decide what are the best interests of the child, it will follow the conditions laid down that must be met if the welfare principle is to be satisfied.

CONTACT ORDER

Definition

Requires the person with whom a child lives, or is to live, to allow the child to visit or to stay with the person named in the order or for that person and the child to have contact with each other. <S8(1)>

Orders can be as wide or as narrow as appropriate. Contact orders provide for the child to visit or to stay with the person named in the order. The person may be any person not just a parent. More than one contact order can be made for a child.

Department of Health guidance indicates that the emphasis has shifted from the adult to the child. Contact can range from long or short visits to contact by letter or telephone. The order is a positive order in the sense that it requires contact to be allowed between an individual and the child and cannot be used to deny contact. (This would require a prohibited steps order, see below). <Vol. 1 (2.29/30)>

Restrictions

Cannot be made if the child is under a care order (see chapter 4) nor can it be made in favour of the local authority. <S9(1/2)>

Where a child is living with one parent and is the subject of an order which allows visits or contact with the other parent, the order will cease to have effect if the parents live together for a continuous period of more than six months. <S11(6)>

Application

Application for a contact order may be made without leave of the court by:

any parent or guardian of the child;

any person holding a current residence order (see below) in respect of the child;

any person who has the consent of each of the persons in whose favour an existing residence order has been made;

any party to a present or previous marriage where the child is a child of the family;

any person with whom the child has lived for at least three years (this period need not be continuous but must not have begun more than five years before, or ended more than three months before, the making of the application);

or any person who has the consent of those holding parental responsibility for the child. <S10(4/5/10)>

Any other person may apply to the court for leave to make an application for a contact order if he can show sufficient connection with the child and good reason for so applying. <S10(9)>

Cannot be made by the local authority. <S9(2)>

In the case of children in care, section 34 (see chapter 4) should be used instead.

In the case of variation and discharge, additional applications may be considered from those not otherwise entitled, so long as they are named in the order. <S10(6)>

PROHIBITED STEPS ORDER

Definition

No step which could be taken by a parent in meeting his parental responsibility for a child, and which is of a kind specified in the order, shall be taken by any person without the consent of the court. <S8(1)>

This order is by nature one which deals with a single issue and is used where contact and residence orders cannot provide the necessary control over a child's upbringing.

Department of Health guidance indicates that the purpose is to impose a specific restriction on the exercise of parental responsibility. <Vol. 1 (2.31)>

Restrictions

Cannot be made if the child is under a care order (see chapter 4). <S9(1)>

Cannot be made with a view to achieving a result which could be achieved by making a residence or contact order.

Cannot be used as a means to circumvent the restrictions upon the use of the inherent jurisdiction of the High Court, that is to place a child in care, place under local authority supervision, accommodate in care or to confer power on the local authority to determine any question which has arisen, or which may arise, in connection with any aspect of parental responsibility for a child. <S9(5)S100(2) /Re P (Times 6/11/92)>

Application

Application may be made without leave of the court by any parent or guardian of the child; and any person holding a current residence order in respect of the child.

Any other person may apply to the court for leave to make an application for a prohibited steps order if he can show sufficient connection with the child and good reason for so applying. <S10(4/9)>

RESIDENCE ORDER

Definition

Settles the arrangements to be made as to the person with whom a child is to live. <S8(1)>

The concepts of residence and parental responsibility are different. For example, on divorce residence may be ordered for one parent but both retain parental responsibility.

> *Department of Health guidance indicates that the order may be used flexibly as it will be able to accommodate various shared care arrangements. The intention is that both parents should feel that they have a continuing role to play in relation to their children. <Vol. 1 (2.23)>*

Shared residence orders are only appropriate in exceptional circumstances. A settled home should be with only with one parent. <Re H 1993 Family Court Reporter. 671, CA.>

Effect

When anybody is in breach of the arrangements settled by a residence order, a person in whose favour the residence order is made may (without prejudice to any other remedy) serve a copy of the residence order on the other person and enforce the order as if it were an order requiring the other person to produce the child to him. <S14>

Restrictions

Cannot be made in favour of the local authority but can be made with respect to a child in care. <S9(1/2)>

The child cannot be removed from the United Kingdom (save for a period of up to one month by the person holding a residence order) without the consent of all persons holding parental responsibility or the leave of the court. <S13>

The child cannot be known by a new surname without the consent of all persons holding parental responsibility or the leave of the court. <S13>

The making of a residence order has the effect of discharging an existing care order (see chapter 4). <S91(1)>

Applications

Application for a residence order may be made without leave of the court by:

any parent or guardian of the child;
any person holding a current residence order in respect of the child;
any person who has the consent of each of the persons in whose favour an existing residence order has been made;
any party to a present or previous marriage where the child is a child of the family;
any person with whom the child has lived for at least three years (this period need not be continuous but must not have begun more than five years before, or ended more than three months before, the making of the application);
or any person who has the consent of those holding parental responsibility for the child. <S10(4/5/10)>

Any other person may apply to the court for leave to make an application for a Residence Order if he can show sufficient connection with the child and good reason for so applying. <S10(9)>

No application can be made by the local authority. <S9(2)>

Conditions

Where an order is made in favour of the father who would not otherwise have parental responsibility for the child, an order will be made under section 4 giving that responsibility. The court shall not bring that order to an end at any time the residence order remains in force.

The Department of Health state that in such cases it will usually be in the child's interests for his father to retain parental responsibility for him in just the same way that a married father does. <Vol. 1 (2.26)>

Where an order is made in favour of a person who is not the parent or guardian of the child concerned that person shall have parental responsibility for the child while the order remains in force.

Parental responsibility does not convey the right here to give consent to adoption, freeing for adoption or appointing a guardian for the child. <S12>

Duration

Where as a result of the order the child lives, or is to live with one of two parents who shall have parental responsibility for him, the order shall cease to have effect if the parents live together for a continuous period of more than six months. <S11(5)>

The Department of Health in its guidance consider examples of how this applies, where the child spends weekdays with one parent and weekends with the other, or term time with one parent and school holidays with the other, or where the child is to spend large amounts of time with each parent. It is not expected that this will be a common order because most children will need the stability of a single home and also where there is shared care it will be less likely that there is a need to make an order at all. There may be benefits in such an arrangement however (including the right to remove the child from accommodation provided by the local authority under section 20 (see chapter 3) and the removal of any impression that one parent is better than the other. <Vol. 1 (2.4-2.9)>

Financial Relief

Section 15 and schedule 1 makes provision for the financial relief of children who are subject to a residence order.

In addition to an order requiring either or both parents of the child to make periodic payments to the applicant or the child himself, schedule 1 (15) provides for the local authority to make contributions towards the accommodation and maintenance of the child except where the person with whom the child lives, or is to live, is a parent of the child or the husband or wife of a parent of the child.

SPECIFIC ISSUE ORDER

Definition

Gives directions for the purpose of determining a specific question which has arisen, or which may arise, in connection with any aspect of parental responsibility for a child. <S8(1)>

Such an order can only be used where orders concerning residence and contact are not sufficient.

The Department of Health suggest that the aim is to enable a particular dispute (for example about education, or medical treatment) to be resolved by the court including the giving of detailed directions where necessary. <Vol. 1 (2.32)>

Restrictions

Cannot be made if the child is under a care order (see chapter 4). <S9(1)>

Cannot be made to achieve a result which could be achieved by making a residence or contact order.

Cannot be used as a means to circumvent the restriction placed upon the use of the inherent jurisdiction of the High Court, that is to place a child in care, place under local authority supervision, accommodate in care or to confer power on the local authority to determine any question which has arisen, or which may arise, in connection with any aspect of parental responsibility for a child. <S9(5)/S100(2)>

Application

Application may be made without leave of the court by any parent or guardian of the child; and any person holding a current residence order in respect of the child. <S10(4)>

Any other person may apply to the court for leave to make an application for a Specific Issue Order if he can show sufficient connection with the child and good reason for so applying. <S10(9)>

SECTION 16: FAMILY ASSISTANCE ORDERS

Definition

An order making a probation officer or a local authority officer available to advise, assist and (where appropriate) befriend any person (parent or guardian, person holding a contact order, or the child himself) named in the order. <S16(1/2)>

The order provides short term assistance, on a consensual basis, to families or individuals experiencing a breakdown of domestic relationships. It can be used by the court as a preventive measure or to promote the upbringing of a child by its family. It is not to be confused with supervision orders (see chapter 4) which apply to more serious cases where there is an element of child protection.

Effect

The order may direct the person, or some of the persons, named in the order to take such steps as may be so specified to enable the officer concerned to be kept informed of the address of any person named in the order and to be allowed to visit any such person. <S16(4)>

Requirements to Be Met by the Court

The circumstances of the case must be exceptional, and the consent of every person to be named in the order other than the child must be obtained. <S16(4)>

> *The Department of Health indicate that it should not be made as a matter of routine. It is a voluntary order. The court will have to be clear why family assistance is needed and what it is hoped to achieve by it. <Vol. 1 (2.52)>*

Where a section 8 order is also in force the officer concerned may refer to the court the question whether the section 8 order should be varied or discharged. <S16(6)>

The order shall not be made so as to require a local authority to make an officer of theirs available unless: the authority agree, and the child concerned lives or will live in their area.

In the case of a probation officer being made available, the officer shall be selected in accordance with arrangements made by the probation committee for the area in which the child lives or will live, as will any arrangements for the substitution of another probation officer. <S16(7-9)>

Duration

Six months unless a shorter period is specified. <S16(5)>

There is no restriction on further orders being made.

3
PROVISION OF SERVICES FOR CHILDREN AND THEIR FAMILIES

The provision of a child care service to children in need and their families is a fundamental part of a strategy to enable viable preventive help. The act places a clear duty upon local authorities to provide services, where necessary, to enable parents to carry out their responsibilities and to avoid any proceedings that would otherwise transfer parental responsibility to the local authority (except where provisions are made for the protection of the child (see chapter 4 on care and supervision and chapter 5 on child protection)).

The wide range of services include day care and accommodation (about which specific detailed provision is made in the Act). The local authority may in certain circumstances charge for providing services under the Act. The authority is required to set up procedures for representation and complaint so that the quality of the service may be maintained. Where a situation may involve more than one authority or department, requirements are stated in the Act for co-operation and consultation.

SECTION 17: PROVISION FOR CHILDREN IN NEED, THEIR FAMILIES AND OTHERS

The Duties of Local Authorities

It shall be the general duty of every local authority to safeguard and promote the welfare of children within their area who are in need; and (so far as is consistent with that duty) to promote the upbringing of such children by their families, by providing a range and level of services appropriate to those children's needs. <S17(1)>

Department of Health guidance indicates that one of the key principles of the Act is the protection of children from harm which arises from family breakdown or abuse within the family, but unwarranted intervention in families' lives or unnecessary weakening of family ties should be avoided. In carrying out these responsibilities local authorities must have regard to the wishes and feelings of the child, parents, any other person with parental responsibility and other relevant persons. Due consideration must be given to the child's religious persuasion, racial origin and cultural and linguistic background. <Vol. 2 (1.12)>

Partnership with parents is the guiding principle for the provision of services within the family home and where children are accommodated under voluntary arrangements. Such arrangements are intended to assist parents and enhance, not undermine, the parent's authority and control. <Vol. 2 (2.1)>

Services may be provided for the family of a particular child in need or for any member of his family, if it is provided with a view to safeguarding or promoting the child's welfare.

The family includes any person who has parental responsibility (see chapter 2) and any other person with whom the child has been living. <S17(3/10)>

Every local authority shall facilitate the provision of services for children and families by others (including in particular voluntary organisations). These services include the whole range of those provided under this section and the provision of day care, accommodation, maintenance, advice and assistance. <S17(5)>

The Department of Health advises authorities to produce and publish plans for children's services. The process should create the foundation for the the planning, management and review of child care services including residential care. It should encourage local authorities to make explicit their policies, and to recognise the resource implications; it should make clear the extent that the services of the voluntary and private sectors are required and encourage collaboration and filling of gaps; and it should enable the more effective monitoring of service provision ensuring that policies are dynamic and adaptable to meet changing needs. Guidance on the content of plans is given. <Circular LAC(92)18>

Every local authority shall take reasonable steps to identify the extent to which there are children in need within their area.

They shall publish information about services provided by them (and where they consider it appropriate, about the provision by others including voluntary organisations) and take such steps as are practicable to ensure that those who might benefit from services receive the information relevant to them. <Schedule 2 (1)>

The Department of Health indicate that any publicity materials should take account of ethnic minorities' cultural and linguistic needs and the needs of those with sensory disabilities. As far as possible publicity should encourage parents to seek help if it is needed. The importance of availability of information in making informed choices about use of facilities in the area is highlighted. <Vol. 2 (2.36/2.37)

Every local authority shall take reasonable steps, through the provision of services, to prevent children within their area from suffering ill-treatment or neglect.

Where they believe that a child, at any time, within their area is likely to suffer harm but lives or proposes to live in the area of another local authority they shall inform that local authority specifying the harm that they believe he is likely to suffer; and (if they can) where the child lives or proposes to live. <Schedule 2 (4)>

Every local authority shall provide services for children with disabilities designed to minimise the effect of their disabilities and give them the opportunity to lead lives which are as normal as possible. <Schedule 2 (6)>

Department of Health guidance indicates that social services departments should have a specific policy on the integration of services for children with disabilities, which meets their general duties and powers towards children and their families. Policies should take account of the wishes and views of the local community including user groups. Every effort should be made to work collaboratively in team and multi-agency structures to avoid the creation of separate and segregated services. Work with children with disabilities should be based on the following principles:

the welfare of the child should be safeguarded and promoted by those providing services;

a primary aim should be to promote access for all children to the same range of services;

children with disabilities are children first;

recognition of the importance of parents and families in children's lives;

partnership between parents and local authorities and other agencies;

and the views of children and parents should be sought and taken into account. <Vol. 6 (1.5/1.7)>

Social services departments will need to develop clear assessment procedures for children in need which take into account the child's and family's needs and preferences, racial and ethnic origins, their culture, religion and any special needs. Assessments under the Act may be combined with those under the Education Act 1993 the Disabled Persons Act 1986 and the Chronically Sick and Disabled Persons Act 1970. This is particularly important for children with disabilities that will need continuing services through their lives. A smooth seamless transition when the young person reaches 18 and comes within the provisions of the NHS and Community Care Act 1990 should be the objective. <Vol. 6 (5.1-5.17)>

Every local authority shall open and maintain a register of children with disabilities within their area. (This may be kept on computer.) <Schedule 2 (2)>

Department of Health guidance indicates that registers should be kept with other authorities and under other legislation (e.g. education and health) to be complete and to avoid duplication.

Registration is voluntary and not a precondition of service provision.

Well planned services will be of assistance to parents and their children and help in planning services when children become adults.

The Act makes it possible to bring together in one process assessment for several different services where this is appropriate

Assistance may be given in kind or, in exceptional circumstances, by cash.

Assistance may be unconditional or subject to conditions as to the repayment of the assistance or its value (in whole or in part).

Before giving assistance or imposing any conditions, a local authority shall have regard to the means of the child concerned and of each of his parents.

Repayment by a person is not possible at any time when he is in receipt of income support or family credit. <S17(6-9)>

Assistance (may be given in cash) to obtain alternative accommodation, where it appears that a child is likely to suffer ill treatment at the hands of another person who is living on the premises where the child is living. Assistance may then be given to that other person. <Schedule 2 (5)>

It is intended that local authorities integrate service provision for all children who are in need, for whatever reason.

SECTION 18: DAY CARE FOR PRE-SCHOOL AND OTHER CHILDREN

Definition

Any form of care or supervised activity provided for children during the day (whether or not it is provided on a regular basis). <S18(4)>

Duties of the Local Authority

To provide day care for children in need who are: aged five or under and not yet attending school, as is appropriate.

May also be provided for children even though they are not in need. (S18(1/2)>

The Department of Health state that in considering whether or not to offer day care services full consideration should be given to the views of parents and children. There should be a variety of day care facilities; parents should be involved in discussions about preferences and meeting children's needs. Local authorities may discharge their general duty either through their own provision or by making arrangements with private firms or individuals. <Vol. 2 (3.4-7)>

Every local authority shall in making arrangements for the provision of day care have regard to the different racial groups to which children in need in their area belong. <Schedule 2 (11)>

The Department of Health state that people working with young children should value and respect different racial origins, religions, cultures and languages in a multi-racial society so that each child is valued as an individual without racial or gender *stereotyping. Local authorities should have approved equal opportunities policies including arrangements for monitoring and reviewing progress towards implementation. They should have available data on the ethnic origins of the local population which is essential to policy assessment. <Vol. 2 (6.9-11)>*

Every local authority shall provide for children in need within their area who are attending any school such care or supervised activities (supervised by a responsible person) as are appropriate: during school hours, or during school holidays.

May also be provided even though children are not in need. <S18 (57)>

They may provide facilities (including training, advice guidance and counselling) for those caring for children in day care or who at any time accompany such children while they are in day care. <S18(3)>

Department of Health guidance indicates that this power enables help in the process of raising standards and improving parenting skills. It includes help for childminders (see chapter 7) and those with parental responsibility (see chapter 2). <Vol. 2 (3.34)>

Local authorities should develop an agreed policy about the extent that they wish to use powers such as those concerning training as part of their policies on family support, day care and educational provision for young children. <Vol. 2 (3.35)>

To review:

their provision for day care and supervised activities;

the availability of child minders for children under eight within their area;

and the provision of day care, and registered child minders provided by others.

The review shall be conducted together with the local education authority and shall have regard to the provision made for children under eight in relevant establishments (hospitals, schools and other establishments exempt from the registration requirements that apply in relation to the provision of day care) within their area.

Reviews shall be conducted at least once in the first year of operation of this section of the Act and each subsequent period of three years.

Representations shall be considered from any relevant health authority or any other people the local authority consider to be relevant.

The results shall be published together with any proposals. <S19/ Schedule 9 (3/4)>

Department of Health guidance explores ways that the co-ordination and duty to review day care services may be fulfilled. Three levels are highlighted: policy making, day-to-day operation *of services and between staff working in different settings. <Vol. 2 (1.16)>*

The guidance on implementation includes: machinery, levels, joint arrangements and inter-agency approaches, processes, consultations, analysis of information, contents of review reports, dissemination and follow up. The agenda is the coherent and efficient use of services and their co-ordination and oversight. Further guidance is given on these issues in DoH publications. <Vol. 2 (4.7/9.1-19)>

SECTION 20: PROVISION OF ACCOMMODATION

Definition

Accommodation provided for a continuous period of more than 24 hours <S22(2)>.

Department of Health guidance indicates that the Act presupposes a high degree of co-operation between parents and local authorities in negotiating and agreeing what form of accommodation can be offered and the use made of it. The Act makes no distinction between the provision of a pre-planned short term, periodic placement and longer term provision of accommodation. <Vol. 2 (2.25/2.26)>

Department of Health guidance also indicates that the partnership with the child's family is based upon provision for the child's needs by voluntary arrangement that builds upon the family's strengths and minimises any weakness. The service provision should be based upon voluntary agreement by the parents to take an appropriate service and continuing participation in and agreement to the arrangements for the child. <Vol. 2 (2.26-2.30)>

A clear distinction is made between local authorities providing accommodation under this provision, whereby parents retain their parental responsibility, and orders placing the child "in care" (see chapter 4) where parental responsibility is the prerogative of the local authority.

Grounds

Accommodation shall be provided for any child in need as a result of:

there being no person who has parental responsibility for him;

his being lost or having been abandoned;

or the person who has been caring for him being prevented (whether or not permanently, and for whatever reason) from providing him with suitable accommodation or care. <S20(1)>

The Department of Health indicate that the responsibility of local authorities is to provide accommodation for children in need who *require it. It does not have the unhelpful connotations of parental shortcomings. The local authority are "looking after" children in partnership with parents; providing a service without pressure or prejudice. <Vol. 2 (2.14/2.15)>*

If the child is 16 or over accommodation shall be provided if his welfare is otherwise likely to be seriously prejudiced. <S20(3)>

May be provided if it would safeguard or promote the child's welfare (even though a person who has parental responsibility for him would be able to provide him with accommodation). <S20(4)>

May not be provided if any person who has parental responsibility objects and is willing and able to provide or arrange accommodation, unless all people who have a residence order in respect of the child (see chapter 2) agree to the child being looked after in accommodation, the child is over 16 and agrees to being provided with accommodation, or the child is under wardship. <S20(7/9-11)>

For 16-20 year olds, accommodation may be provided in a community home which takes children who have reached the age of 16. <S20(5)>

Accommodation may not be provided under S20 if any person who has parental responsibility for the child objects unless all people who have a residence order (see chapter 2) in respect of the child agree to the child being looked after in accommodation, or the child is over 16 and agrees to being provided with accommodation. <S20(7-10)>

Provision for reception and accommodation shall be made for children in police protection or detention or the subject of a supervision order with a residence requirement or on remand. <S21/Schedule 12 (23/26)>

Conditions to Be Met

To ascertain the child's wishes and give due consideration to be met (having regard to his age and understanding) to such wishes. <S20(6)>

Duties to Be Observed

To safeguard and promote the child's welfare; and to make use of services available for children cared for by their own parents. <S22(3)>

To ascertain the wishes and feelings of:
the child;
his parents;
any person who is not a parent of his but who has parental responsibility;
and any other relevant person. <S22(4)>

Department of Health guidance indicates that sensible agreements should be made between the local authority and persons with parental responsibility to cover ways of terminating use of the service the timetable of which will not mitigate against the child's best interests. These will reflect the need to minimise disruption to the child. The agreement will require careful negotiation and should be framed so as to enhance the parent's role in their child's life.

The plan for the arrangements will set out (amongst other things) the reason for, purpose and anticipated length of the child's stay in local authority or other accommodation, and the arrangements for contact with the child.

The guidance also states the provision of accommodation by agreement is to be viewed as a service to parents who, in the best interests of the child, voluntarily agree to the arrangements before accommodation is provided. So far as it is reasonably practicable and consistent with the child's welfare the authority will give due consideration to such wishes of the child as they have been able to ascertain. This requirement must be kept in mind when planning arrangements for the child. The importance of the assessment of need being made in consultation with the child before a particular type of accommodation is provided or plans made cannot be over-emphasised. <Vol. 2 (3.28-3.32)>

In making any decision (except where necessary to protect the public from serious injury) the authority shall give due consideration to:

the child's age and understanding;

the wishes and feelings of the child, his parents, any person who may have parental responsibility, and any other relevant person;

and to the child's religious persuasion, racial origin, cultural and linguistic background. <S22(5-8)>

Guidance from the Department of Health indicates that section 3 (5) (see scope of parental responsibility in chapter 2) applies to children accommodated by local authorities. Here a person who has the care of the child but who does not have parental responsibility may do what is reasonable in the particular circumstances of the case. <Vol. 1 (2.11)>

To provide accommodation and to maintain the child by:

placing him with a family, a relative of his, or any other suitable person;

maintaining him in a community, voluntary, or registered children's home, or in a home provided in accordance with arrangements made by the Secretary of State;

or by making any other arrangements that seem appropriate. <S23(1/2)/ Courts and Legal Services Act 1990, Schedule 16(12)>

The Department of Health states that when a local authority places a child under S23 and delegates its functions to a voluntary organisation, the local authority remains responsible *for how these tasks are carried out. The local authority has to satisfy itself that the proposed arrangement is suitable and is likely to promote and safeguard the child's welfare. <Circular LAC(94)20>*

If the child is disabled, the accommodation should not be unsuitable to his particular needs. <S23(8)>

In relation to short term or respite care for children with disabilities, the Department of Health state that an appropriate flexible short term service should be provided which offers:

a local service where the child can continue to attend school as if still living at home;

good quality child care in which parents have confidence and which ensures that the child is treated first as a child and then for any disability which may require special provision;

planned availability;

a service which meets the needs of all children (including complex needs);

care which is compatible with the child's family background and culture, racial origin, religious persuasion and language;

age appropriate care;

an integrated programme of family support which sees planned respite care as part of a wider range of professional support services to meet family needs. <Vol. 6 (11.11)>

The local authority, subject to regulations made by the Secretary of State shall make arrangements to enable a child to live with a parent, a person with parental responsibility or a person with a residence order (see chapter 2) .

In respect of families, relatives and suitable persons, terms and payment can be determined by the local authority.

Approval as local authority foster parents will be made in the case of persons other than parents, those with parental responsibility or those who held a residence order immediately before a care order was made.

A child shall be regarded as living with a person if he stays with that person for a continuous period of more than 24 hours. <S23(4-6)/ Courts and Legal Services Act 1990, Schedule 16(12)>

Accommodation should, so far as reasonably practical and consistent with the child's welfare, be near to his home. Siblings should be accommodated together. <S23(7)>

Where accommodation is provided for a child ordinarily resident in the area of another authority, that authority may take over the provision of accommodation within three months of being notified in writing or a longer period if prescribed. <S20(2)>

The receiving authority and initially the transferring authority shall (where reasonably practicable) inform the child's parents or person holding parental responsibility. <Schedule 2(15)>

If the Secretary of State considers it necessary, for the purpose of protecting members of the public from serious injury, to give directions to the local authority with respect to the exercise of their powers, they shall comply with them even if they are inconsistent with their other duties .<S22(7/8)>

Contact with Parents etc.

Where it is reasonably practicable and consistent with the child's welfare, the local authority shall endeavour to promote contact between the child and: his parents; any person with parental responsibility and any relative, friend or other person connected with him. <Schedule 2 (15)>

The authority shall take reasonable practicable steps to secure that his parents, and any person with parental responsibility are kept informed of where he is accommodated and to inform such persons of the need to keep the local authority informed of their address. <Schedule 2(15)>

Where communication has been infrequent between the child and his parent or person with parental responsibility) and he has not been visited by (or lived with) such person during the preceding 12 months, if it is in the child's best interests (and unless he objects and has sufficient understanding to make an informed decision) an independent visitor (see interpretation in chapter 9) shall be appointed to have the duty of visiting, advising and befriending the child. <Schedule 2(17)>

The local authority shall make payments in respect of travelling, subsistence or other visiting expenses to parents, those holding parental responsibility and to any relative, friend or other person connected with him, when circumstances (such as undue financial hardship) warrant the making of payments. (Schedule 2(16)>

Removal by Persons with Parental Responsibility

Any person who has parental responsibility for a child may at any time remove the child from accommodation provided under S20 unless:

any person who has a residence order (see chapter 2) in respect of the child objects;

or the child is over 16 and agrees to being provided with accommodation;

or any person who has the care of the child by virtue of an order made in the exercise of the High Court's inherent jurisdiction with respect to children objects. <S20(8-11)>

This provision includes children placed in secure accommodation under section 20

Review

The Secretary of State has power to make regulations. These may provide that:

the authority be required to seek the views of: the child, his parents, any person who has parental responsibility and any other person whose views are considered to be relevant;

and inform the child of any steps he may take under the act.

The result should be notified to: the child; his parents; any person with parental responsibility; and any other person who ought to be notified. <S26(1/2)>

The Arrangements for Placement of Children (General) Regulations and the Review of Children's Cases Regulations are discussed in this book in chapter 8. These two provisions should be read in conjunction with each other and in relation to this section. The regulations concerning placements place a duty on responsible authorities to draw up an individual plan for the child before making arrangements for placement. The regulations concerning reviews require that the plan is reviewed (and amended as necessary) on a regular basis.

The two sets of regulations were introduced to provide local authorities, voluntary organisations and registered children's homes with a statutory framework within which to meet their duty to contribute to a well planned, well organised arrangement: to plan review and monitor the case of every child they are looking after. Planning is required from the earliest time after recognition of need. The plan should be reviewed on an ongoing basis so that all necessary considerations for the child's welfare, including the child's wishes and views and the views of parents are given due attention.

Preparation for After Care

It is the duty of the local authority to advise, assist and befriend any child being looked after by the authority, with a view to promoting his welfare when he ceases to be looked after by them. <S24(1)>

Preparation for leaving care starts well before a person ceases to be looked after or accommodated and is likely to continue until well after he has done so.

The Department of Health state that planning after care services for individual children will help the child to adjust during the transition from child to adult. <Vol. 2 (3.32)>

After Care

The local authority shall advise and befriend those formerly looked after by them (aged 16 to under 21) and may also give assistance in kind, or in exceptional circumstances cash. This may include living expenses near where he is employed, or receiving education or training, or a grant to meet education or training expenses. <S24(2-9)>

If the child proposes to live or are living in the area of another local authority they shall inform that local authority. <S24(11)>

The local authority have a duty to advise and befriend and may also give assistance (in kind or in exceptional circumstances in cash) where:

a person (aged 16 to under 21) is looked after by another local authority;

or a person (aged 16 to under 21) is accommodated by or on behalf of a voluntary organisation, is located in the local authority's own area, is no longer so looked after, or accommodated, has asked for advice and assistance in the absence of facilities being available, and is in such need and does not have such facilities. <S24(4-7)>

Where a person (aged 16 to under 21) accommodated in a registered children's home; accommodated by a health or education authority or any residential care, nursing, or mental nursing home or any accommodation provided by a National Health Service trust for a consecutive period of at least three months; or privately fostered,

is located in the local authority's own area,

is no longer so looked after, accommodated or fostered,

has asked for advice and assistance,

is in such need and does not have such facilities,

the local authority may advise and befriend the person concerned. <S24(4-7) as amended by The National Health Service and Community Care Act 1990 (Schedule 9 paragraph 36)>

CO-OPERATION AND CONSULTATION BETWEEN AUTHORITIES

Where it appears to a local authority that any other local authority, local education authority, local housing authority, health authority or national health service trust, or any authorities authorised by the Secretary of State for these purposes could, by taking specified action, help in the exercise of any of their functions in relation to support for children and families, they may request the help of that other authority specifying the action in question.

Any request shall be complied with if it is compatible with that authority's own statutory or other duties and obligations and does not unduly prejudice the discharge of any of their functions. <S27(1-3)/ Courts and Legal Services Act 1990, Schedule 16(14)>

Attention is drawn to the Document "Homelessness Code of Guidance for Local Authorities" issued by the Department of The Environment, Department of Health and the Welsh Office (HMSO 1991) under Part III of the 1985 Housing Act. This indicates that the social services authority may seek the help of the housing authority in the provision of accommodation for young persons aged 16 and over who are at risk (e.g. from violence or sexual abuse *at home or the likelihood of drug or alcohol abuse or prostitution). Whilst there is no formal correlation with the definition of vulnerability under the Housing Act 1985 and "serious prejudice" or "need" under section 20 of the Children Act (see above: provision of accommodation) the two might be expected to arise in similar circumstances. The code of practice expresses the need for a corporate approach and clear departmental policies to ensure collaboration at all levels. <Paragraphs 6.14-6.16>*

The Department of Health draw attention to the Joint Circular DES 22/89 (Assessments and Statements of Special Educational Needs: Procedures within the Education, Health and Social Services) which clearly acknowledges that assessment cannot be seen as a single agency approach. The exchange of information between departments and authorities on provision and individual needs, is a key part of a unified service. A child's special educational needs are related both to abilities and disabilities and to the nature and extent of the interaction of these with his or her environment. The requirement under the Education (Special Educational Needs) Regulations 1994 for local education authorities to seek advice on individual cases from social services departments and others is also part of this process. The Department of Health suggests that services can be provided in tandem. <Vol. 6 (9.1/9.17)>

Where a child is being looked after by the local authority; and they propose to provide accommodation for him in an establishment at which education is provided, they shall, so far as is reasonably practicable, consult the appropriate local education authority before doing so.

Where such a proposal is carried out the local education authority shall be informed as soon as reasonably practicable.

When such accommodation ceases the education authority shall be informed. <S28>

RECOUPMENT OF COSTS

Where a local authority provides any service for children and their families (including day care but excluding advice, guidance and counselling) they may recover from each of the child's parents (when he is under 16); the child himself, when over 16; and where it is provided for a member of the child's family, that person, such charge for the service as they consider reasonable. <S29(1/4)>

Local authorities are given discretion to decide whether or not to impose reasonable charges for services, assistance in kind or cash.

Department of Health guidance indicates that in deciding

whether or not to impose charges it should be borne in mind that in some cases parents may accept the provision of services more readily if they are given the opportunity to contribute towards the cost. Others may be deterred from seeking support before a crisis if their liability for repayment is unclear. <Vol. 2 (3.39)>

When satisfied that a person's means are insufficient for it to be practicable for him to pay the charge, he shall not be expected to pay more than is reasonable.

No person shall be liable for any charge at any time when he is in receipt of income support or family credit.

Any charge may be recovered summarily as a civil debt.

In relation to children being looked after by local authorities schedule 2 part III gives details of liability of parents and children, how contributions will be agreed and arrangements to be made (where necessary) for contribution orders (including applications to the court and enforcement of orders). <S29(2/3/5/6)>

The procedure for recovery of contributions is simple.

A contribution notice is served upon the contributor, specifying a weekly sum not greater than that which a local authority would be prepared to pay foster parents for looking after a similar child and which it would be reasonable to expect the contributor to pay.

The notice must also state the proposed arrangements for payment.

If the contributor does not agree with the sum and the arrangements, or if they withdraw their agreement, the authority may apply to the court for a contribution order based upon revised arrangements.

Failing agreement, a contribution order may be varied or discharged on the application of the contributor or the local authority.

A charge for accommodation for a child who (immediately prior to being looked after) was ordinarily resident within the area of another local authority may be recovered from that authority.

A charge in respect of help by a local authority in relation to support for a child or person not ordinarily resident in their area may be similarly recovered. <S29(5-9)>

SECTION 26: PROCEDURES FOR REPRESENTATIONS AND COMPLAINTS

Every local authority shall establish a procedure for considering any representations (including any complaints) made to them by:

any child being looked after by them or who is not being looked after by them but is in need;

any parent of his;

any person with parental responsibility;

any local authority foster parent;

any other person the authority considers has sufficient interest in

the child's welfare to warrant his representations being considered by them;
and any person qualifying for advice and assistance about the discharge of their functions concerning support for children and their families. <S26(3)/Courts and Legal Services Act 1990, Schedule 16 (13)>

The procedure shall ensure that at least one person who is not a member or officer of the authority takes part in the consideration and in any discussions held by the authority about the action (if any) to be taken in relation to the child in the light of the consideration. <S26(4)>

Every local authority shall give such publicity to their procedure for considering representations under this section as they consider appropriate. <S26(8)>

In considering any representation under the procedures established, the local authority shall:
have due regard to the findings of those considering the representation;
and take such steps as are reasonably practicable to notify (in writing):
the person making the representation;
the child (if the authority consider that he has sufficient understanding);
and such other persons (if any) as appear to the authority to be likely to be affected;
of the authority's decision on the matter and their reasons for taking that decision and of any action which they have taken, or propose to take. <S26(7)>

The Secretary of State may make regulations requiring local authorities to monitor the arrangements that they have made with a view to ensuring that they comply with any regulations also made for the purpose of regulating the procedure to be followed. <S26(5/6)>

Department of Health guidance states that, in the case of children with disabilities, complaints and representations are likely to focus around assessment and the delivery of (or failure to deliver) certain services. Because of the multi-professional support needed by the majority of children with disabilities, the consideration of such complaints should:
consider whether there is a need to consult a range of relevant expert opinion, for example from the health authority or education department;
ensure that the child is given appropriate support;
and consider whether the complaint is really about another agency's services and should be directed to a different procedure. <Vol. 6 (14.6)>

REPRESENTATIONS PROCEDURE (CHILDREN) REGULATIONS 1991

Scope

The Department of Health in the explanatory note to the regulations state that these regulations establish a procedure for considering representations made to a local authority about the discharge of their duties relating to their support for children and families of children they are looking after, advice and assistance for children aged 18 to 21 and any person exempted (or seeking to be exempted) from limits on the number of foster children (see chapter 7).

The regulations also apply the procedure for considering representations (including complaints) made to voluntary organisations where accommodation is provided for a child and he is not looked after by a local authority.

Similarly they apply to persons carrying on registered children's homes where accommodation is provided for a child and he is not looked after by a local authority nor accommodated on behalf of a voluntary organisation. <Regulation 11>

These regulations shall not apply to representations made by a child or a person in respect of a child who is being provided with accommodation (except by a local authority or a voluntary organisation) in an independent school which is a children's home in the meaning of the Act, or a special school which is not maintained by a local education authority or otherwise out of public funds. <Regulation 11A as inserted by The Children (Homes, Arrangements for Placement, Reviews and Representations) (Miscellaneous Amendments) Regulations, 1993>>

Although the regulations do not apply to children who are accommodated in independent schools for more than 295 days a year, schools will be expected, in the special consideration they will wish to give to the arrangements for the care of these children, to have regard to the principles and practice recommended in the regulations and in volume 4 of the Children Act guidance. Local authority inspectors should look specially at the welfare provision made by schools for these children.

Schools who are however registered as children's homes should follow the guidance in respect of children accommodated. <Circular LAC(93)24>.

A complaint is a written or oral expression of dissatisfaction or disquiet which may arise as a result of an unwelcome or disputed decision, concern about the quality or appropriateness of services or about their delivery or non-delivery in respect of individual children. Representations will include statements about the availability, delivery and nature of service and will not necessarily be critical.

Department of Health guidance indicates that the Act envisages a high degree of co-operation between parents and authorities in negotiating and agreeing what form of action will best meet a child's needs and promote his welfare. It also calls for the informed participation of the child and his parents in decision making about services for the child. Sometimes, the required co-operation will not be achieved or will break down or delays will occur. The Act requires that authorities establish a procedure which provides an accessible and effective means of representation or complaint about such matters. <Vol. 3 (10.1-10.56) & Vol. 4 (5.1-5.56)>

Consideration of Representations

Action required

The local authority (voluntary organisation, or person carrying on a registered children's home) shall appoint one of their officers to assist them in the co-ordination of all aspects of their consideration of representations.

They shall take all reasonable steps to ensure that everyone involved in the handling of the representations, including "independent persons" are familiar with the procedure set out in these regulations.

(In relation to these regulations an independent person is one who:
is neither a member nor an officer of the local authority;
a person (or their spouse) who is not an officer of the voluntary organisation, nor a person (or their spouse) engaged in any way in furthering its objects;
or in relation to a registered children's home, a person who is neither involved in the management or operation of that home nor financially interested in its operation, nor the spouse of any such person.) <Regulations 2/3/11>

Preliminaries

Where a local authority (voluntary organisation, or person carrying on a registered children's home) receive representations from:
any child who is looked after by them or provided with accommodation (or in the case of a local authority, is not being looked after by them but is in need);
a parent of his or person who has parental responsibility;
any local authority foster parent;
they shall send to the complainant an explanation of the procedure set out in these regulations, and offer assistance and guidance on the use of the procedure, or give advice on where he may obtain it. <Regulation 4 1)>

Where oral representations are made, the authority (organisation or person carrying on a registered children's home) shall forthwith cause them to be recorded in writing, and sent to the complainant who shall be given the opportunity to comment on the accuracy of the record.

The authority shall consider any comments made by the complainant concerning the accuracy of the record and shall make any amendments to the record which they consider necessary.

For the purpose of these regulations the written record, as amended shall be deemed to be the representations. <Regulation 4 (2/2A/3) as amended by The Children (Representations, Placements and Reviews: Miscellaneous Amendments) Regulations 1991 (Regulation 2)>

In the case of any other person the authority (organisation or person carrying on a registered children's home) may consider has sufficient interest in the child they shall:

forthwith consider whether the person has a sufficient interest in the child's welfare to warrant his representations being considered;

if this is the case, cause the representations to be dealt with in accordance with the provisions of these regulations, and send to the complainant an explanation of the procedure set out in the regulations, and offer assistance and guidance on the use of the procedure, or give advice on where he may obtain it. (The date that the authority conclude that the person has a sufficient interest shall be treated for the purpose of these regulations as the date of the receipt of the representations.);

if they consider that he has not got a sufficient interest they shall notify him accordingly in writing, and inform him that no further action will be taken;

if they consider it appropriate to do so having regard to his understanding, they shall notify the child of the result of their consideration. <Regulation 4 (4)>

A complaints procedure should be understood and accepted by service users and their representatives, authority's staff and local authority's elected members.

Appointment and consideration of independent person

The local authority (voluntary organisation, or person carrying on a registered children's home) shall appoint an independent person to take part in the consideration of representations (except for a notification to the child). <Regulations 5/11>

The local authority (voluntary organisation, or person carrying on a registered children's home) shall consider the representations with the independent person and formulate a response within 28 days of their receipt.

The independent person shall take part in any discussions which are held by the local authority (voluntary organisation, or person carrying on a registered children's home) about the action (if any) to be taken in relation to the child in the light of the consideration of the representations. <Regulations 6/11>

Withdrawal of representations

The representations may be withdrawn at any stage by the person making them. <Regulation 7>

Notification to complainant and reference to panel

The local authority (voluntary organisation, or person carrying on a registered children's home) shall give notice in writing (may be sent by post) within 28 days of the receipt of the representations to:

the complainant;

the person on behalf of whom the representations were made (if different from the complainant) unless the local authority (voluntary organisation or person carrying on a registered children's home) consider that he is not of sufficient understanding or it would be likely to cause serious harm to his health or emotional condition;

the independent person;

any other person whom the local authority (voluntary organisation or person carrying on a registered children's home) consider has sufficient interest in the case;

of the proposed result of their consideration of the representations and the complainant's right to have the matter referred to a panel (see below). <Regulations 8 (1)/11>

If the complainant informs the authority (organisation or person carrying on a registered children's home) in writing within 28 days of the date on which the notice is given that he is dissatisfied with the proposed result and wishes the matter to be referred to a panel for consideration of the representation, a panel shall be appointed by the local authority (voluntary organisation or person carrying on a registered children's home) for that purpose.

The panel shall consist of three members, and include at least one independent person.

The meeting of the panel shall consider any oral or written submissions that the complainant or the local authority (voluntary organisation or person carrying on a registered children's home) wish to make.

If the independent person first appointed is different from the independent person on the panel, the panel shall consider any oral or written submissions which the first independent person wishes to make.

If the complainant wishes to attend the meeting of the panel he may be accompanied throughout the meeting by another person of his choice, and may nominate that other person to speak on his behalf. <Regulations 8(2-6)/11>

Department of Health guidance indicates that meetings should be informal. Consideration should be given to provision for those whose first language is not English and to mobility or communication difficulties for disabled persons. <Vol. 3 (10.46) & Vol. 4 (5.46)>

The panel shall decide upon their recommendations and record them with their reasons in writing within 24 hours of the end of the meeting. The panel shall give notice of their recommendations to:

the local authority (voluntary organisation, or person carrying on a registered children's home);

the complainant;

the independent person first appointed if different from the independent person on the panel;

and any other person whom the local authority (voluntary organisation or person carrying on a registered children's home) considers has sufficient interest in the case.

The local authority (voluntary organisation, or person carrying on a registered children's home) shall together with the independent person appointed to the panel consider what action should be taken in relation to the child in the light of the representation, and that independent person shall take in any discussions about such action. <Regulations 9/11>

Monitoring of operation of review procedure

Each local authority (voluntary organisation or person carrying on a registered children's home) shall monitor the arrangements that they have made with a view to ensuring that they comply with the regulations by keeping a record of each representation received, the outcome of each representation, and whether there was compliance with the time limits specified in the regulations.

For the purposes of such monitoring, each local authority (voluntary organisation or person carrying on a registered children's home) shall, at least once in every period of twelve months, compile a report on the operation in that period of the procedure set out in these regulations. <Regulations 10/11>

4
CARE AND SUPERVISION

> *The Department of Health indicate that civil care and supervision proceedings are founded upon a number of principles:*
>
> *Compulsory intervention in the care and upbringing of a child is possible only by court order following proceedings in which the child, his parents and others who are connected with the child will be able to participate fully;*
>
> *The proceedings should establish what action, if any, is in the child's interests and the proceedings should be as fair as possible to all concerned;*
>
> *A care or supervision order should be sought only when there appears to be no better way of safeguarding and promoting the welfare of a child suffering, or likely to suffer, significant harm;*
>
> *Voluntary arrangements through the provision of services to the child and his family should always be explored. Where a care or supervision order is the appropriate remedy because control of the child's circumstances is necessary to promote his welfare, applications in the proceedings should be part of a carefully planned process;*
>
> *There is an emphasis on representing the views, feelings and needs of the child in proceedings;*
>
> *Where a care order is in force the local authority and parents share parental responsibility for the child subject to the authority's power to limit the exercise of such responsibility by the parents in order to safeguard the child's welfare;*
>
> *The Act establishes a presumption of reasonable parental contact with children in care, subject to court orders and limited local authority action in emergencies. <Vol. 1 (3.1-3.5)>*

"Care" is used in the act in relation to a child subject to a care order, not to a child accommodated under the voluntary arrangements of section 20 (see chapter 3).

Supervision orders made in criminal proceedings are subject to the separate provisions of the 1969 Children and Young Person's Act.

ASPECTS COMMON TO BOTH CARE AND SUPERVISION ORDERS

Aspects common to the making of both care and supervision orders under the Act (except for Education Supervision Orders) apply irrespective of the route by which cases proceed.

Grounds

The grounds provide the threshold(s) that have to be proved in court before a care order can be made. If the grounds are unsubstantiated or not accepted by the court then no order can be made.

The child is suffering, or is likely to suffer significant harm; and that the harm, or likelihood of harm is attributable to :

the care given to the child, or likely to be given to him if the order were not made, not being what it would be reasonable to expect a parent to give him;
or the child being beyond parental control. <S31(2)>

Department of Health guidance indicates that the likelihood of suffering significant harm allows proceedings where, significant harm has been suffered in the past and may be likely to re-occur, or where the welfare of a child being accommodated voluntarily under section 20 (see chapter 3) would be at risk if the parents went ahead with plans to return him to an unsuitable home environment. <Vol. 1 (3.22)>

If there is a risk of significant harm the court should try to assess that risk in the light of all available evidence rather than the balance of probabilities of harm occurring. Action should be taken by the court to protect the child where that is indicated. <Newham LB v AG (19/3/93 Court of Appeal)>

HARM means ill-treatment or the impairment of health or development; *DEVELOPMENT* means physical, intellectual, emotional, social or behavioural development; *HEALTH* means physical or mental health; and *ILL-TREATMENT* includes sexual abuse and forms of ill-treatment which are not physical. <S31(9)>

Department of Health guidance highlights that these are alternatives. Only one of these conditions needs to be satisfied but proceedings may refer to all three. <Vol. 1 (3.19)>

Ill-treatment is sufficient proof of harm in itself and it is not necessary to show that impairment of health or development followed. It is additionally necessary to show that the ill-treatment is significant (i.e. noteworthy or important). The "significance" could exist in the seriousness of the harm or the implication of it. This will be a finding of fact for the court. <Vol. 1 (3.19)>

Where the question of whether harm suffered by a child is significant turns on the child's health or development, his health and development shall be compared with that which could reasonably be expected of a similar child. <S31(10)>

The Department of Health indicate that this may need to take into account environmental, social and cultural characteristics of the child. The standard would be that which it is reasonable to expect for that particular child, rather than the best which could be achieved. It will be necessary to show a deficit in the standard to be expected. Minor shortcomings (in heath care or physical or social development) should not require compulsory intervention unless cumulatively they are having, or likely to have, serious or lasting effects on the child. As with ill-treatment it will be necessary to show that the impairment in any or all the aspects of the child's health or development is significant. The court will have to establish what standard of health and development it would be reasonable to expect for a child with similar attributes, assess the shortfall against that standard and decide whether the difference represents significant harm. <Vol. 1 (3.20/21)>

Applications to the Court

Applications may be made by any local authority, the NSPCC, or person or body authorised by the Secretary of State, on their own or in any family proceedings. <S31(1/4/6/7/9)>

In commenting upon the fact that only authorised persons or authorities may bring care proceedings, the Department of Health draws attention to the special responsibilities of the local authority in establishing full agency co-operation including sharing information and participating in decision making. A multi-agency case conference should be held and parents, the child (if of sufficient age and understanding) and others with legitimate interest be involved wherever possible. No decision to initiate proceedings should be taken without clear evidence that provision of services to the child and his family (including provision of accommodation under section 20) has failed or would be likely to fail to meet the child's needs adequately and that there is no suitable person prepared to apply to take over the child under a residence order (see chapter 2). <Vol. 1 (3.10)>

The question should be asked what compulsory powers will add in safeguarding the child and is the gain sufficient to justify the use of compulsion and the trauma that may result? Options should be discussed with the parents or others having parental responsibility and with the child himself (unless very young) in language appropriate to his understanding. Care or supervision proceedings should not be presented as a threat, but the parents should always understand where, in the absence of adequate parenting and co-operation, exercise of the authority's responsibilities and duties will lead. <Vol. 1 (3.11)>

Department of Health guidance also indicates that before proceeding with an application the social services department should always seek legal advice on:

whether in the circumstances of the case the court is likely to be satisfied that criteria are met, and that an order would be better for the child than making no order at all;

the implications of any party to the proceedings opposing the application and applying for a section 8 order (see chapter 2) instead;

whether the application falls within the criteria of transfer of cases to a higher court (and whether representations about this should be made);

whether the court should be asked for an interim care or supervision order and the desired length of the initial interim order and what directions should be sought;

the matters to be provided for in the authority's advance statement of the case including copies of witnesses statements that can be available and the broad outline of the authority's plans for the child;

notification and other procedural requirements and matters likely to be considered at a directions appointment;

whether the court is likely to consider in all the circumstances of the case that a guardian ad litem (see chapter 1) does not need to be appointed;

and whether use of a residence order (see chapter 2) linked to a supervision order would be an appropriate alternative to a care order. <Vol. 1 (3.12)>

Applications by an authorised person will not be entertained if the child is already subject to:

a care order;

a supervision order;

an earlier application not yet disposed of;

or is provided with accommodation by or on behalf of the local authority (see chapter 3). <S31(7)>

It is thus inappropriate to pursue court proceedings if other means have already been found to deal with the issue or if previous proceedings have not yet been completed.

The child must be under 17 (16 if married {for example outside the UK.}). <S31(3)>

Department of Health guidance indicates that the court is likely to look particularly exactingly at a case for making an order for a young person who is approaching his seventeenth birthday (or sixteenth if married). <Vol. 1 (3.15)>

Department of Health guidance also indicates that at the first hearing when the court will usually not be able to fully decide the application, the applicant should be able to tell the court whether he is applying for an interim order.

If so, any directions which may be required are given. The applicant should be ready to tell the court at that directions appointment:

what plans the local authority have made for safeguarding and promoting the child's welfare while the interim order is in force and what type of placement is envisaged;

and what proposals the authority have for allowing the child reasonable contact with his parents and others. <Vol. 1 (3.30)>

Requirements to Be Met by the Court

The child's welfare is of paramount consideration. In particular:

- the ascertainable wishes and feelings of the child (in the light of his age and understanding);
- his physical, emotional and educational needs;
- the likely effect on him of any change in circumstances;
- his age, sex , background and any relevant characteristics;
- any harm suffered or at risk of suffering;
- how capable each parent and any other relevant person is of meeting needs;
- and whether the order is required at all. <S1>

The welfare of the child is the essential principle that the court will uphold.

In care proceedings the court has a duty to critically scrutinise the care plan to satisfy itself that it will promote the child's welfare. If not so satisfied it may refuse to make the order. <Re T (A Minor)(Care Order: Conditions)(1994) 2 FLR 423 and (1994)2 FLR 721>

Where risk is a factor in deciding between care or supervision, the court will assess future risk by careful scrutiny of past events. The local authority's duty to safeguard the child's welfare only arises when a care order is made and is not present in a supervision order. The court should look at the case as a whole to assess the risk of physical and emotional harm to the child and make a decision in the light of the seriousness of the case. <Re S(J)(a minor)(care or supervision order) 1993, 2FLR 919>

Where all parties agree to a care order, the court will still need to satisfy itself that the criteria have been met. <Re G (A Minor)(Care Proceedings) (1994)2FLR 69>

SECTION 33: CARE ORDER

Definition

A court order placing a child in the care of a designated local authority. <S31(1a/11)>

Effect

The local authority have parental responsibility but shall not:

bring up the child in any religious creed other than that in which he would have been brought up in;

or have the right to consent or refuse to consent to adoption, freeing for adoption, or appoint a guardian. <S33>

The local authority can determine the extent to which a parent may meet their parental responsibility so long as they safeguard or promote the child's welfare.

Parents may continue to do what is reasonable in all the circumstances of the case to safeguard or promote the child's welfare and what may be promoted by any other legislation or order of a court. <S33(3-6)>

Department of Health guidance indicates that the designated local authority acquire parental responsibility for the child so long as the order is in force. It also has the power to determine the extent to which parents or guardians (who do not lose their parental responsibility on the making of the order) may meet their responsibility. The authority may deal with any conflict that may arise between the authority and the parent in exercising their respective parental responsibilities. <Vol. 1 (3.67)>

Applies until 18 unless discharged earlier. <S91(12)>

The court has no continuing role in the future welfare of the child when an order is made, unless a further substantive issue comes before it. <Re B 1993 1 Family Court Reporter 363, BCC, CA>

Courts have no power to add directions to a care order. < Re CN 1992 2 Family Court Reporter 401, FD>

The role of a guardian ad litem ceases on the making of a care order. <Kent County Council v C 1993 1FLR 308, FD>

The child cannot be removed from the United Kingdom for more than one month without the written consent of every person who has parental responsibility or the leave of the court, similarly the child cannot be known by a new surname. <S33(7/8)>

Where an emergency protection order (see chapter 5) is made with respect to a child who is in care, the care order shall have effect subject to the emergency protection order. <S91(6)>

The making of a care order automatically discharges any existing: contact order; prohibited steps order; residence order; wardship; supervision order; school attendance order; or specific issue order. <S91(1-5)>

The Local Authority alone is thus responsible for the oversight of the child's welfare.

Duties to Be Observed

To safeguard and promote the child's welfare; and to make use of services available for children cared for by their own parents. <S22(3)>

So far as is reasonably practical, to ascertain the wishes and feelings of: the child; his parents; any person who has parental responsibility; and any other relevant person. <S22(4)>

In making any decision with respect to the child, (except where necessary to protect the public from serious injury) the authority shall give due consideration to:

the child's age and understanding, to such wishes and feelings of the child, his parents, any person who may have parental responsibility, and any other relevant person;

and to the child's religious persuasion, racial origin, cultural and linguistic background. <S22(5-8)>

To provide accommodation and to maintain the child by:

placing him with a family, a relative, or any other suitable person;

maintaining him in a community, voluntary or registered children's home, or in a home provided by the Secretary of State;

or by making any other arrangements that seem appropriate. <S23(1-6)>

Accommodation should, so far as reasonably practical and consistent with the child's welfare, be near to his home, and siblings be accommodated together. <S23(7)>

If the child is disabled, the accommodation should not be unsuitable to his particular needs. <S23(8)>

The Act details a number of principles of sound child care practice that social workers should follow in providing a service to the court.

If the Secretary of State considers it necessary, for the purpose of protecting members of the public from serious injury, to give directions to the local authority with respect to the exercise of their powers, they shall comply with them even if they are inconsistent with their other duties. <S22(7/8)>

Contact with Parents etc.

The local authority shall allow the child reasonable contact with: his parents or guardian; and if applicable, the persons in whose favour a residence order (see chapter 2) was made immediately before the care order. <S34(1)> This should be read in the light of the long term plans which the local authority have for the child. <Re B (Times 31/12/92)>

Where it is reasonably practicable and consistent with the child's welfare, the local authority shall endeavour to promote contact between the child and such persons and any other person connected with him. <Schedule 2 (15)>

Department of Health guidance indicates that courts will consider contact arrangements before making a care order. The underlying principle is that the authority, child and other persons should as far as possible seek reasonable arrangements before the care order is made, but should be able to seek the court's assistance if agreement cannot be reached or the authority want to deny contact to a person who is entitled to it under the Act. These provisions limit the authority's power to control and deny contact. Where contact may be detrimental to the child's welfare this should be considered at the pre-court stage. <Vol. 1 (3.76)>

Contact may be refused if necessary to safeguard or promote the child's welfare and the refusal is decided upon as a matter of urgency and does not last for more than seven days. <S34(6)>

Where contact is refused to the child's parents or guardian (and if applicable, the persons in whose favour a residence order (see chapter 2) was made immediately before the care order) any of the following information as the authority considers those persons need to know shall be notified to them as soon as the decision has been made:

the local authority's decision;
the date of decision;
the reasons for the decision;
the duration (if applicable);
and remedies available in case of dissatisfaction.

Information shall also similarly be given to:

the child, if he is of sufficient understanding;
any person who had care of the child by virtue of wardship immediately before the care order was made;
and any other person whose wishes and feelings the authority consider to be relevant. <Contact with Children Regulations 1991,

Regulation 2/ Schedule>

Department of Health guidance indicates that the principle that should be applied here is that contact should only be denied in order to safeguard or promote that child's welfare. In non-urgent cases the local authority should give notice to the person concerned. This should also be discussed with the child if he is of sufficient age and understanding. The person concerned should be made aware of the representations procedure (see chapter 3) and informed of their right to apply to the court to make an application for an order for contact. If agreement cannot be reached, particularly if the person had previously enjoyed contact with the child, the authority should apply for an order as quickly as possible or encourage the person concerned to do so, so that the impact of refusal of contact on the child can be tested in court. <Vol. 1 (3.82)>

On application to the court by the local authority, or the child, an order to allow contact between the child and any named person can be made. <S34(2)>

Subject to any court order, it is for the authority to decide what is reasonable contact under the circumstances. They should take into account that their proposals may be scrutinised or challenged.

An application to the court to allow contact may be made by the child's parents, any guardian of his, any person previously holding a residence order, or any person who has obtained the leave of the court to do so. <S34(3)>

In the case of unmarried fathers contact is at the local authority's discretion. Relevant factors here are: the child's interest; how much commitment the father has shown to the child; what attachment existed between father and child; and why the father is applying for parental responsibility. <G (a minor)(parental responsibility order) (1994)1 FLR 504.CA.>

A contact order under section 34 as discussed here is separate from private law
provisions under section 8 (see chapter 2). Section 8 orders for contact cannot be made when a child is in local authority care.

An application to the court may be made by the local authority, or the child, to make an order to refuse contact between the child and his parents, any guardian of his or any person previously holding a residence order. <S34(4)>

Any orders which place conditions on contact can be varied or discharged at any time. <S34(7/10)>
However, if an application for contact, or change in contact, has been refused, no further application for such an order may be made without

leave of court for a further six months. <S91(17)>

Department of Health guidance indicates that the court would expect to hear of a change in circumstances sufficient to justify a departure from a rule designed to discourage frequent rehearings of the same case. Local authorities are not exempt from this restriction. <Vol. 1 (3.83)>

The local authority may depart from the terms of any order for parental contact etc. with children in care, by agreement between the local authority and the person in relation to whom the order is made, where the child is of sufficient understanding and has also given his agreement. Written notification shall be sent within seven days of the agreement to:

the child's parents or guardian;
if applicable, the persons in whose favour a residence order (see chapter 2) was made immediately before the care order;
the child, if he is of sufficient understanding;
any person who had care of the child by virtue of wardship immediately before the care order was made;
and any other person whose wishes and feelings the authority consider to be relevant.

Any parts of the following information as the authority considers those persons need to know shall be included in the notification:

the local authority's decision;
the date of decision;
the reasons for the decision;
the duration (if applicable);
and remedies available in case of dissatisfaction. <Contact with Children Regulations 1991, Regulation 3/ Schedule>

These notifications also apply where a local authority varies or suspends any arrangements made (other than a court order) with a view to affording any person contact with a child in their care. <Contact with Children Regulations 1991, Regulation 4/ Schedule>

The local authority, subject to regulations made by the Secretary of State shall make arrangements to enable a child to live with a parent, a person with parental responsibility or a person with a residence order (see chapter 2). <S23(4-6)>

In respect of families, relatives and suitable persons, terms and payment can be determined by the local authority; approval as local authority foster parents will be made in the case of persons other than parents, those with parental responsibility or those who held a residence order immediately before a care order was made. <S23(4-6)>

The authority shall take reasonable practicable steps to secure that his parents, and any person with parental responsibility are kept informed of where he is accommodated and to inform such persons of the need to keep the local authority informed of their address. <Schedule 2(15)>

Where communication has been infrequent between the child and his parent or person with parental responsibility and he has not been visited by (or lived with) such person during the preceding twelve months, if it is in the child's best interests (and unless he objects and has sufficient understanding to make an informed decision) an independent visitor (see interpretation in chapter 9) shall be appointed to have the duty of visiting, advising and befriending the child. <Schedule 2(17)>

Department of Health guidance indicates that regular contact between parents, relatives and friends will usually be an important part of the child's upbringing in his new environment and is essential to successful rehabilitation. The presumption is that contact for certain named people is allowed and the court will take a pro-active role reflecting the importance of this subject. <Vol. 1 (3.77)>

The local authority may make payments to assist contact <Schedule 2(16)>; this is intended mainly to help with costs incurred in making visits. This may be given to the person making contact or to the child. The general duty of the local authority to promote contact between a child and his parents should be borne in mind when determining whether such assistance should be provided. Thus the local authority should ensure that the parents and child are aware that assistance is available when plans for contact are discussed. <Vol. 1 (3.85)>

Specific guidance is given for children with special needs. For children who have difficulty in communicating and where distances are involved, letters and telephone contact may need facilitating. Particular consideration must also be given to the needs of children for whom their first language (or that of their parents) is not English. <Vol. 1 (3.86)>

Appeals

Appeal against a Magistrates' Court making a care order/any other order, or the refusal to make an order, may be made to the High Court who shall make any orders as may be necessary to determine the appeal. <S94>

Rules of court provide that any one who had party status in the original proceedings may make an appeal.

Appeals against decisions in care proceedings heard in the County Court or High Court go to the Court of Appeal. <County Courts Act 1984 S77/ Supreme Court Act 1981 S16>

Where a court dismisses an application for a care order and at the time the child concerned is the subject of an interim care order, the court may make a care order to have effect subject to such directions (if any) as the court may see fit to include in the order.

Where a court dismisses an application for a care order, and at the time the child concerned is the subject of an interim supervision order, the court may make a supervision order to have effect subject to such directions (if any) as the court may see fit to include in the order.

Where a court grants an application to discharge a care order it may order that: the decision is not to have effect; or the care order is to continue to have effect but subject to such directions as the court sees fit to include in the order.

Such orders shall only have effect for a period as may be specified that should not exceed the appeal period. (The period between the making of the decision and the determination of the appeal; or the period during which an appeal may be made against the decision.) <S40>

Thus, in particular circumstances, the court has the additional facility of imposing requirements which must be observed by the parties concerned.

> *The Department of Health indicate that the court's basic approach will be to allow the immediate status quo to be maintained in order to provide continued protection for the child or to prevent interruption in the continuity of his care until the appeal is heard. <Vol. 1 (3.61)>*

Review

The Secretary of State may make regulations. <S26(1/2)> These may provide that:

the authority be required to seek the views of:

the child;

his parents, any person who has parental responsibility, and any other person whose views are considered to be relevant;

and consider whether an application should be made for discharge.

The child shall be informed of any steps he may take under the act. The result should to be notified to: the child; his parents; any person with parental responsibility; and any other person who ought to be notified.

The Arrangements for Placement of Children (General) Regulations and the review of Children's Cases Regulations are discussed in this book in chapter 8. They should be read in conjunction with each other and in relation to this section.

The regulations concerning placements place a duty on responsible authorities in making arrangements to place a child to draw up an individual plan for the child.

The regulations concerning reviews require that the plan is reviewed (and amended as necessary) on a regular basis.

Application for Discharge

Applications may be made by any person with parental responsibility, the child, or the local authority.

A supervision order can be substituted or any other order made.

The court may make directions if the care order is to be continued. <S39(1/4)/S40(3)>

The court is required under section 1(5) to ensure the minimum amount of intervention in the lives of children and parents.

Department of Health guidance indicates that the principles contained in the checklist concerning the welfare of children in section 1(3) (see the earlier discussion) will be applied again by the court. The court's concern will focus upon on what, if any, alternative provisions can be made to safeguard and promote the welfare of the child. <Vol. 1 (3.55)>

If an application for discharge (or for the substitution of a supervision order) has been refused, no further application may be made without leave of the court for a further six months. <S91(15)>

The making of a residence order (see chapter 2) has the function of discharging the care order. <S91(1)>

As a residence order determines where the child is to live, a care order will no longer be relevant.

This provides the means for persons not having parental responsibility (e.g. local authority foster parents, an unmarried father, a person with whom the child has lived with for three years or a person who has the local authority's consent) to apply for a residence order and thus discharge the care order.

A supervision order can also be made in these circumstances. The court would wish to have regard to the local authority's plans for the child's future and the wishes and feelings of the child's parents.

When there has been an appeal and where a court agrees to discharge a care order, it may order that pending the appeal the decision is not to have effect, or that the order should remain in force subject to directions it makes.

The order lasts only until the appeal is determined, or where no appeal is made, the period during which it could be made expires.

If the court makes a residence order (see chapter 2) it can postpone the coming into effect of the order or impose temporary requirements pending an appeal. <S40(3-6)/S11(7)>

Placement with Parents and Others

The authority may only allow the child to live with a parent, a person who has parental responsibility, or a person who has held a residence order, in accordance with regulations made by the Secretary of State. <S23(5)>

The Placement of Children with Parents etc. Regulations 1991

Scope

The regulations apply to every child who is in the care of a local authority and who is or is proposed to be placed with a parent, a person with parental responsibility or a person holding a residence order that was in force immediately before a care order was made.

They do not apply to a placement made under the Adoption Act of 1976 or if they are incompatible with a court order made in respect of parental contact.

The temporary removal of a child (pending a placement decision) from the person with whom he is already living and with whom he may be placed is not required by the regulations. <Regulation 1/2>

Department of Health guidance indicates that the regulations seek to provide a framework for good practice. Local authorities should consider carefully whether a placement under these regulations is the only means to achieve placing a child with a parent or person who has had parental responsibility. It may be that an arrangement can be negotiated between the parent and the local authority (involving the child and other significant individuals) that would enable an application to discharge the care order. If such an agreement can be reached and the court agrees to the local authority's application, then these regulations will not apply. <Vol. 3 (5.2)>

The regulations reflect the position that after a care order is granted parents do not lose parental responsibility although a local authority acquires it and the power to limit the parents' exercise of their responsibility. <Vol. 3 (5.4)>

The regulations must be complied with before a placement is made (except in some cases where the child is aged over 16, or where intermediate placements are involved). <Vol. 3 (5.10)>

Children on remand and accommodated by a local authority (see chapter 3) are not in the care of the local authority and are therefore not governed by these regulations.

Placements under the regulations include stays of 24 hours or more for the purpose of contact.

Placement with relatives or friends will be subject to The Foster Placement (Children) Regulations 1991 (see chapter 7).

The regulations also apply to a series of short term placements with the same person where all the placements occur within a period which does not exceed one year, no placement is of more than four weeks duration and the total duration of the placements does not exceed 90 days.

Any such series of short term placements may be treated as a single placement for the purpose of the regulations. <Regulation 13>

Enquiries and Assessments

Before a decision to place a child under 16 is made by the director of social services or nominated person (a "placement decision") under regulation 5 (see below) a local authority shall make all necessary enquiries in respect of:

the health of the child;

the suitability of the person with whom it is proposed the child should be placed;

the suitability of the accommodation, including the sleeping arrangements;

the educational and social needs of the child;

and the suitability of all other members of the household aged 16 and over, in which it is proposed a child will live.

In considering the suitability of all persons in the household, account will be taken of the following:

age;

health;

personality;

marital status and particulars of any previous marriage;

the result of any application to have a child placed with him or adopt a child and application for registration as a child minder and details of prohibition on acting as a child minder, providing day care, or caring for foster children privately or children in a voluntary or registered children's home;

past and present employment and leisure activities and interests;

any criminal convictions (subject to the provisions of the Rehabilitation of Offenders Act 1974).

In respect of the person with whom the child is to be placed account will be taken of the following:

previous experience of looking after and capacity to look after children and capacity to care for the child;

details of children in his household, whether living there or not;

religious persuasion and degree of observance, racial origin and cultural and linguistic background;

details of the living standards and particulars of accommodation of his household. <Regulation 3/ Schedule 1>

Duties of Local Authorities

A local authority shall satisfy themselves that the placement of a child is the most suitable way of performing their general duty to safeguard and promote his welfare and to make use of services available, and that the placement is the most suitable having regard to all the circumstances. <Regulation 4>

A placement shall only be made after a "placement decision" has been made on behalf of the local authority by the director of social services or an officer nominated in writing for that purpose by the director. <Regulation 5>

Intermediate Placements

An intermediate placement is possible where the local authority considers it necessary and in accordance with their general duty to safeguard and promote the child's welfare and to make use of services available. In such a case they shall take steps to ensure that the provisions of these regulations that would otherwise have to be complied with before the placement decision is made are complied with as soon as practicable thereafter.

Before an intermediate placement is made a local authority shall arrange to interview the person whom the child is to be placed with a view to obtaining as much of the information required under regulation 3 (see above) as can be readily ascertained.

This regulation does not apply to a child who is to be placed aged 16 or over. <Regulation 6>

The Department of Health give an example of an intermediate placement where the unforeseen breakdown of a foster placement requiring the child's immediate removal to a parent is the least traumatic move for the child. <Vol. 3 (5.11)>

Provision of Agreements

Following a placement decision for a child under 16, the local authority shall seek to reach agreement (so far as practicable) with the person with whom the child is to be placed concerning:

the authority's plans and the objectives of the placement;

the arrangements for support of the placement;

arrangements for visiting in connection with supervision, and the frequency of visits and reviews;

arrangement for contact if any (including prohibition of contact) by parents and others;

the duty of the local authority to remove the child under certain circumstances;

the need to notify the local authority of relevant changes in circumstances of the person with whom the child is placed, including intention to change address, changes in the household and any serious occurrence involving the child such as injury or death;

the provision of a statement concerning the health of the child, the need for health care and surveillance, and the child's educational needs and the local authority's arrangements to provide for all such needs;

any arrangements for delegation of responsibility for consent to medical examination or treatment;
the need to ensure that any information relating to any child or his family or other person given in confidence to the person with whom the child is placed in connection with the placement is kept confidential and that such information is not disclosed to any person without the consent of the local authority;
the circumstances in which it is necessary to obtain in advance the approval of the local authority for the child living, even temporarily, in a household other than the household of the person with whom the child has been placed;
the arrangements for requesting a change in the agreement.

For a child under age 16, the placement shall not be put into effect unless and until such an agreement has been reached and recorded in writing and a copy of it has been given or sent to that person. <Regulation 7>

Department of Health guidance indicates that the placement agreement will be based upon the plan required by the Arrangements for Placement of Children (General) Regulations 1991 (see chapter 8). The plan and the agreement should be reviewed and amended as necessary. <Vol. 3 (5.41)>

The placement agreement should indicate the extent of the carer's delegated responsibility. It should define clearly to what degree the parent should exercise his parental responsibility without reference back to the local authority. <Vol. 3 (5.16)>

Notification of Placements

The local authority (in respect of a child under 16) shall (so far as practicable and subject to any enquiries and assessment that they undertake, and their duty to safeguard and promote the child's welfare) notify the placement decision, and details of where the child is to be placed, in writing to: all the persons (the child, his parents, persons with parental responsibility and significant others) whose wishes and feelings have been sought in relation to the decision to place the child.

Notice is not required in the case of a person whose whereabouts are unknown, or cannot be readily ascertained. <Regulation 8 (1/3)>

Where the child is placed with a person other than a parent the notice shall contain the name and address of the person with whom the child is placed; the arrangements for contact; and any other particulars relating to the care and welfare of the child which appears ought to be supplied. <Regulation 8 (2)>

Persons notified shall include the district health authority, the local education authority, the child's registered medical practitioner, the local authority in whose area the child is to be placed, and any person who has been caring for the child immediately before the placement. Where there was a residence order (see chapter 2) in force before the care order was made, the person concerned shall also be notified. <Regulation 8 (4)>

Support and Supervision of Placements

A local authority shall satisfy themselves that the welfare of each child under 16 who has been placed continues to be appropriately provided for by his placement. The local authority shall:

give such advice and assistance as appears necessary to the person with whom the child is placed as appears to the local authority to be necessary;

and make arrangements for a person authorised by the local authority to visit the child from time to time as necessary but in any event:

within one week of the beginning of the placement;

at intervals of not more than six weeks during the first year of the placement;

thereafter at intervals of not more than three months and also whenever reasonably requested by the child or person with whom the child is placed.

(In the case of a series of short term placements visiting will be as above during the first of the series of placements, and on one other occasion while the child is in fact placed during the series.)

The person authorised to make the arrangements shall, so far as practicable, on each visit see the child alone.

A written report shall be prepared of each visit. <Regulations 9/13(3)>

Department of Health guidance indicates that the supervisor of the placement should have knowledge of the child before placement, be involved in the plan for the placement, and the child should know the particular worker. <Vol. 3 (5.51)>

Guidance continues: the child should be seen alone on visits whenever practicable and if necessary a further visit arranged at short notice. It is important for the supervisor to study the interaction between the child, carer and family and clear messages of expectations and feedback given. The aim should be to enhance the carer's ability to cope, and to build upon strengths within the family. The supervisor will need to be aware how accommodation is utilised and will need to see the child's room (while being mindful of the issues of privacy if it is shared). <Vol. 3 (5.52-5.54)>

Placement Outside England and Wales

In making any such arrangements the local authority shall, so far as is reasonably practicable, ensure that these regulations are complied with. <Regulation 10>

Under schedule 2 (19) of the Act no placement of a child in care outside England and Wales is permitted without the approval of the court. This is because such a placement may be regarded as an emigration, or may become an emigration.

In cases where placement of the child has been made in Northern Ireland Guernsey and the Isle of Man, The Children (Prescribed Orders) Regulations 1991, provide for equivalent orders to be available and to have effect there (and in certain circumstances to cease to have effect in England and Wales). There is currently no provision for the transfer of care orders from the mainland to Jersey.

Termination of Placements

A local authority shall terminate a placement made by them (and shall remove the child) if it no longer promotes or safeguards the welfare of the child or would prejudice his safety.

Where a child has been placed in the area of another local authority and it appears to that authority that it would be detrimental to the welfare of the child if continued to be so placed, the area authority may remove the child forthwith from the person with whom he is placed. They shall then notify the other authority forthwith of that fact and make other arrangements for the care of the child as soon as is practicable. <Regulation 11>

A local authority shall, so far as is reasonably practicable (if the child is under 16) give notice in writing of any decision to terminate the placement (before the termination takes place) to:

the child (having regard to his age and understanding);
the other persons (his parents, persons with parental responsibility and significant others) whose wishes and feelings have been sought in relation to the decision;
the person with whom the child is placed;
the district health authority;
the local education authority;
the child's registered medical practitioner;
the local authority in whose area the child is to be placed;
any person who has been caring for the child immediately before the placement;
where there was a residence order in force before the care order was made (see chapter 2), the person concerned.

Notice shall be given to all these person (other than the child and the person with whom the child was placed) in writing of the termination of the placement. <Regulation 12>

Department of Health guidance indicates that it is essential that *social workers should recognise when the placement is no longer in the best interests of the child. In most cases removal should be planned for so as to minimise stress and counteract a sense of failure in the carer of the child. <Vol. 3 (5.57-5.60)>*

Preparation for After Care

It is the duty of the local authority to advise, assist and befriend any child being looked after by the authority, with a view to promoting his welfare when he ceases to be looked after by them. <S24(1)>

Guidance from the Department of Health indicates that a continuing care plan should be formulated with the young person, parents, agencies involved and other persons. The plan should specify the type of help available and contain contingency arrangements in the event of a breakdown of arrangements. <Vol. 3 (9.18) & Vol. 4 (7.18)>

After Care

The local authority shall advise and befriend those formerly in their care (aged 16 to under 21) and may also give assistance in kind (or in exceptional circumstances cash). <S24(2-9)>

The local authority shall make payments in respect of travelling, subsistence or other visiting expenses to parents, those holding parental responsibility and to any relative, friend or other person connected with him, when circumstances (such as undue financial hardship) warrant the making of payments. <(Schedule 2(16)>

This may include living expenses near where he is employed, or receiving education or training, or a grant to meet education or training expenses. <S24(2-9)>

If the child proposes to live or is living in the area of another local authority they shall inform that local authority. <S24(11)>

SECTION 35: SUPERVISION ORDERS

Definition

Places the child under the supervision of a designated local authority or of a probation officer. <S31(1/11)>

Effect

May require the supervised child to comply with any directions decided and given from time to time by the supervisor, specifically:

to live at a specified place or places;

to present himself to a specified person(s) at a specified place(s) and on specified day(s);

to participate in specified activities on specified day(s). <Schedule 3 (2)>

Lasts for one year unless application is made to the court to extend the order.

The court may extend for such period as it may specify but not more than three years.

Any order in force when the child reaches the age of 18 will automatically expire. <S39(2)/ S91(13)/ Schedule 3 (6)>

May require the supervised child and/or the responsible person (ie. any person who has parental responsibility for the child and any other person with whom the child is living) to allow the supervisor to visit him at his home address. <Schedule 3 (8)>

May require the supervised child to keep the supervisor informed of any change in this address. <Schedule 3 (8)>

Conditions attached to a supervision order must relate to a child or person with whom a child lives <Croydon London Borough Council v. A (No.3) 1992 2FLR 350, FD.>

If, on application to the court, it appears that a person attempting to apply these powers has been prevented from doing so by being refused entry to the premises concerned, or access to the child concerned; or that they are likely to be prevented from exercising such powers, a warrant authorising any constable to assist that person, using reasonable force if necessary, may be issued.

The court may direct that the constable be accompanied by a registered medical practitioner, registered nurse or registered health visitor if the person so chooses. <S102>

Psychiatric and Medical Examinations and Treatment

These are dealt with separately.

The order may require the supervised child to submit to medical or psychiatric examination (as directed by the court or by the supervisor).

The court will need to be satisfied that the child has sufficient understanding to make an informed decision, has consented and satisfactory arrangements are made for the examination.

The name of the registered medical practitioner or the place for attendance as a non-resident patient may be specified by the court.

Residence as a patient will only be permitted by the court on the required evidence of a registered medical practitioner. <Schedule 3 (4)>

The court may specify resident or non-resident treatment for a mental disorder at a specified place or under a specified registered medical practitioner, on the evidence of a medical practitioner approved under the 1983 Mental Health Act. The condition should require and be susceptible to treatment and not warrant detention under a Hospital Order.

Similarly, the court may specify a period of resident or non-resident treatment for a specific physical condition at a specified place or under a specified registered medical practitioner. The evidence of a registered medical practitioner is required and the condition should require and be susceptible to treatment.

Where it appears to a medical practitioner under whose direction treatment is being given that a variation in requirements needs to be made, he will make a report in writing to the supervisor who shall refer it to the court who may make an order cancelling or varying the requirement. <Schedule 3 (5)>

Duties to be Observed

The supervisor shall advise, assist and befriend the child; take such steps as are reasonably necessary to give effect to the order; and consider (if appropriate) application for variation or discharge of the order. <S35(1)>

Contact with Parents etc.

A supervision order may require any person who has parental responsibility or any other person with whom the child is living, to keep the supervisor informed of his address, if it differs from the child's. <Schedule 3(1/3)>

Applications for Variation or Discharge

May be made by any person with parental responsibility the child or the supervisor. <S39(2)>

It shall be the duty of the supervisor to consider whether or not to apply to court for variation or discharge where the order is not wholly complied with, or where the order may no longer be necessary. <S35(2)>

Where a previous application has been made for discharge no further application may be made without the leave of the court, unless the period between the disposal of the previous application and the making of a further application exceeds six months. <S91(15)>

SECTION 38: INTERIM ORDERS

Circumstances

If in any proceedings relating to an application for a care order or supervision order and the proceedings are adjourned, an interim care order or an interim supervision order may be made by the court.

Similarly an interim order can be made in any family proceedings in which a question arises in relation to the welfare of the child (and it appears to the court that it may be appropriate for a care or supervision order to be made) and a direction is made for the appropriate authority to undertake an investigation of the child's circumstances. <S38(1)/ S37(1)>

There must be reasonable grounds for believing that the circumstances correspond with the grounds for a care or supervision order. <S38(2)/ S31(2)>

Department of Health guidance indicates that this test is not the same as the proof required for a full order (that the child is suffering or likely to suffer significant harm). Court findings of fact leading to the making of interim orders are not binding upon the court at the final hearing, and should not be regarded as prejudicial to any of the parties to the final hearing. In making a decision, the court will need to have regard to the welfare of the child <S1(1-3)> and to the presumption against making an order <S1(5)>. <Vol. 1 (3.36/7)>.

Where in proceedings for a care order the court makes a residence order (see chapter 2) it shall also make a supervision order with respect to the child unless satisfied that his welfare will be satisfactorily safeguarded without an interim order being made. <S38(3)>

The Department of Health state that although a residence order (linked to an interim supervision order) is an alternative to a care order, the residence order cannot be made out to the local authority. The objectives are to enable the child to be suitably protected while proceedings are progressing and to see that interim measures operate only so long as necessary. Questions of contact can be settled by contact orders and other matters (e.g. education) can be settled by specific issues orders and prohibited steps orders. The authority should ensure that support services are provided as necessary. <Vol. 1 (2.62/3.35/3.41/3.42)>

An interim care order is appropriate if specific additional evidence is awaited. Use is inappropriate to generally review the progress of a child in rehabilitation. <Re CN 1992 2 Family Court Reporter 401, FD/ Re A 1993 1 Family Court Reporter 164, FD>

Duration and Effect

As determined by the court and stated on the order: the order shall cease to have effect after eight weeks, unless it is the second or subsequent such order in the same proceedings when four weeks applies (unless the overall period of all the interim orders in respect of the proceedings constitutes up to no more than eight weeks).

In the case of an application for a care or supervision order, the disposal of the application; or in the case of a direction (made by the court) concerning the finding of information, disposal by the local authority; will result in the interim order ceasing to have effect. <S38(4/5)>

In determining the period for which the order is to be in force, the court shall consider whether any party who was, or might have been, opposed to the making of the order was in a position to argue his case against the order in full. <S38(10)>

The Department of Health indicate that interim orders have the same effect and give the same responsibilities to local authorities as full orders except in duration and directions given with regard to medical or psychiatric examinations or other assessments of the child. These orders represent substantial interventions in the care and upbringing of children and should not be regarded as routine parts of an application for a care order. The interim supervision order should enable effective means of achieving control short of acquisition of parental responsibility and the power to remove the child from the home. <Vol. 1 (3.38)>

Medical or Psychiatric Examinations and Other Assessments

The court may give such directions (if any) as it considers appropriate when making an interim order; but if the child is of sufficient understanding to make an informed decision he may refuse to submit to the examination or other assessment.

A direction may state there is to be no such examination or assessment, or none unless the court directs otherwise. A direction may be given at any time an order is made or whilst an order is in force; and varied at any time on application by a person prescribed in rules of court.

Provisions relating to supervision orders do not apply in interim supervision orders. <S38(6-9)>

The Department of Health indicate that these powers permit courts to avoid repeated examination of children for evidential purposes. Local inter-agency arrangements should establish a pool of professionally trained experts for multi-disciplinary assessments. Considerations of gender, ethnic and cultural identity of the child will play a part in determining the programme of assessment and the manner in which it is undertaken. <Vol. 1 (3.48)>

Relationship of Interim Orders to Appeals

Where a court dismisses an application for a care order and at the time the child concerned is the subject of an interim care order, the court may make a care order to have effect subject to such directions (if any) as the court may see fit to include in the order.

Where a court dismisses an application for a care order, or an application for a supervision order and at the time the child concerned is the subject of an interim supervision order, the court may make a supervision order to have effect subject to such directions (if any) as the court may see fit to include in the order.

Such orders shall only have effect for a period as may be specified that should not exceed the appeal period. (The period between the making of the decision and the determination of the appeal; or the period during which an appeal may be made against the decision.) <S40(1/2/4-6)>

SECTION 36: EDUCATION SUPERVISION ORDERS

Definition

Places the child under the supervision of a designated local education authority. <S36(1/2)>

> *The Department of Health indicate that the intention is to ensure that a child who is subject to the order receives efficient full-time education suited to his or her age, ability, aptitude and any special educational needs, and that sufficient support, advice and guidance are provided to the parents and the child. <Vol. 7 (3.2)>*

Effect

For the duration of an Education Supervision Order the legal duties placed upon parents under the Education Act 1944 (to secure the education of children and to secure regular attendance of registered pupils) are superseded by their duty to comply with any directions in force under the order.

Similarly provisions enabling children to be educated in accordance with their parent's wishes do not apply whilst an Education Supervision Order remains in force.

Any school attendance order also ceases to have effect. <Schedule 3 (13)>

In this provision the word "Parent" is defined so as to include any person who is not a parent of a child but has parental responsibility for him or has the care of him. <Schedule 3 (21)/ Schedule 13 (10)/ Education Act 1944 S114 (1D)>

May require the parent to keep the supervisor informed of any change in the child's address (if it is known to him); and if he is living with the child, allow the supervisor reasonable contact with the child. <Schedule 3 (16)>

Lasts for one year unless the supervisor applies to the court to extend or further extend the order.

No one extension may be for a period of more than three years. <Schedule 3 (15)>

An order ceases to have effect when the child becomes above school leaving age, or a care order is made. <Schedule 3 (15)>

An education supervision order may not be made if the child is already subject to a care order. <S36(6)>

Applications

To the court may be made by the local education authority only. <S36(1)>

Department of Health guidelines highlight other options available under the 1944 Education Act (whereby the parents of a child may be prosecuted) and the need for attempts to resolve a problem of poor attendance without the use of legal sanctions. <Vol. 7 (3.18/3.19)>

The Department of Health state that an order should be sought in full consultation with both the child and the family. <Vol. 7 (3.16)>
The guidelines also state that a report should be submitted to the court including:
the child's record of attendance;
relevant details of the child's circumstances;
an assessment of the causes of poor attendance;
the reasons why an order is being requested including an assessment of any likely educational disadvantage to the child should an order not be made;
and an outline of the intended intervention.
The report should detail a programme of intended work, indicating the role of the child, the parents and the school. <Vol. 7 (3.15)>

Where there are particular factors relating to the child's religious persuasion, racial origin, or cultural and linguistic background that may have a bearing on the application, or the manner in which the order is conducted, these should be drawn to the attention of the court. <Vol. 7 (3.17)>

Grounds

The child is of compulsory school age and is not being properly educated (i.e. receiving efficient full time education suitable to his age, ability and aptitude and any special educational needs he may have). <S36(3/4)>

Where a child is the subject of a school attendance order which has not been complied with, or is not attending regularly at a school he is a registered pupil at, then, unless it is proved that he is being properly educated it shall be assumed that he is not. <S36(5)>

Conditions to Be Met

Before making the application the Local Education Authority shall consult with the appropriate local authority. <S36(8/9), as amended by The Education Act 1993 (Schedule 19)>

The child's welfare is of paramount consideration. In particular:
 the ascertainable wishes and feelings of the child (in the light of his age and understanding);
 his physical, emotional and educational needs;
 the likely effect of any change in circumstances;
 age, sex, background and any relevant characteristics;
 any harm suffered or at risk of suffering;
 how capable each parent and any other relevant person is of meeting needs;
 and whether the order is required at all. <S1>

Duties to Be Observed

The supervisor shall advise, assist and befriend and give directions to: the supervised child, and his parents, to secure that he is properly educated. <Schedule 3(12)>

Department of Health guidance indicates that a supervising officer should ideally be already known to the child and the family .<Vol. 7 (3.13)>

The religious, cultural, racial and linguistic background of the child's family should influence the choice of supervising officer. <Vol. 7 (3.14)>

Guidelines indicate that they should be sensitive to the educational needs of the child including any special educational needs that may be required under the 1993 Education Act. <Vol. 7 (3.20-3.29)>

Before giving any directions, the supervisor shall ascertain the wishes and feelings of: the child; and his parents; (in particular their wishes with regard to the school the child should attend).

When giving the terms of any directions the supervisor shall give due consideration to the child's age and understanding. <Schedule 3(12)>

Department of Health guidance indicates that directions need to be made with care and only where necessary. They should be explained to the parent or child and confirmed in writing.

They may include, for example, requirements for parents to *attend meetings at the school to discuss the child's progress, or cover assessment by an educational psychologist. <Vol. 7 (3.31-3.35)>*

A parent shall be guilty of an offence if they persistently fail to comply with a direction given under an education supervision order.

It shall be a defence in such proceedings if they took all reasonable steps to ensure that the direction was complied with; or the direction was unreasonable; or in their compliance with requirements, directions appear to be unreasonable. <Schedule 3 (18)>

Where the child appears to persistently fail to comply with any direction given under the order, the Local Education Authority will notify the appropriate Social Services Department who shall investigate the circumstances of the child. <Schedule 3 (19)>

Applications for Variation or Discharge

Applications for discharge may be made by:

the child;

a parent;

or the local education authority.

The court may direct the local authority to investigate the circumstances of the child.

Application for extension can be made by the local education authority three months before the expiry date.

Extensions can be made on more than one occasion. <Schedule 3 (15/17)>

Where a previous application has been made for discharge no further application may be made without the leave of the court, unless the period between the disposal of the previous application and the making of a further application exceeds six months. <S91(15)>

5
CHILD PROTECTION

The measures for child protection are short-term and time limited. They may, or may not lead to further action for care or supervision (see chapter 4) or they may be a prelude to services being provided for children and their families (see chapter 3).

Department of Health guidance in "Working Together" highlights the close working relationship required between social services departments, the police service, medical practitioners, community health workers, schools, voluntary agencies and others (and their respective roles). Area Child Protection Committees provide a recognised joint forum for developing, monitoring and reviewing child protection policies. Such committees also provide a mechanism whereby procedures are laid down to share information between agencies whenever one individual agency becomes concerned that a child may be at risk. Co-operation between agencies will be determined by shared agreement on the handling of individual cases.

The child protection conference is an essential stage in joint work. It is the prime forum for professionals and the family to share information and concerns, analyse and weigh up the level of risks and make recommendations for action. An initial conference should only be called after an investigation under section 47. Guidance is given on the function, organisation, and process of these conferences, the designation of a keyworker and mechanisms for case reviews.<Working Together (5.15.1-4/6.1-6.34/8.1-8.21)>

Additional guidance on approach to assessment can be found in the Department of Health's Publication "Protecting Children - A Guide for Social Workers Undertaking a Comprehensive Assessment" (HMSO, 1989).

Details of requirements for child protection registers are contained in "Working Together" (6.36-6.54).

The Emergency Protection Order has strict grounds, clearly defined responsibilities for the person holding the order and specified time limits. The Child Assessment Order applies where significant harm is suspected and attempts to have the child examined or assessed by voluntary means have failed. Police powers to detain a child for the purposes of protection are defined, as are powers of entry and search.

Except when a child is in acute physical danger it is essential that the timing of the removal of children from their home is agreed following consultation with all appropriate professionals. <Working Together (3.8)>

The Department of Health guidance states that proceedings

under this part of the Act are not classified as family proceedings. This means that the court must either make or refuse to make the order applied for and cannot make any other kind of order. (Except that the court may make an emergency protection order instead of a child assessment order.)

The child's welfare is paramount. Although the court is not required in these proceedings to consider the checklist of relevant factors concerning the welfare of the child (see chapter 1) as information is unlikely to be available, such consideration should be given as far as is reasonably practicable. <Vol. 1 (4.1- 4.5)>

It is essential when considering court proceedings to understand the difference between criminal prosecutions by the police (where the burden of proof rests with the prosecution, i.e. the defendant does not have to prove his innocence) and proceedings for the protection of children (where there is a lesser standard of proof based upon the balance of probabilities). In child protection the consideration is what is in the interests of the child.

SECTION 43: CHILD ASSESSMENT ORDER

Definition

An order of up to seven days for the assessment of the child. <S43(2/5)>

Department of Health guidance indicates that this order is not for emergencies. It deals with the narrow issue of enabling an examination or assessment of the child in circumstances of non co-operation by the parents and lack of evidence of the need for a different order or action. Significant harm may be suspected but the child is not thought to be at immediate risk. <Vol. 1 (4.4 / 4.6)>

Guidance continues by stating that the purpose of the order is to ascertain the child's health or development or the way in which he has been treated so as to decide what further action is required. <Vol. 1 (4.6)>

The order should be used sparingly. This is a lesser order in terms of the scale of intervention, yet could lead to further intervention. It should be contemplated only when there is reason for serious concern for the child. <Vol. 1 (4.23)>

Effect

Directs any person to produce the child and to comply with such directions relating to the assessment of the child as may be specified. <S43(6/7)>

Department of Health guidance indicates that the order will usually be most appropriate where the harm to the child is long *term and cumulative rather than sudden and severe. It is used where an assessment is needed to help establish basic facts about the child's condition. <Vol. 1 (4.9)>*

The applicant should know enough about the circumstances to satisfy himself that the child is not in immediate danger. If possible he should have been seen recently by someone competent to judge this. Persistent refusal to allow a child (about whom there is serious concern) to be seen will usually justify an application for an emergency protection order. <Vol. 1 (4.19)>

Guidance continues: assessments should be planned so that the work (including multi- disciplinary work) can be achieved within the limitations of timescale. The best way to involve the parents and minimise trauma to the child should be considered. <Vol. 1 (4.10/4.11)>

The Department of Health also indicate that a deliberate refusal to produce the child (without legitimate reason) would add to the concern for the child's welfare and an emergency protection order may be applied for. If the developing situation is urgent and an immediate application cannot be made for an emergency protection order, it may be possible and appropriate for the police to use their powers of protection under section 46. <Vol. 1 (4.19)>

Only authorises assessment in accordance with the terms of the order.

Regardless of these terms, if the child is of sufficient understanding to make an informed decision he may refuse to submit to a medical or psychiatric examination or other assessment. <S43(7/8)>

Department of Health guidance indicates that the order does not transfer parental responsibility . <Vol. 1 (4.13)>

Only authorises the child to be kept away from home if directions are specified. <S43(9)>

Department of Health guidance indicates that this is intended for use only in exceptional circumstances, and if used (e.g. for special needs dictating 24 hour assessment) the number of overnight stays be kept as low as possible.

Guidance continues: the assessment should be conducted with as little trauma for the child as possible. The court must in these circumstances give directions about contact and may consider that person(s) connected with the child should be allowed to stay with the child overnight. The applicant should consider offering this facility.

If the child is kept away from home for the purposes of assessment and the situation revealed is such that the child cannot be allowed to return home then an emergency protection order should be sought. <Vol. 1 (4.15-4.17)>

Applications to the Court

May be made by any local authority, the NSPCC or authorised person. <S43(13)/S31(9)>

It should be noted that there is no provision for an ex-parte hearing.

> *Department of Health guidance indicates that the applicant must consider that a decisive step is required to obtain an assessment to show whether their concern is well founded or further action is not required and informal arrangements have failed.*
>
> *Guidance continues: applications by the local authority should always be preceded by an investigation under section 47. The court will expect to be given details of the investigation including the applicant's attempts to satisfy themselves as to the welfare of the child. <Vol. 1 (4.11)>*
>
> *Since applications involve non-emergency situations, there is no justification for superficial investigations under section 47. <Working Together (5.14.5)>*

Grounds

The court must be satisfied that there is reasonable cause to suspect that:

the child is suffering or is likely to suffer significant harm;
an assessment of the child's health or development, or of the way in which he has been treated, is required to enable the applicant to determine whether or not the child is suffering, or is likely to suffer, significant harm;
and it is unlikely that such an assessment will be made, or be satisfactory, in the absence of an order under this section. <S43(1)>

Conditions to Be Met

The child's welfare shall be the court's paramount consideration. <S1>

The court must be satisfied that making the order would be better for the child than making no order at all.

Duties to Be Observed

The applicant shall take such steps as are reasonably practical to give notice before the hearing to:

the child's parents;
any person with parental responsibility;
any other person caring for the child;
any person with a contact order (see chapter 2);
and the child. <S43(11)>

> *Guidance from the Department of Health indicates that these requirements indicate the non-emergency nature of the order. The*

application should always be considered on notice at a full hearing in which the parties are able to participate. <Vol. 1 (4.18)>

Other Powers of the Court

May treat as an application for an Emergency Protection Order; a Child Assessment Order will not be made if the court is satisfied that there are grounds for making an Emergency Protection Order and such an order ought to be made. <S43(3/4)>

Contact with Parents etc.

Where the child is to be kept away from home, the court will give directions. <S43(10)>

Variation or Discharge

Rules of court may make provision for applications by:
- the child's parents;
- any person with parental responsibility;
- any other person caring for the child;
- any person with a contact order (see chapter 2);
- the child;
- and other persons. <S43(12)>

Unless the court is satisfied that it is not necessary the court will appoint a guardian ad litem under section 41 (see chapter 1).

Where a previous application has been made for discharge no further application may be made without the leave of the court, unless the period between the disposal of the previous application and the making of a further application exceeds six months. <S91(15)>

SECTION 44: EMERGENCY PROTECTION ORDER

Definition

An emergency order of up to eight days for the protection of the child. <S45(1)>

Effect

Directs any person to produce the child; authorises removal and retention in accommodation, prevents removal from hospital (or other place); and gives the applicant parental responsibility. <S44(4)>

An order provides immediate short-term protection for the child in a genuine emergency.

Department of Health guidance indicates that it is not to be used as a routine response to allegations of child abuse or as a first step to initiating care proceedings. <Vol. 1 (4.30)>

In relation to a child in police protection <S46(7)> the eight days begin with the first day of police protection. <S45(3)>

A person who intentionally obstructs any person exercising powers of removal or prevention of removal shall be guilty of an offence. <S44(15)>

Where the last day of the eight day period falls upon a Sunday or bank holiday the court may specify a period that ends at noon on the first later day which is not a holiday. <S45(2)>

Where an emergency protection order is made with respect to a child who is in care, the care order (see chapter 4) shall have effect subject to the emergency protection order. <S91(6)>

Department of Health guidance indicates that where the need for emergency action centres on alleged abuse of the child the local authority will want to explore the possibility of providing services to and/or accommodation for the alleged abuser as an alternative to the removal of the child. Schedule 2(5) gives authorities the discretion to provide assistance with finding alternative housing or cash assistance to the person who leaves the family home. The non-abusing parent may agree to apply to the county court for a short term ouster injunction under the Domestic Violence and Matrimonial Proceedings Act 1976 (S1) or for an exclusion order under the Domestic Proceedings and Magistrates' Court Act 1978 (S16) forcing the alleged abuser out of the home. <Vol. 1 (4.31)>

The needs of children are only one factor amongst others in the operation of this legislation. The Children Act Advisory Committee Annual Report 1992/3 draws attention to inadequacy of law and procedures in this area.

Powers of Entry and Search

May authorise the applicant to enter premises specified by the order and search for the child. <S48(3)>

Where the court is satisfied that there is reasonable cause to believe that there may be another child on those premises with respect to whom an emergency protection order ought to be made, it may make an order authorising the applicant to search for the other child on those premises.

Where the child is then found on the premises and the applicant is satisfied that the grounds for making an emergency protection order exist with respect to him, the order shall have effect as if it were an emergency protection order. The applicant shall then notify the court of its effect. <S48(4-6)>

A person shall be guilty of an offence if he intentionally obstructs any person exercising powers of entry and search. <S48(7/8)>

Where entry to premises or access is refused, or likely to be refused, a warrant may be issued by the court authorising any constable to assist using reasonable force if necessary.

A court may direct that the applicant may be accompanied, in executing the warrant, by a registered medical practitioner, registered nurse or registered health visitor. <S48(9-13)>

Department of Health guidance indicates that (should the circumstances appear to require it) the possibility of applying for a warrant should be thought of at the time of application to the court. The emergency nature of the case should always be borne in mind and whether difficulties of gaining entry are foreseen, or if the applicant believes that he is likely to be threatened, intimidated or physically prevented from carrying out this part of the order. If necessary the advice of the local police should be sought before proceeding with such an application.

In dire emergencies the police can exercise their powers under the Police and Criminal Evidence Act 1984 (S17) to enter and search premises without a warrant for the purpose of saving life and limb. Similarly the police can under section 25 of the same Act, arrest without a warrant a person who has committed any offence where the arrest is necessary to protect the child from that person. <Vol. 1 (4.57)>

Applications to the Court

May be made by any person ("the applicant"). <S44(1)>

The Department of Health indicate that this could include a concerned relative or neighbour, or teacher and may include the police. (Although they could use their powers under section 46: Police Protection in Cases of Emergency <see below>.) Rules of court require the applicant to notify the local authority, amongst others, so that the case may be investigated under section 47 (see below). <Vol. 1 (4.32/4.45)>

Wherever it is reasonably practicable to do so, the order shall name the child; and where it does not name him it shall describe him as clearly as possible. <S44(14)>

The Department of Health indicate that ex-parte hearings will (because of their emergency nature and the need to protect the child from danger) be the norm. Full inter-partes hearings with others present who wish to attend, are however provided for in rules of court, should these be desirable. <Vol. 1 (4.46)>.

Rules of court will require the applicant to serve a copy of the order on the parties to the proceedings, any person who is not a party to the proceedings but has actual care of the child and the *local authority in whose area the child is normally resident (if that authority is not the applicant). This should take place within 48 hours. <Vol. 1 (4.47)>*

Grounds

The court must be satisfied that there is reasonable cause to believe that the child is likely to suffer significant harm if:

he is not removed to accommodation provided by or on behalf of the applicant;

or if he does not remain in the place in which he is then being accommodated. <S44(1)>

The applicant has to convince the court that these circumstances pertain. There does not have to have been previous harm to the child for the order to be made.

The Department of Health indicate that in applying the criteria of the welfare of the child and the requirements under S1(5) (see chapter 1) that the court should not make an order unless it would be better for the child to make the order than no order. Thus they will want to know what it is that necessitates urgent action and whether alternatives such as the removal of the child by provision of accommodation (see chapter 3) with the agreement of the parents have been explored. They will also want to know whether a decision can wait until the parents can present a properly prepared case at an interim hearing. The applicant will be expected to give as much of the information as possible either orally or in the application. The court may take account of any statement in the report to the hearing or any evidence presented (e.g. relevant hearsay, opinions, health visiting or social work records and medical reports). <Vol. 1 (4.43)>

The Department of Health also indicate that where a child is at a refuge (see section 51, chapter 6) the organisation can apply for an emergency protection order or ask the police to take the child into police protection. The grounds here would be that the organisation believes that the child is likely to suffer significant harm if he does not remain in the refuge. <Vol. 1 (4.70)>

Additional grounds exist, when enquiries are being made and these are frustrated by access to the child being unreasonably refused to a person authorised to seek access, and that person has reasonable cause to believe that access to the child is required as a matter of urgency. <S44(1)>

The applicant has to convince the court of the urgency and that the refusal of access is unreasonable.

Department of Health guidance indicates that generally an application under the "frustrated access" provision is made by the *local authority, although the enquiries may have been conducted by persons from other voluntary or statutory agencies acting on their behalf. These grounds only apply to an emergency (where access is required as a matter of urgency) where enquiries cannot be completed because the child cannot be seen but there is enough cause to suspect the child is suffering or likely to suffer significant harm. <Vol. 1 (4.36/4.38/4.39)>*

An application can be made in the same circumstances by a person who has been making enquiries on the local authority's behalf, and who is authorised to apply under section 44 (1). They must also satisfy the court as to their reasonable cause for suspicion. <Vol. 1 (4.37/4.39)>

The local authority is required to respond positively to refusal of access or denial of information about the child's whereabouts when they are conducting enquiries: they must apply for an emergency protection order or take other specified action unless satisfied that such action is unnecessary. <Vol. 1 (4.40)>

Conditions to Be Met

The child's welfare shall be the court's paramount consideration. <S1>

When information concerning the child's whereabouts is withheld, the person involved may be ordered by the court to supply that information. <S48(1/2)>

Where an order has been made, and the applicant was not the local authority in whose area the child is ordinarily resident (and that local authority is of the opinion that it would be in the child's best interests for the applicant's responsibilities under the order to be transferred to them) the authority shall be treated as if they had applied for (and been granted) the order. In forming such an opinion the local authority shall have regard to:

the ascertainable wishes of the child having regard to his age and understanding;
the child's physical, emotional and educational needs for the duration of the order;
the likely effect on him of any change in his circumstances which may be caused by the transfer of responsibilities;
his age, sex, family background;
the circumstances which gave rise to the application for the order;
any directions of the court and other orders made in respect of the child;
the relationship (if any) of the applicant for the order to the child;
and any plans which the applicant may have in respect of the child.

These regulations do not apply where a child is in a refuge (see section 51, chapter 6) and a Secretary of State's certificate is in force under that section of the Act provided that the person carrying on the home or the foster parent providing the refuge (having taken into account the wishes and feelings of the child) has decided that the child should continue to be provided with a refuge for the duration of the order. <The Emergency Protection Order (Transfer of Responsibilities) Regulations 1991 (Regulations 2/3/5)>

Where the local authority form an opinion that it would be in the child's best interests for them to be treated as if they had applied for (and been granted) the order. They shall give notice in writing (which may be sent through the post) of the date and time of the transfer to:

the court which made the emergency protection order;
the applicant for the order;
and those (other than the local authority) to whom the applicant for the order gave notice of it.

The time at which the transfer of responsibility takes place shall be the latter of: the time stated in the notice, or of the time at which the notice is given to the applicant. <The Emergency Protection Order (Transfer of Responsibilities) Regulations 1991 (Regulations 3/4)>

The Department of Health indicate that the intention of these regulations is to ensure that in an emergency any individual can seek immediate and protective intervention and not be deterred or prevented by his inability to comply with any or all directions that the court may make. Application by any authorised person (e.g. the NSPCC) are not exempt from these regulations. <Vol. 1 (4.33)>

Duties to Be Observed

Any person who has parental responsibility shall only take such action as is reasonably required to safeguard and promote the child's welfare.

Powers of removal or prevention of removal are included in such action. <S44(5)>

The Department of Health in exploring these limitations on the exercise of parental responsibility give an example: if on obtaining access the applicant finds that the child is not harmed and not likely to suffer significant harm because a suspected abuser had vacated the home, the applicant may not remove the child. The powers only apply to safeguarding the welfare of the child. If removal is necessary the child is entitled to an explanation (of why he is being removed and what will happen to him) appropriate to his age and understanding. <Vol. 1 (4.58)>

The local authority shall make enquiries to enable them to decide and take what action they need to safeguard or promote the child's welfare.

In particular to establish whether the authority should make any application to the court, or exercise any of their powers under the act, with respect to the child. <S47(2/3)>

Powers authorising the removal of the child to accommodation or the prevention of the child's removal from any hospital, or other place in which he was accommodated immediately before the making of the order shall only be exercised in order to safeguard the welfare of the child. <S44(5)>

In the case of a child not in accommodation provided by or on behalf of the authority, the authority should establish whether it would be in the child's best interests to be in such accommodation. <S47(3)>

Other Powers of the Court

The court may give directions re medical or psychiatric examination (or other assessment) of the child.

Directions can be varied at any time on application. Where the child is of sufficient understanding to make an informed decision he may refuse to submit to the examination or other assessment. <S44(6-9)/ The Family Proceedings Rules 1991 (Rule 4.18)/The Family Proceedings Courts (Children Act 1989) Rules 1991 (Rule 18)>

Department of Health guidance indicates that in promoting the welfare of the child the court will ensure that the child is not subject to unnecessary assessments. As a matter of good practice a local authority should always seek directions on assessment or examination of the child where this is likely to be an issue. Where possible it is anticipated that assessments will be undertaken by professionals agreed between the parties or arranged by the guardian ad litem. The court may direct, and the parents, if present, may request that the child's GP observe or participate in the assessment. Directions of the court do not override the right of the child who is of sufficient understanding to make an informed decision to refuse to submit to an examination or assessment. <Vol. 1 (3.50/3.51/4.63/4.64)>

A court may direct that the applicant may be accompanied (when exercising powers given by the order) by a registered medical practitioner, registered nurse or registered health visitor. <S45(12)>

These proceedings are not family proceedings as defined under the act. Thus the court must either make or refuse to make the order applied for and cannot make any other kind of order. There can be no appeal against a refusal to make an order.

Contact with Parents etc.

The court may give directions or conditions regarding contact which is to be allowed or not allowed between the child and any named person.

These may be varied on application to the court. <S44(6/8/9)>

Subject to any directions, the applicant shall allow the child reasonable contact with:

his parents;

any person with parental responsibility;
any person with whom he was living immediately before the making of the order;
any person in whose favour a contact order (see chapter 2) is in force;
and any person acting on behalf of those persons. <S44(13)>

The Department of Health indicate that in considering what is reasonable contact, the authority will need to explore fully the wishes and feelings of the child. Where the authority wish to limit or control contact with families they believe to be troublesome and contact needs to be supervised, they should seek a direction from the court defining contact. Where such a direction has been given they will need to inform other agencies who may have regular dealings with the child (e.g. the child's school). <Vol. 1 (4.62)>

Where an order is made while the child is subject to a care order (e.g. if a serious situation arises during placement) the emergency protection order takes precedence enabling appropriate action to safeguard the child.

Review

Where it appears to the applicant that it is safe for the child to be returned, or for him to be removed from the place in question, he shall return the child or allow him to be removed.

If it is not reasonably practical to return him to the care of the person previously caring for him, the applicant shall return him to:
a parent of his;
any person holding parental responsibility;
or such other person the applicant (with the agreement of the court) considers appropriate. <S44(10/11)>

At any time while the emergency protection order remains in force the applicant may again exercise his powers if it appears necessary. <S44(12)>

Applications for Variation etc.

Directions can be varied on application. <S44(8/9)>

An application for extension can be made by the original applicant or any person entitled to apply for a care order. <S45(4)>

Can only be extended once, and for a period of up to seven days, and if the court has reasonable grounds to believe that the child concerned is likely to suffer significant harm if the order is not extended. <S45(4-6)>

The Department of Health indicate that rules of court will require an application for extension to be on notice in a full inter-partes hearing. <Vol. 1 (4.66)>

Applications for discharge may be made at any time but will not be heard until after 72 hours.

Applications can be made by: the child; a parent; a person holding parental responsibility; or any person with whom he was living immediately before the making of the order.

This does not apply in cases where the person concerned was given notice (in accordance with rules of court) of the hearing at which the order was made, and was present at that hearing, or cases where the order has been extended. <S45(8/9/11)>

> *The Department of Health indicate that the 72 hours gives time to clarify any confusion that has arisen from the making of the order and the people involved time to prepare a case. It is not expected that the 72 hours will substantially change the authority's timetable for assessment (although they will be expected to go as far and as fast as is reasonably practicable). If an application comes to court for the discharge of the order and the assessment has not been completed the authority will advise the court accordingly. Unless the circumstances have so changed as to allay any concerns the authority may have had for the safety of the child it is unlikely that the court will agree to discharge the order. <Vol. 1 (4.69)>*

No appeal may be made against:

the making of, or refusal to make, an order;
the extension of, or refusal to extend, the period during which such an order is to have effect;
the discharge, or refusal to discharge, an order;
or the giving of, or refusal to give, any direction in connection with an order. <S 45(10)/ Courts and Legal Services Act 1990, Schedule 16(19)>

SECTION 46: POLICE PROTECTION IN CASES OF EMERGENCY

Definition

Removal and accommodation, for up to 72 hours, in cases of emergency. <S46(2/6)>

Effect

Authorises a constable to remove the child to suitable accommodation and keep him there; or take such steps as are reasonable to ensure that the child's removal from any hospital (or other place) is prevented. <S46(1)>

The police do not hold parental responsibility. <S46(9)>

Grounds

The constable must have reasonable cause to believe that a child would otherwise be likely to suffer significant harm. <S46(1)>

Duties to Be Observed

The constable shall:

take such steps as are reasonably practicable to discover the wishes and feelings of the child;

inform the local authority (of the steps taken/ proposed, the reasons for taking them and the place of accommodation);

inform the child if he appears capable of understanding (of the steps taken/proposed and the reasons for taking them);

secure that the case is enquired into by a designated officer;

secure the removal of the child to local authority accommodation or to a refuge for children at risk;

inform:

the child's parents;

every person with parental responsibility;

and any person with whom the child was living immediately before being taken into police protection;

of the steps taken, the reasons for taking them and the further steps that may be taken. <S46(3/4) S51>

The designated officer shall do what is reasonable for the purpose of safeguarding or promoting the child's welfare (having regard to the period involved). <S46(9)>

The local authority shall make, or cause to be made, enquiries to enable them to decide any action they need to take to safeguard or promote the child's welfare; in particular whether it would be in the child's best interests to apply for an emergency protection order (see above) or a care or supervision order (see chapter 4). <S47(1/3-12)>

Department of Health guidance indicates that local authorities will find it necessary to ensure that channels of communication with the police are reviewed at regular intervals so that effective inter-agency working is achieved. Good and effective channels of communication should mean that the police never make an application under section 46 without the local authority's knowledge and agreement. <Vol. 1 (4.74/4.77)>

Contact with Parents etc.

The designated officer (or if the child is in local authority accommodation: that authority) shall allow such contact (if any) as appears to them reasonable and in the child's best interests between the child and:

his parents;

any person with parental responsibility;

any person with whom he was living immediately before the making of the order;

any person in whose favour a contact order (see chapter 2) is in force;

and any person acting on behalf of those persons. <S46(10/11)>

Review

On completing enquiries the officer shall release the child from police protection unless he considers that there is still reasonable cause for believing that the child would be likely to suffer significant harm if released. <S46(5)>

Applications etc.

The designated police officer may apply on behalf of the appropriate authority for an emergency protection order to be made. <S46(7)>

SECTION 47: DUTY TO INVESTIGATE

Where a local authority have reasonable cause to suspect that a child lives, or is found in their area suffering, or is likely to suffer, significant harm (or are informed that a child who lives, or is found, in their area is the subject of an emergency protection order; or is in police protection the authority shall make, or cause to be made, such enquiries as they consider necessary to enable them to decide whether they should take any action to safeguard or promote the child's welfare. <S47(1)>

Department of Health guidance indicates that action to investigate under section 47 should be seen as the usual first step when a question of child protection arises. <Vol. 1 (4.78)>

The enquiries shall be directed towards establishing:

whether the authority should make any application to the court or exercise any of their powers under the Act;

whether, in the case of a child under an emergency protection order (and who has been in accommodation provided for or on behalf of the authority) it would be in the best interests of the child for him to be in such accommodation;

and whether in the case of a child who has been taken into police protection, it would be in the child's best interests for the authority to ask for an application to be made for an emergency protection order (see above). <S47(2)>

The local authority shall take such steps as are reasonably practicable to obtain access to the child or to ensure that access to him is obtained, on their behalf, by a person authorised by them unless they are satisfied that they already have sufficient information with respect to him. <S47(4)>

Where matters in relation to the child's education appear to need investigation, the local education authority shall be consulted. <S47(5)>

The Department of Health indicate that this may include

situations such as the child's non-attendance at a named school, the fact that the child is not registered at any school, or where the school raises questions about the child's behaviour. <Vol. 1 (4.84)>

It shall be the duty (unless it is unreasonable) of:
any local authority;
local education authority;
housing authority;
health authority or national health service trust;
and any person authorised by the Secretary of State
to assist a local authority in their enquiries; in particular by providing relevant information and advice if called upon to do so. <S47(9-11)/ Courts and Legal Services Act 1990, Schedule 16(20)>

The Department of Health indicate that the definition of unreasonable will depend upon local circumstances. Where appropriate that local authority will also wish to consult with other agencies including the police and probation service, building upon existing inter-agency networks and co-operation. <Vol. 1 (4.87)>

Where the child appears to be ordinarily resident in the area of another local authority that authority shall be consulted and may undertake the necessary enquiries in their place. <S47(12)>

Where any officer or authorised person is refused access to the child or is denied information as to his whereabouts, the authority shall apply for an emergency protection order, a child assessment order, a care order, or a supervision order unless they are satisfied that his welfare can be satisfactorily safeguarded without their doing so. <S47(6)>

If on the conclusion of enquiries or review an application for an order is not made the authority shall consider whether it would be appropriate to review the case at a later date; and when that date is. <S47(7)>

If the authority conclude that they should take action to safeguard or promote the child's welfare they shall take that action (so far as it is both within their power and reasonably practicable to do so). <S47(8)>

SECTIONS 49 & 50: ABDUCTION AND RECOVERY OF CHILDREN IN CARE

ABDUCTION <S49>

In relation to a child in care, the subject of an emergency protection order, or in police protection, a person shall be guilty of an offence if he knowingly and without lawful authority or reasonable excuse:
takes a child away from the responsible person (i.e. a person who for the time being has care of him);

keeps a child away from the responsible person;
or induces, assists or incites a child to run away or stay away from the responsible person. <S49>

Where a voluntary home, registered children's home, or local authority or voluntary organisation foster parents provide a refuge under section 51 (see chapter 6) for children who appear to be at risk of harm, and have been issued with a certificate by the Secretary of State the organisation are exempt from these provisions. <S51 (5-7)>

RECOVERY ORDERS <S50>

Definition/Effect

A recovery order:
directs any person who is in a position to do so to produce the child on request to any authorised person;
authorises their removal;
requires any person who has information as to the child's whereabouts to disclose that information, if asked to do so, to a constable or an officer of the court;
authorises a constable to enter any premises specified in the order and search for the child using reasonable force if necessary. <S50(3)>

An authorised person means:
any person specified by the court;
any constable;
and any person who is authorised to exercise any power under a recovery order after the recovery order is made and has parental responsibility by virtue of a care order or an emergency protection order (in these cases the authorisation shall identify the recovery order and duly authenticated documents are required to be produced on request). <S50(7/8)>

Premises may only be specified if it appears to the court that there are reasonable grounds for believing the child to be on them. <S50(6)>

The order will name the child and the applicant(s). <S50(5)>

Grounds

The court may make a recovery order where it appears that there is reason to believe that a child has been unlawfully taken away or is being unlawfully kept away from the responsible person; has run away or is staying away from the responsible person; or is missing. <S50(1/2)>

The Department of Health indicate that although the authority should promptly notify the police of all children looked after who abscond or are abducted, so that enquiries to trace the child may be instigated, the court's powers to make a recovery order are *restricted to those children who are in care are the subject of an emergency protection order or are in police protection <Vol. 1 (4.90)>*

Applications

Can only be made by:

any person who has parental responsibility for the child by virtue of a care order or emergency protection order;

or, where the child is in police protection, the designated officer under that section of the Act. <S50(4/7)>

Offences

Intentional obstruction of an authorised person exercising powers under the order to remove the child. <S50(9)>

6
RESIDENTIAL PROVISION

Part VI of the Act defines a system for the provision and management of community homes by the statutory and voluntary sectors. Detailed regulations are framed to govern social work and managerial practice by both the local authority and voluntary organisations in these institutions.

Part VII governs the provision of services including accommodation by voluntary organisations. The registration and inspection of voluntary homes by the local authority is subject to this part of the Act.

Part VIII similarly governs the private sector in relation to registered children homes provision. Registration, inspection by the local authority and the duties of persons carrying on the home are outlined.

The Children's Homes Regulations apply to Parts VI, VII and VIII. These regulations set out detailed practice and managerial requirements. Some parts of the regulations are specific to particular types of homes.

Further regulations concerning review and placement of all children provided with accommodation are discussed in chapter 8. Chapters 6 and 8 should be read in conjunction with each other. (The regulations concerning placements place a duty on responsible authorities in making arrangements to place a child to draw up an individual plan for the child. The regulations concerning reviews require that the plan is reviewed (and amended as necessary) on a regular basis.)

Section 25 and the associated regulations outline specific additional requirements for secure accommodation in residential establishments. Similarly section 51 outlines the provision made for refuges for children at risk.

The inspection of private residential schools is governed by section 87 and associated regulations. Basic practice requirements are set out including the duties of proprietors or persons conducting schools.

PART VI COMMUNITY HOMES

Definition

A home provided, managed, equipped and maintained by a local authority; or provided by a voluntary organisation (and managed, equipped and maintained by either the local authority [a "controlled community home] or the voluntary organisation [an "assisted community home"]). <S53<3-5)>

Duties of Local Authorities

Every local authority shall make appropriate arrangements for securing that community homes are available:

for the care and accommodation of children looked after by them;

and for purposes connected with the welfare of children (whether or not looked after by them);

and may do so jointly with one or more other local authorities.

Provision shall have regard to the need for ensuring accommodation of different descriptions; and which is suitable for different purposes and the requirement of different descriptions of children. <S53(1/2)>

Instruments of Management

For controlled and assisted community homes, the Secretary of State may make an order providing for the constitution of a body of managers.

Where two or more voluntary homes are designated as controlled or assisted; those homes are, or are to be, provided by the same voluntary organisation and the same local authority is to be represented on the body of managers; a single instrument may be made constituting one body of managers. <Schedule 4 (1-3)>

A date the instrument comes into force, the designation of the home and any such provisions as the Secretary of State considers appropriate, will be specified.

Nothing in the instrument shall affect the purposes for which the premises comprising the home are held. It may contain provisions: specifying the purpose of the home, or each of the homes; specifying numbers or proportion of places to be made available to local authorities and any other stated body; and relating to the charging of fees.

In the event of any inconsistency between the instrument of management and provisions of the trust deed, the instrument of management shall prevail.

Provisions in the instrument of management may be varied or revoked by the Secretary of State after consultation with the voluntary organisation and the local authority. <Schedule 4 (7-9)>

The number of persons specified in the instrument shall be a multiple of three.

In the case of a controlled community home two thirds of these shall be appointed by the local authority; in the case of an assisted community home, one third.

The voluntary organisation's membership shall be appointed to represent the interests of that organisation and to secure, so far as practicable, the character of the home as a voluntary home; and the observation of any terms of any trust deed relating to the home. <Schedule 4 (4-6)>

Determination of Disputes

Where any dispute arises between the local authority specified in the instrument of management and the voluntary organisation by which the home is provided; or any local authority who have placed, desire or are required to place a child looked after by them in the home; the dispute may be referred by either party to the Secretary of State for his determination.

The Secretary of State may give such directions as he thinks fit to the local authority or voluntary organisation. <S55(1-4)>

Where any trust deed (i.e. any instrument other than an instrument of management regulating the maintenance, management, or conduct of the home; or the constitution of a body of managers or trustees) relating to a controlled or assisted home contains a provision whereby an ecclesiastical or denominational authority has power to decide questions relating to religious instruction given in the home these shall not be referred to the Secretary of State if capable of being dealt with in accordance with that provision. <S55(5/6)>

Management of Homes

"The responsible body" is the local authority or (as the case may be) the voluntary organisation responsible for the management, equipment and maintenance of a home.

In the case of a controlled community home it is the responsibility of the local authority specified in the instrument of management; in the case of an assisted community home it is the voluntary organisation by which the home is provided.

The functions of a home's responsible body shall be exercised through the managers. Anything done, liability incurred or property acquired by a home's managers shall be done, incurred or acquired by them as agents of the responsible body.

Where a matter is reserved for the decision of the home's responsible body (such as employment of persons at the home, the service by the body on the managers <or on any of them> of a notice reserving any matter and any items mentioned in the instrument of management) that matter shall be dealt with by the responsible body not by the managers. <Schedule 4 (3)>

Where the instrument of management of a controlled community home provides, the responsible body may enter into arrangements with the voluntary organisation (on such terms as may be agreed) that persons who are not in the employment of the responsible body shall undertake duties at the home. <Schedule 4 (3)>

Except in cases or circumstances, specified by notice in writing by the local authority (in relation to the employment of any persons or class of persons stated in the instrument of management): where the responsible body for an assisted community home proposes to engage a person in employment (or terminate a person's employment without notice) it shall consult the local authority specified in the instrument of management.

If that local authority so direct, the responsible body shall not carry out its proposal. <Schedule 4 (3)>

The managers shall submit to the responsible body, as they require, estimates of expenditure and receipts for the next accounting year the dates of which the responsible body shall specify.

Any expenses incurred by the managers with the approval of the responsible body shall be defrayed by that body.

The managers shall keep proper accounts and financial records in relation to the home. Where the instrument of management relates to more than one home, sets of accounts may be kept in respect of all the homes. <Schedule 4 (3)>

Regulations Applicable to Community Homes

Regulations may be made as to the placing of children in community homes; the conduct of such homes; and for securing the welfare of children in such homes. They may prescribe:

standards to which the premises should conform;
requirements as to accommodation, staff and equipment;
arrangements for protecting the health of children;
provide for the control and discipline of children;
state required records to be kept and notices to be given;
impose requirements as to facilities for religious instruction;
authorise the Secretary of State to give and revoke directions requiring the responsible body to accommodate in the home a child looked after by a local authority for whom no places are available in the home, or take action in relation to a child accommodated in the home;
provide for consultation with the Secretary of State as to applicants for appointment to the charge of the home;
empower the Secretary of State to prohibit the appointment of any particular applicants;
and require the approval of the Secretary of State for the provision and use of secure accommodation in addition to requirements contained elsewhere in the Act.

These regulations may confer additional functions on the local authority. <Schedule 4 (4)>

The Children's Homes Regulations 1991 apply in relation to conduct, administration, and Secretary of State's directions (see below).

Directions specific to a particular home (which vary from those in the regulations) may be made in respect of:

standards to which the premises should conform;
requirements as to accommodation, staff and equipment;
arrangements for protecting the health of children.

Directions may be varied or revoked. <Schedule 4 (4)>

Discontinuance of Provision by Voluntary Organisations

The voluntary organisation by which a controlled or assisted community home is provided shall not cease to provide the home except after giving the Secretary of State and the local authority not less than two years' notice in writing of their intentions , specifying the date from which the voluntary organisation will cease to provide the home. <S56(1/2)>

Where such notice is not withdrawn, the instrument of management shall cease to have effect on the date specified and the home shall cease to be a controlled or assisted community home. <S56(3)>

Where the voluntary organisation give notice and also inform the Secretary of State that they are unable to continue as managers the Secretary of State may by order revoke the homes' instrument of management and require the local authority to conduct the home, until a date he specifies, as if it were a community home provided by the local authority.

The home shall cease to be a community home on that date: and nothing in the trust deed shall affect the conduct of the home.

The Secretary of State may provide, for the purpose of specific directions given, treatment as a controlled or assisted community home. <S56(4/5)>

Closure by a Local Authority of an Assisted or Controlled Community Home

The local authority mentioned in the instrument of management may give the Secretary of State and the voluntary organisation not less than two years' notice in writing of their intention to withdraw their designation of the home. The notice shall specify the date involved. <S57(1/2)>

Where the home's managers then give notice to the Secretary of State that they are unable or unwilling to continue as managers; the Secretary of State may (if the managers' notice is not withdrawn) after consulting with the local authority and voluntary organisation by order revoke the home's instrument of management by a specified date. On that date the home shall cease to be a community home. <S57(3-5)>

Directions that Premises Are to Be No Longer Used

Where it appears to the Secretary of State that:

any premises used for the purposes of a community home are unsuitable for those purposes;

or the conduct of a community home is not in accordance with the regulations;

or is otherwise unsatisfactory;

he may by notice in writing served upon the responsible body direct that the premises shall not be used for the purpose of a community home.

He may also at any time by order revoke the instrument of management for the home concerned. <S54>

Financial Provisions on Cessation or Disposal of Premises

In all the above cases where any premises used for the purpose of a home are disposed of, or put to uses other than the purpose of a home, the proprietors shall pay compensation.

In the case of a controlled community home (or an assisted community home previously a controlled community home) the compensation will be a sum equal to the expenditure related to the premises, incurred by the responsible authority while the home was designated as a controlled community home.

In the case of an assisted community home (or community home previously assisted) compensation relating to the premises will be equivalent to the grants paid. <Further details may be found in section 58>

Grants by Secretary of State

The Secretary of State may make grants to local authorities in respect of expenditure incurred by them in providing secure accommodation in community homes other than assisted community homes.

Where the grant is not used for the purpose for which it was made or the accommodation is not used or ceases to be used as secure accommodation the Secretary of State may require the authority to repay the grant in whole or in part. <S82(2/3)>

The Secretary of State may arrange for the provision, equipment and maintenance of homes for the accommodation of children who are in particular need of facilities and services which are or will be provided in those homes; and in the opinion of the Secretary of State are unlikely to be readily available in community homes. <S82(5)>

The Secretary of State may make grants to voluntary organisations towards expenditure incurred by them in connection with the establishment, maintenance or improvement of voluntary homes (which, at the time when the expenditure was incurred, were assisted community homes, or designated as assisted community homes) or expenses incurred in respect of the borrowing of money to defray any such expenditure. <S82(4)>

PART VII VOLUNTARY HOMES AND ORGANISATIONS

Provision of Accommodation

Where a voluntary organisation provide accommodation for a child, they shall do so by:

placing him with a family, a relative of his, or any other suitable person (on such terms as to payment by the organisation as they may determine);

maintaining him in a voluntary home, a community home registered children's home, or a home provided by the Secretary of State;

making other arrangements as seem appropriate to them (subject to regulations made by the Secretary of State including regulations for placement with foster parents). <S59(1-3)>

Persons who, without reasonable excuse, contravene or fail to comply with regulations may be guilty of an offence. <S59(6)>

Duties of Voluntary Organisations

Where a child is accommodated by or on behalf of a voluntary organisation it shall be the duty of the organisation to safeguard and promote his welfare; to make such use of the services and facilities available for children cared for by their own parents as appears to the organisation to be reasonable and to advise assist and befriend him with a view to promoting his welfare when he ceases to be so accommodated. <S61(1)>

Before making any decision with respect to a child accommodated the organisation shall, so far as is reasonably practicable, ascertain the wishes and feelings (regarding the matter to be decided) of:

the child;
his parents;
any person with parental responsibility;
and any other person whose wishes and feelings the organisation consider to be relevant.

In making any such decision the organisation shall give due consideration:

to such wishes and feelings of the child as they have been able to ascertain (having regard to his age and understanding);
to such other wishes and feelings of other relevant people they have been able to ascertain;
and to the child's religious persuasion, racial origin and cultural and linguistic background. <S61(2/3)>

Regulations will be made requiring voluntary organisations to review cases and consider any representations (including any complaint) made to them by prescribed classes of persons. <S59(4/5)>

Registration of Voluntary Homes

A "Voluntary Home" is any home or institution providing care or accommodation for children which is carried on by a voluntary organisation.

Exceptions include: a nursing home, mental nursing home or registered care home; a school; any health service hospital; any community home; any home or other institution provided, equipped and maintained by the Secretary of State; or any home which is exempted under the regulations. <S60>

All homes are required to be registered with the Secretary of State. The register may be kept by means of a computer. <S60(1/2)>

An application for registration shall be made by the person intending to carry on the home; and be made in such manner, and be accompanied by such particulars as the Secretary of State may prescribe.

The Secretary of State may grant or refuse that application (as he thinks fit) or grant the application subject to such conditions as he considers appropriate.

Conditions may be varied from time to time by the Secretary of State, or additional conditions imposed.

Registration may be cancelled (and the home removed from the register) where at any time, it appears that the conduct of the home is not in accordance with the regulations or is otherwise unsatisfactory.

Any person who, without reasonable excuse, carries on a voluntary home without registration, or contravenes a condition imposed shall be guilty of an offence.

Registration or the cancellation of registration by the Secretary of State shall be notified to the local authority. <Schedule 5 (1)>

Procedures with regard to: notice of proposals and conditions are given in schedule 5 (2); the right to make representations concerning notices in schedule 5 (3); decision making and appeals in schedule 5 (4/5); and requirements for the notification to the Secretary of State of particulars prescribed with respect to the home in schedule 5 (6).

Regulations as to Voluntary Homes

The Secretary of State may make regulations: as to the placing of children in voluntary homes; as to the conduct of such homes; and for securing the welfare of children in such homes. These may in particular:

- prescribe standards to which the premises used for such homes are to conform;
- impose requirements as to the accommodation, staff and equipment to be provided in such homes, and the arrangements to be made for protecting the health of children;
- provide for the control and discipline of children;
- require the furnishing to the Secretary of State of information regarding facilities provided (to visit and communicate with the children) for parents, people with parental responsibility, and other persons connected with children;
- authorise the Secretary of State to limit the number of children who may be accommodated;
- prohibit the use of accommodation for the purpose of restricting the liberty of children;
- impose requirements as to the keeping of records and giving notices with respect to children;
- impose requirements as to the facilities which are to be provided for giving religious instruction;

and require notice of any change of the person carrying on or in charge of a voluntary home or of the premises used by such a home.

Contravention of, or failure to comply with any specified provision of the regulations without reasonable excuse may be specified therein as an offence.

The regulations may also make provision for disqualifying certain persons from the management or having a financial interest in a voluntary home. (Schedule 5 (7/8)>

The Children's Homes Regulations 1991 apply in particular in relation to conduct, administration, registration, notification of particulars, and local authority visits (see below).

A person who is disqualified from privately fostering a child (see chapter 7) shall not carry on, or otherwise be concerned in the management of, or have any financial interest in, a voluntary home unless he has disclosed to the Secretary of State the fact that he is so disqualified and obtained his written consent.

No person shall employ a person who is so disqualified in a voluntary home unless he has disclosed to the Secretary of State the fact that he is so disqualified and obtained his written consent.

Where the Secretary of State refuses to give consent he shall inform the person carrying on or intending to carry on the voluntary home by a written notice which states the reason for the refusal and the right (including timescale) to appeal to a Registered Homes Tribunal.

Any person who contravenes such a disqualification shall be guilty of an offence. <The Disqualification for Caring for Children Regulations 1991 (Regulation 3)>

Duties of Local Authorities

Every local authority shall satisfy themselves that any voluntary organisation providing accommodation within the authority's area for any child; or outside that area for any child on behalf of the authority; are satisfactorily safeguarding and promoting the welfare of the children so provided with accommodation.

Every local authority shall arrange for children who are accommodated (other than in community homes) within their area by or on behalf of voluntary organisations to be visited, from time to time, in the interests of their welfare. <S62(1/2/4)>

If, on application to the court it appears that a person attempting to apply these powers has been prevented from doing so by being refused entry to the premises concerned, or access to the child concerned; or that they are likely to be prevented from exercising such powers, a warrant authorising any constable to assist that person, using reasonable force if necessary, may be issued.

The court may direct that the constable be accompanied by a registered medical practitioner, registered nurse or registered health visitor if the person so chooses. <S102>

The Secretary of State may make regulations requiring every child who is accommodated within a local authority's area, by or on behalf of a voluntary organisation, to be visited by a officer of the authority in prescribed circumstances, and on specified occasions or within specified periods.

Regulations may impose requirements which must be met by any local authority or officer of a local authority. <S62(3)>

Under regulations 15/16 of The Foster Placement (Children) Regulations 1991 (see chapter 7) local authorities have a duty to visit (in certain circumstances and within specified periods) a child placed by a voluntary organisation with a foster parent.

Where a local authority are not satisfied that the welfare of any child who is accommodated by or on behalf of a voluntary organisation is being satisfactorily safeguarded or promoted, they shall take such steps as are reasonably practicable (unless they consider that it would not be in the best interests of the child) to secure that the care and accommodation of the child is undertaken by:

a parent, a person with parental responsibility;

or a relative;

and consider the extent to which (if at all) they should exercise any of their functions with respect to the child. <S62(5)>

Any person authorised by a local authority may enter, at any reasonable time, and inspect the premises in which children are being accommodated; inspect any of the children there; require any persons to furnish him with records of a kind required to be kept by the regulations, or allow him to inspect such records as he may at any time direct.

Duly authenticated documents shall be produced by persons acting under these powers showing their authority to do so.

In the case of computerised records, they shall be entitled at any reasonable time to have access to, and inspect and check the operation of, any computer and any associated apparatus or material which is or has been in use in connection with the records; and may require such assistance with the operation of the computer, apparatus or material as he reasonably requires.

A person who intentionally obstructs another in the exercise of any power under this section shall be guilty of an offence. <S62(6-9)>

Where a person looked after by a voluntary organisation is located in the local authority's own area and would qualify for advice and assistance, has asked for such help, is in such need and does not have such facilities, the local authority have a duty to advise and befriend and may give assistance (in kind or in exceptional circumstances in cash). <S24(4-7)>

Guidance from the Department of Health suggests that preparation for this process should be incorporated in the plan for the young person, as soon as he is looked after or accommodated. The voluntary organisation does not have a statutory duty to provide after care once he has ceased to be accommodated by the organisation or on its behalf. As a matter of good practice the provision of appropriate after care services should however be considered by the voluntary organisation. It should inform the local authority as early as possible, i.e. as soon as it is known on what date the young person will cease to be accommodated. <Vol. 3 (chapter 9)>

Grants by Secretary of State

The Secretary of State may arrange for the provision, equipment and maintenance of homes for the accommodation of children who are in particular need of facilities and services which: are or will be provided in those homes; and in the opinion of the Secretary of State are unlikely to be readily available in community homes. <S82(5)>

The Secretary of State may make grants to voluntary organisations towards expenditure incurred by them in connection with the establishment, maintenance or improvement of voluntary homes (which, at the time when the expenditure was incurred were assisted community homes; or designated as assisted community homes) or in connection with expenses incurred in respect of the borrowing of money to defray any such expenditure. <S82(4)>

PART VIII REGISTERED CHILDREN'S HOMES

Definition

A home or institution which is registered to provide (or usually provide, or is intended to provide) care and accommodation wholly or mainly for more than three children at any one time; but does not include a home which is exempted from these provisions by the Secretary of State. <S63(3/8/9)>

The following are excluded:

a community home;
a voluntary home;
a residential care home, nursing home or mental nursing home;
a health service hospital;
a home provided, equipped and maintained by the Secretary of State;
or a school (but an independent school is a children's home if it provides accommodation for more than 3 children for more than 295 days in a year and is not approved by the Secretary of State under the Education Act 1993 S189). <S63(5) Education Act 1993 S292>

In the case of children accommodated in lodgings arranged by the school they will be regarded as accommodated by the school and the arrangements will accordingly affect whether the school is determined to be a children's home or not.

If a child under the age of 16 is cared for and accommodated by someone other than a parent and the accommodation is not arranged by a school the child will be regarded as privately fostered.

The use of "guardians" to look after, or have some responsibility for children accommodated by independent schools has no basis in the Children Act. Schools should clarify whether such accommodation is arranged by the parent or the school. The provisions of the Children Act governing independent schools (or private fostering) will apply, regardless of the existence of a "guardian".

Although section 87 (Welfare of children accommodated in independent schools: see below) does not apply in respect of any children accommodated in schools that are children's homes the standards expected by the guidance on section 87 schools are considered appropriate and should be used in inspections. <Circular LAC(93)24>

Where a child is accommodated by a parent, a person with parental responsibility, or a relative; he shall not be treated as cared for and accommodated in a children's home.

Where a parent, or person with parental responsibility are living at a registered children's home (or the person caring for the child is doing so in a personal capacity and not in the course of his duties in relation to the home) the child concerned shall not be treated as cared for and accommodated in a children's home. <S63(4/7)>

In relation to fostering (unless the circumstance of exemption apply) if a person exceeds "the usual fostering limit", or where exempted he fosters a child not mentioned in the exemption, he shall be treated as carrying on a children's home. Thus except where the children are all siblings, a person may not normally foster more than three children.

In granting any exemptions, the local authority shall have particular regard to:

the number of persons it is proposed to foster;
the arrangements for care and accommodation;
the intended and likely relationship between the person and the fostered children;
the period of time proposed for fostering;
and whether the welfare of the fostered children (and any other children who are or will be living in the accommodation) will be safeguarded and promoted. <S63(12)/ Schedule 7>

The boundaries between foster homes, children homes and other institutions are thus clearly set. This determines which set of requirements and regulations apply to which situations.

Registration

An application for registration shall be made by the person carrying on or intending to carry on the home, to the local authority for the area in which it is situated.

It shall be made in the prescribed manner and be accompanied by such particulars as may be prescribed, together with such reasonable fee as the local authority may determine.

The Secretary of State may make regulations concerning the manner and particulars.

The local authority may grant the application if it meets the prescribed requirements or grant the application subject to conditions. If the local authority are not satisfied they shall refuse the application. <S63(11)/ Schedule 6(1)>

Conditions may be varied from time to time or additional ones imposed. <Schedule 6(2)>

Regulations made in relation to prescribed requirements may make provision as to the purpose of inspection. <Schedule 6(1)>

The responsible authority shall annually review the home's registration to determine whether it should remain in force or be cancelled. <Schedule 6(3)>

Procedures with regard to notice of proposals and conditions are given in schedule 6(5); the right to make representations concerning notices in schedule 6(6); decision making and appeals in schedule 6(7/8) and prohibitions on further applications in schedule 6(9).

The Secretary of State may make regulations: as to the placing of children; the conduct of homes; and for securing the welfare of children in homes.

In particular they may:

prescribe the standards as to the accommodation, staff and equipment to be provided;

impose requirements as to the arrangements to be made for protecting the health of children;

provide for the control and discipline of children;

require the furnishing of information to the local authority as to facilities provided (to visit and communicate with the children) for the parents of children, persons with parental responsibility and other persons connected with the children;

impose requirements as to the keeping of records and giving notices with respect to children;

impose requirements as to facilities for giving religious instruction;
make provision for annual reviews;
authorise the authority to limit the number of children who may be accommodated;
prohibit the use of accommodation for the purposes of restricting liberty;
require notice to be given of any change of the person carrying on or in charge of the home, or of the premises used;
make provision for the review of cases and inquiries and representations. <Schedule 6 (10)>

The Children's Homes Regulations 1991 apply in relation to conduct, administration, registration, and local authority visits (see below).

Duties of Persons Carrying on Registered Children's Homes (In Relation to the Welfare of the Child)

Where a child is accommodated in a children's home it shall be the duty of the person carrying on the home to: safeguard and promote the child's welfare; make use of such services and facilities available for children cared for by their parents as appears to be reasonable; and advise, assist and befriend the child with a view to promoting his welfare when he ceases to be so accommodated. <S64(1)>

Guidance from the Department of Health suggests that preparation for this process should be incorporated in the plan for the young person, as soon as he is looked after or accommodated. Social services departments should encourage the provision of appropriate after care services by all registered children's homes in their areas. The person carrying on the home should keep the young person informed at all stages by telling him as soon as possible when he is likely to cease to be accommodated and by letting him know what provision for after care will be made and by which agency. <Vol. 3 (9.15-9.17)>

Where a child ceases to be accommodated after reaching the age of sixteen, the person carrying on the home shall inform the local authority within whose area the child proposes to live.

Before making a decision with respect to any child accommodated; so far as is reasonably practicable the person carrying on the home shall ascertain the wishes and feelings of: the child; his parents; any person with parental responsibility; and any person considered relevant.

In making any such decision due consideration shall be given to the child's age and understanding, to such wishes and feelings of the child as has been ascertained; and to the child's religious persuasion, racial origin and cultural and linguistic background. <S64(2/3)>

Duties of Local Authorities

Every local authority shall satisfy themselves that any registered children's home providing accommodation within the authority's area for any child (or outside that area for any child accommodated on behalf of the authority) are satisfactorily safeguarding and promoting the welfare of the children so provided with accommodation. <S64(4)/S62(1)>

If, on application to the court it appears that a person attempting to apply these powers has been prevented from doing so by being refused entry to the premises concerned, or access to the child concerned; or that they are likely to be prevented from exercising such powers, a warrant authorising any constable to assist that person, using reasonable force if necessary, may be issued.

The court may direct that the constable be accompanied by a registered medical practitioner, registered nurse or registered health visitor if the person so chooses. <S102>

The Secretary of State may make regulations requiring every child who is so accommodated within a local authority's area to be visited by a officer of the authority: in prescribed circumstances; and on specified occasions or within specified periods; and imposing requirements which must be met by any local authority or officer of a local authority. <S64(4)/S62(3)>

Where a local authority are not satisfied that the welfare of any child who is accommodated is being satisfactorily safeguarded or promoted they shall take such steps as are reasonably practicable (unless they consider that it would not be in the best interests of the child) to secure that the care and accommodation of the child is undertaken by:

a parent,
a person with parental responsibility;
or a relative;

and consider the extent to which (if at all) they should exercise any of their functions with respect to the child. <S64(4)/S62(5)>

Any person authorised by a local authority may:

enter at any reasonable time, and inspect the premises in which children are being accommodated;
inspect any of the children there;
require any persons to furnish him with records of a kind required to be kept by the regulations, or allow him to inspect such records as he may at any time direct.

Duly authenticated documents shall be produced by persons acting under these powers showing their authority to do so.

In the case of computerised records, they shall be entitled at any reasonable time to have access to, and inspect and check the operation of, any computer and any associated apparatus or material which is or has been in use in connection with the records; and may require such assistance with the operation of the computer, apparatus or material as he reasonably requires. <S64(4)/S62(6-9)>

Disqualification

A person who is disqualified from private fostering under the act and associated regulations (see chapter 7) shall not carry on, or be otherwise concerned in the management, or have any financial interest in, a children's home unless he has disclosed to the responsible authority that he is so disqualified, and has obtained their written consent.

The regulations for private fostering may, in particular provide for disqualification of a person where:

a specified order has been made at any time in respect to him or the child who has been in his care;

a specified requirement has been imposed at any time with respect to a child who has been in his care;

he has been convicted, placed on probation, discharged absolutely or conditionally for any specified offence with respect to a child;

a prohibition has been imposed at any time with regard to private fostering;

or his rights or powers with respect to a child have been vested in a specified authority under a specified enactment. <S65(1) /S68(1/2)>

Full details are given in The Disqualification for Caring for Children Regulations 1991 <Regulations 1/1/Schedule> (see chapter 7).

Similarly, a person shall not foster a child privately, and therefore may not carry on, or otherwise be concerned with a children's home, if he lives in the same household as a person who is himself prevented from fostering a child or he lives in a household at which such person is employed; unless he has disclosed the fact to the appropriate local authority and obtained their written consent. <S65(1)/S68(4/5)>

No person shall employ a person who is similarly disqualified in a children's home unless he has:

disclosed to the responsible authority the fact that the person is so disqualified;

and obtained the authority's written consent.

Where an authority refuse to give their consent they shall inform the applicant by written notice stating:

the reason for the refusal;

the applicants right to appeal to a Registered Homes Tribunal;

and the time within which he may do so. <S65(2/3)>

Offences

Where a child is at any time cared for and accommodated in a children's home which is not registered the person carrying on the home shall be guilty of an offence unless he has a reasonable excuse. <S63(10)>

A person who intentionally obstructs another in the exercise of any powers of inspection shall be guilty of an offence. <S64(4)/S62(9)>

A person who is disqualified from private fostering and yet carries on a children's home, is involved in the management of a children's home or has a financial interest in it shall be guilty of an offence; unless he has disclosed to the responsible authority that he is so disqualified and has obtained their written consent. <S65(2/4)>

A person who knowingly employs a person in a children's home who is disqualified from private fostering, unless he has disclosed to the responsible authority that the person is so disqualified and has obtained their written consent shall be guilty of an offence. <S65(2/4)>

Contravention of or failure to comply with any specified provision of the regulations concerning the placing of children, the conduct of homes and securing the welfare of children in homes, without reasonable excuse shall be an offence. <Schedule 6 (10)>

CHILDREN'S HOMES REGULATIONS 1991

Scope

These regulations apply to "Children's Homes" whether a registered children's home, a community home (maintained, controlled or assisted), a voluntary home, or a qualifying school. <Regulations 1/2 as amended by The Children (Homes, Arrangements for Placement, Reviews and Representations) (Miscellaneous Amendments) Regulations, 1993>

Department of Health guidance indicates that homes should exercise the concern that a good parent would be providing a safe environment which promotes the child's development and protects him from exposure to harm in his contacts with other people or experiences in the community. Residential care is seen as a vital resource that should be used in a planned way and when it is in the best interests of the individual child. Although the administrative arrangements for the different kinds of homes are different, the aim is that the requirements with regard to the welfare of each child in the home and the conduct of the home should be subject to the same standards of provision and child care practices. <Vol. 4 (1.1 / 1.2 / 1.6)>

The regulations shall not apply to premises used by a local authority only to accommodate children for the purpose of holiday periods of less than 28 days at a time in the case of any one child. <Regulation 3(2) as amended by The Children (Homes, Arrangements for Placement, Reviews and Representations) (Miscellaneous Amendments) Regulations, 1993>

Interpretation

"Registration Authority" means the Secretary of State (in the case of a voluntary home) or the local authority (registered children's homes).

"Responsible Authority" means the authority providing the home: i.e. the local authority (in the case of a maintained community home); the local authority or the voluntary organisation providing the home (controlled or assisted community home); the voluntary organisation (providing a voluntary home) or the person carrying on a registered children's home.

"Qualifying School" means an independent school which is a children's home within the meaning of the Act <Regulation 2 as amended by The Children (Homes, Arrangements for Placement, Reviews and Representations) (Miscellaneous Amendments) Regulations, 1993>

For the purposes of these regulations, a voluntary Home or a children's home does not include:

any home used only to accommodate children for the purpose of a holiday for periods of less than 28 days at a time in the case of any one child;
an approved probation hostel or an approved bail hostel
a hostel run by or on behalf of a professional football club to provide care and accommodation exclusively for professional footballers or trainee professional footballers who are under the age of 18; or
an institution of further education. <Regulation 3A, as inserted by The Children (Homes, Arrangements for Placement, Reviews and Representations) (Miscellaneous Amendments) Regulations, 1993

Part II Conduct of Children's Homes

Statement of purpose and function

The responsible authority shall within three months of the regulations coming into force, and keep up to date a written statement of the following particulars:

the purpose and objectives of the home (in relation to the children accommodated);
the name and address of the responsible body, and of the person in charge;
details of the children for which accommodation is provided (age range, sex, number, and criteria of selection);
organisational structure of the home;
the experience of the person in charge, the staff and persons working there including details of relevant qualifications;
facilities and services to be provided;
arrangements made to protect and promote the health of the children accommodated;

fire precautions and associated emergency procedures;
arrangements for religious observance by the children accommodated;
arrangement for contact between children and parents, those with parental responsibility, relatives and friends;
methods of control and discipline, their circumstances of use including authorisation;
procedure for dealing with unauthorised absence of a child accommodated;
arrangements for dealing with any representation (including any complaint);
arrangements for education of any child accommodated;
and arrangements for reviews as required under the Act. <Regulation 4/ Schedule 1>

Guidance indicates the overall purpose of the statement is to describe what the home sets out to do for children and the manner in which care is provided. It is designed for those making placements, staff and parents and for the management of the home. It would be expected to include a brief statement of broad intentions or aims and a description of the ethos of the home (the values the approach to care emphasises) and may embrace a philosophy or set of guiding principles. The practical arrangements (e.g. the procedures for admissions) which follow from the home's aims, objectives and ethos and the limitations on the home's provision would also be described. <Vol. 4 (1.16-1.26)>

This statement shall be made available for inspection (in addition to those who have a statutory right of inspection) by:
the person in charge;
the staff and any other person working there;
the children accommodated;
parents;
persons with parental responsibility for a child accommodated;
any local authority looking after or having the care of a child accommodated;
any voluntary organisation providing accommodation for a child accommodated in the children's home;
and any local education authority which has placed a child in the children's home or is considering doing so. <Regulation 4/ Schedule 1>

These particulars shall be brought to the notice of all staff by the responsible authority. <Regulation 5 (2)>

Staffing

The responsible authority shall ensure that, so far as reasonably practicable, the number of staff and their qualifications and experience are adequate to secure and promote the welfare of children accommodated there at all times. <Regulation 5, as amended by The Children (Homes, Arrangements for Placement, Reviews and Representations) (Miscellaneous Amendments) Regulations, 1993>

Department of Health guidance indicates that staff should be engaged in numbers which are at least adequate to support the aims and objectives of the home and provide both adequate supervision and activities appropriate to the age, sex and characteristics of the children accommodated. <Vol. 4 (1.28)>

Guidance indicates ways of pursuing formal mechanisms such as police checks on appointment and proof of qualifications / assessment of experience. <Vol. 4 (1.34-1.37)>

The guidance also indicates the importance of staff support through supervision, development and training, written guidance, meetings and external consultancy. Written guidance for example, should include matters such as:

admission and reception;
methods of care and control;
case recording and access to records;
log book and diary recording;
confidentiality;
administration of finance (petty cash) and security;
purchasing;
repairs and maintenance;
fire precautions and emergency procedures;
the extent to which all (or any part) of the premises may be locked as a security measure;
statement of safety policy;
child protection;
arrangements for checking lodgings etc;
HIV / AIDS awareness, confidentiality and infection control;
dealing with disclosure of sexual abuse;
treatment of children who have been abused;
rostering shift handovers;
sleeping in, bed time and night supervision;
care practices towards children of the opposite sex to staff;
particular needs of children from ethnic minority groups and practices within the home to combat racism;
disciplinary and grievance procedures;
delegated authority and notifications to senior staff;
placements;
reviews;
dealing with aggression and violence;
risk taking;

and dealing with sexuality and personal relationships and working with parents. <*Vol. 4 (1.38 / 1.39)*>

Supervision should be on a one-to-one basis, in private. Staff should be encouraged to express their feelings and helped to understand these. Practical guidance should be given to ensure that responses are appropriate to the methods employed and personal involvement with children is appropriate. Similar guidance is given to establishing sound practice through other strategies. <*Vol. 4 (1.42-1.52)*>

Accommodation

Department of Health guidance indicates that the welfare of each child is to be provided for. Those responsible for the home must ensure that each child's accommodation is designed to secure the child's welfare and development, as well as taking account of general management needs. The location of the home should be one which clearly support the aims and objectives. <*Vol. 4 (1.57)*>

In respect of children with disabilities the Department of Health state that such children should have access to all the accommodation and the same rights to privacy as their able-bodied counterparts. Homes which accommodate children with a disability are required to provide the necessary equipment, facilities and adaptations. The aim should be to integrate the child in every aspect of the life of the home, not merely the physical aspects. <*Vol. 6 (13.1)*>

The responsible authority shall ensure that within the home (for children accommodated):

So far as is reasonably practicable, each child accommodated shall be provided with an area which is suitable for their needs and is equipped with furniture, bedding and furnishings appropriate to their needs. Where the child is disabled, the area is equipped with what is necessary for the child to live as normal a life as possible. <Regulation 6, as amended by The Children (Homes, Arrangements for Placement, Reviews and Representations) (Miscellaneous Amendments) Regulations, 1993>

Department of Health guidance indicates that decor and furnishings should emphasise informality. Children should be able to personalise areas of the home that are regarded as their own. <*Vol. 4 (1.71 / 1.72)*>

There are sufficient washbasins, baths and showers (with hot and cold water), and lavatories for the number of children. <Regulation 7(1)>

All areas used by children are: adequately lit, heated and ventilated; and kept in good structural repair, clean and reasonably decorated and maintained. <Regulation 7(2)>

Guidance indicates that resident children should have a say in the decor and upkeep of the home if they wish; particularly in relation to their own rooms. <Vol. 4 (1.73)>

There are provided suitable facilities for any child to meet privately: his parents; persons with parental responsibility; relatives; friends; his solicitor; his guardian ad litem; any independent visitor required under the act; any person authorised to conduct an inspection by the Secretary of State, responsible authority or local authority (as appropriate to the situation). In the case of a refuge for children at risk, the facilities for meeting these persons privately may be at a different address. <Regulation 7(3) as amended by The Children (Homes, Arrangements for Placement, Reviews and Representations) (Miscellaneous Amendments) Regulations, 1993>

Guidance indicates the importance of welcoming in a congenial setting. <Vol. 4 (1.65)>

There are adequate facilities for laundering linen and clothing used by children, and for children wishing to do so to wash, dry and iron their own clothes. <Regulation 7(4)>

There is a telephone available for children in a setting where it is possible to make and receive calls in privacy. <Regulation 7(5) as amended by The Children (Homes, Arrangements for Placement, Reviews and Representations) (Miscellaneous Amendments) Regulations, 1993>

Control and discipline

Department of Health guidance indicates that responsible authorities should ensure that control of homes is maintained in accordance with sound management and good professional practice. They should have regard to the role and purpose of each home and the nature and characteristics of the children accommodated therein, to develop sound written policies for each home and for the officer in charge to implement these in the day to day management of the home. Control is unlikely to be achieved unless there is an established framework of general routines and individual boundaries of behaviour are well defined. Control is much more likely to be achieved in homes where children are routinely involved in decision making about their care. They should be encouraged to accept responsibility appropriate to their age and understanding. <Vol. 4 (1.82-1.88)>

The aim must be to create an environment which gives a firm structure and sense of order to the lives of volatile young people. Control will be achieved through constructive relationships, and *a positive and professional ethos. The implications of behaviour should be discussed and examined prospectively with individuals and groups of children. They should be left in no doubt as to their responsibilities. Discontents may be aired at an early stage before they develop into formal complaints, and so contribute both to good order and the prevention of abuse. The authority and responsibility of the staff should always be clearly defined. Staff should take into account the relevant histories of the child in making judgements about appropriate interventions. This history should be noted in care plans which may include agreed approaches to the control of individual children. Issues of control should be examined in staff meetings and team approaches formulated (eg. in relation to defusing tension and diverting aggression). A written statement of permissible sanctions (eg. extra domestic chores or removal of privileges) is required to delineate the boundaries of acceptable behaviour. Staff need to respond in the way most likely to maintain or restore control. <Circular LAC(93)13, Guidance on Permissible Forms of Control in Children's Homes, 1993 (1.2 / 7.1-7) >*

The guidance draws attention to the child's age and competence as factors in the ability to understand danger to himself, others and property. Holding or physical intervention may be more necessary with smaller younger children. The need for physical intervention may be more frequent in the case of children with impairments such as autism, learning difficulties or severe emotional disorders. Access to unsafe areas such as the outside of the house or grounds will also need to be supervised for these children. Care should be taken to lock away dangerous objects and materials. The reasonable application of domestic security such as locking doors at night will not constitute restriction of liberty but should not be used as an easy means of saving staff time etc. Children should not be locked in their bedrooms at night whatever their age and competence, although in some circumstances close night time supervision may be necessary. <Circular LAC(93)13, Guidance on Permissible Forms of Control in Children's Homes, 1993 (8.1-6) >

Except where otherwise directed by the Secretary of State only such sanctions as are for the time being approved by the responsible authority shall be used on children accommodated. <Regulation 8(1) as amended by The Children (Homes, Arrangements for Placement, Reviews and Representations) (Miscellaneous Amendments) Regulations, 1993>

The Department of Health state that it is recognised that some form of sanction will be necessary where there are instances of *behaviour which would in any family or group environment reasonably be regarded as unacceptable. There should also be a system of rewards (commendations, extension of privileges, etc.). Where sanctions are felt necessary, good professional practice indicates that these should be contemporaneous, relevant and above all, just. The responsible body should detail in writing the sanctions available to staff; other measures may not be used. <Vol. 4 (1.90)>*

The guidance gives general principles governing interventions to maintain control. This gives a framework in which to exercise sound judgement and to act with discretion in particular circumstances:

> *The distinction between "one off" intervention, appropriate to the particular circumstances and repeated using as a regular feature of a regime is to be maintained.;*
> *Staff must be able to show that the method of intervention was in keeping with the incident that gave rise to it;*
> *The degree and duration of any force applied must be proportional to the circumstances;*
> *The potential for damage to persons and property in applying any form of restraint must always be kept in mind;*
> *Escalation should be avoided if at all possible, especially if it would make the overall situation more destructive and/or unmanageable. The failure of one form of intervention should not automatically signal the use of a more forceful approach;*
> *The age and competence of the child should be taken into account in deciding what degree of intervention is necessary;*
> *In developing individual care plans, consideration should be given to approaches to control that would be appropriate. <Circular LAC(93)13, Guidance on Permissible Forms of Control in Children's Homes, 1993 (9.1) >*

The following are not to be used on children accommodated:

any form of corporal punishment;

The Department of Health indicate that this covers any intentional application of force as punishment including slapping, throwing missiles, rough handling and punching or pushing in the heat of the moment in response to violence. It does not prevent taking necessary physical action to avert immediate danger or personal injury. The use of "holding" as a helpful containing experience is not excluded. <Vol. 4 (1.91)>

any deprivation of food or drink;

any restriction on visits to or by any child or any restriction on or delay in communications by telephone or post with: his parents, any person with parental responsibility, relatives or friends, and

independent visitor under the Act, any social worker assigned to him by the local authority or voluntary organisation, any guardian ad litem of the child, and any solicitor acting for the child or whom the child wishes to instruct;
any requirement that a child wear distinctive or inappropriate clothes;
the use or withholding of medication or medical or dental treatment;
the intentional deprivation of sleep;
the imposition of fines (except by way of reparation);
and any intimate physical examination of the child. <Regulation 8(2) as amended by The Children (Homes, Arrangements for Placement, Reviews and Representations) (Miscellaneous Amendments) Regulations, 1993>

Department of Health guidance also draws attention to the prohibition of the use of accommodation in community homes to restrict the liberty of any child (except where approved by the Secretary of State <and under criteria in the act> as secure accommodation (see below). <Vol. 4 (1.91)>

Action may however be taken:

by or in accordance with the lawful instructions of a registered medical practitioner or which is necessary to protect the health of the child;
if immediately necessary to prevent injury to any person or damage to property;
to impose a requirement to wear distinctive clothing, for purposes connected with education or with any organisation whose members customarily wear uniform in connection with its activities;
by the responsible authority, or person in charge (having obtained a court order where necessary) to restrict (or place conditions on) contact between the child and any person, if it is necessary to protect or promote the child's welfare. <Regulation 8(3)>

The Department of Health state that local authorities should seek legal advice in formulating guidance to staff on the use of measures which fall short of locking up children but which clearly restrict their liberty. In considering measures to avoid "injury to any person", Department of Health guidance defines injury to mean significant injury eg. grievous bodily harm, physical or sexual abuse, risking the lives of, or injury to, the self or others by wilful or reckless behaviour, and self poisoning. It must be shown that, unless immediate action had been taken, there were strong indicators that injury would follow. <Circular LAC(93)13, Guidance on Permissible Forms of Control in

Children's Homes, 1993 (4.2/5.1)>

Guidance on the use of physical restraint (positive application of force with the intent of overpowering the child) indicates that this may be used to protect the child from harming themselves or others or seriously damaging property. The use of physical restraint requires skill and judgement. The onus is on the worker to determine the degree of restraint appropriate and when it should be used. Staff should be careful not to overreact. Physical restraint should avert danger by preventing or deflecting a child's action, or perhaps by removing a physical object which could be used to harm themselves or others. Physical restraint applied may be eased by degrees as the child calms down in response to the physical contact. The following principles apply:

Staff should have good grounds for believing that immediate action is necessary to prevent a child from significantly injuring themselves or others, or causing serious damage to property;

Staff should take steps in advance to avoid the need for physical restraint, eg. through dialogue and diversion; and the child should be warned orally that physical restraint will be used unless they desist;

Only the minimum force necessary to prevent injury or damage should be applied;

Every effort should be made to secure the presence of other staff before applying restraint. These staff can act as assistants and witnesses;

As soon as it is safe, restraint should be gradually relaxed to allow the child to gain self control;

Restraint should be an act of care and control, not punishment;

Physical restraint should not be used purely to enforce compliance with staff instructions when there is no immediate risk to people or property. <Circular LAC(93)13, Guidance on Permissible Forms of Control in Children's Homes, 1993 (5.2/6)>

The guidance details methods of care and control falling short of physical restraint and the restriction of liberty which are acceptable. A dialogue with the child is essential here. This may be reinforced with persuasive (rather than coercive) actions such as standing in the way of a child wishing to leave, placing a hand on the child's arm or holding the child if they are highly distressed.

The use of the worker's physical presence will reinforce authority or concern. Presence in a room should be a deterrent to misbehaviour, a look or gesture may send out signals which help to keep behaviour within acceptable limits. Standing in the way of a child who is ignoring instructions or losing control may be reinforced eg. by restriction of the child's movement by placing a hand on their arm so long as it does not extend into hours. Effectiveness will depend upon the respect the child has for the member of staff and their overall authority. Physical presence should not continue to be used if the child physically resists, a decision will then need to be made about alternatives. It must be used in the context of a discussion with the child about the significance and implications of the behaviour.

The use of holding may successfully divert a child from destructive or disruptive behaviour by being led away by the hand, arm, or by means of an arm around their shoulder. A fight or argument may be diffused by firm holding and guiding away. The degree of force here discourages but does not prevent action. Holding should emphasis concern and reinforce attempts to reason. It should be based in established relationships, provide the basis for explanation, not arouse sexual expectations or feelings (and cease if it gives any indication of this). It should involve appropriate location of contact (particularly not around breasts or genitals). Demonstrable objections should result in consideration of other means of intervention and consultation with other staff if circumstances or time permit.

Touching is often an important part of care and parenting. Parental affection should be expressed to children and comfort given to ease distress. In order that physical contact is not misinterpreted, on admission checks should be made regarding possible previous sexual or physical abuse, and comfort (or otherwise) with physical contact. This should be taken into account as should culture, age and gender. Physical contact should not be in response, or be intended to arouse sexual expectations or feelings. Where it is thought inappropriate to respond to a child seeking comfort, the reasons for denying this should be explained and verbal comfort given as necessary. There should be no expectation of privacy for physical affection or comfort although in some circumstances (eg. a bereavement) this may be appropriate. Touching should form part of induction training. <Circular LAC(93)13, Guidance on Permissible Forms of Control in Children's Homes, 1993 (10.1-7) >

Full particulars of the use made of any disciplinary measures (including the date, the reason and the person by whom they were used) shall be recorded in permanent form in the home, by a duly authorised person on behalf of the responsible authority, within 24 hours of their use and the record signed by him. <Regulation 8(4)>

The Department of Health guidance states that the frequency with which physical means of control are employed should be *examined. Information to and from children, and staff involved, should underpin line management policy, practice and training programmes. Good practice will require interpretation of the guidance rather than assumptions that policies have been implemented. <Circular LAC(93)13, Guidance on Permissible Forms of Control in Children's Homes, 1993 (12.1/2)>*

When physical restraint has been used, the following procedural points should be observed:

The circumstances and justification must be recorded immediately;

Afterwards the child should be counselled on why restraint was necessary. They should be given the opportunity to put their side of the story;

The worker's line manager should discuss the incident with the worker within 24 hours;

A full report of the incident should be prepared within 48 hours and submitted by the head of home to their line manager/supervisor;

Senior managers must monitor every such incident , take and action indicated and be prepared to investigate homes where there is a pattern of absconding or frequent use of physical restraint; managers should ensure that arrangements exist for children who run away to be interviewed about the reasons and circumstances by someone not connected with the home (eg. the field social worker);

Where it is clear that the worker needs further advice/support/training the line manager should take prompt action to ensure that it is provided;

Staff meetings should provide an opportunity for a "post mortem" of the incident. Such discussion is essential to prevent the development of a culture where a physical response becomes routine. <Circular LAC(93)13, Guidance on Permissible Forms of Control in Children's Homes, 1993>

Guidance also indicates that In the case of children remanded to (or detained within) local authority accommodation, detention under a court order implies the need for positive intervention if the child indicates that they will leave an open unit, or attempt to leave without authority. Staff will need to take full account of the nature and seriousness of the offence, in considering the kind of intervention and level of physical restraint necessary in order to prevent injury or serious damage. <Circular LAC(93)13, Guidance on Permissible Forms of Control in Children's Homes, 1993 (3.2) >

Guidance suggests that staff in open children's homes should *recognise that there are practical limitations on their ability to prevent young people running away if they are determined to do so. Where there is concern that a child is likely to run away and suffer significant harm or inflict injury, then consideration should be given to whether the criteria for placement in secure accommodation (see below) can be satisfied. The use of physical restraint cannot become a substitute for secure accommodation. The practice of not allowing children out ("gating" or "grounding") is common and acceptable provided the child is not prevented from leaving by being locked in or physically restrained and regulation 8 (2) concerning restrictions on visits and communications (see above) is observed. <Circular LAC(93)13, Guidance on Permissible Forms of Control in Children's Homes, 1993 (4.4) >*

A staff member who has reason to be concerned about a young person who indicates their intention to leave without permission, or run away, should take vigorous action. They should give clear instructions and warn the child about the consequences if they do not comply. The staff member may use their physical presence to obstruct an exit and thereby express an opportunity to express concern and remonstrate with the child, provided the general principles of such intervention are observed. They may also hold the child by the arm to reinforce a point or secure the child's attention. Physical restraint to prevent the child leaving may be used if there is a strong likelihood of injury to themselves or others. Follow up work, probably with additional professional advice, will be needed after the immediate problem has been dealt with, in order to bring about long term stability and prevent repeated use of physical restraint. <Circular LAC(93)13, Guidance on Permissible Forms of Control in Children's Homes, 1993 (5.3/4) >

Arrangements for placements (see chapter 8) and reviews should have regard for the care and control of children when they go outside the home. Normally a child of sufficient age and competence may be allowed to the shops, to school and to visit friends etc. Where risk of harm to themselves or getting into trouble may be involved, those with parental responsibilities should be a party to decision making (which may involve refusing permission to go out). It may be desirable for a child to go out even though there are risks. When a child is on a visit the responsibilities of those visited should be made clear (eg. requirements to report when the child has arrived safely, times of return and escort arrangements). <Circular LAC(93)13, Guidance on Permissible Forms of Control in Children's Homes, 1993 (6.1-3) >

The guidance details aspects of training which may be appropriate for staff in open units. In-service training in the use of restraint should include:

creating a positive child care setting;
pre-emptive discussions regarding the issues of acceptable behaviour;
dealing with hostility constructively to avoid spiralling tension;
defusing aggression; and
managing violence.

Self defence, if taught, should be in relation to training in positive means of control. <Circular LAC(93)13, Guidance on Permissible Forms of Control in Children's Homes, 1993 (11.1-4)>

Storage of medicinal products

(A medicinal product requires a product licence under the Medicines Act 1968 and may only be obtained upon the authority of a medical or dental practitioner.) <Regulation 2>

The responsible authority shall ensure that any medicinal product which is kept in a children's home shall be administered by a member of staff (or a qualified nurse, registered medical practitioner or registered dental practitioner) and stored in a secure place so as to prevent any child accommodated having access except when under supervision of a member of staff (except where the product may be safely stored and self-administered, by the child for whom it is intended, in such a way that others are prevented from using it). <Regulation 9 as amended by The Children (Homes, Arrangements for Placement, Reviews and Representations) (Miscellaneous Amendments) Regulations, 1993>

Department of Health guidance indicates that children of 16 and over should in general be entrusted with the retention and administration of their own medication. Local authorities and voluntary organisations should have laid down procedures in relation to children accommodated on their behalf. These should be included in the child's care plan. The community pharmacist will be able to advise on the safe storage and administration of medications and appropriate methods for recording their use. <Vol. 4 (1.100/1.102)>

Employment and education of older children

Where any child is over the school leaving age, the responsible authority shall assist with the making of, and give effect to, the arrangements made for him in respect of his education, training and employment. (Does not apply to qualifying schools.) <Regulation 10 as amended by The Children (Homes, Arrangements for Placement,

Reviews and Representations) (Miscellaneous Amendments) Regulations, 1993>

> *Guidance indicates that young people who have the ability should be encouraged most strongly to continue their education beyond compulsory school age. The importance of preparing young people for working life and in assisting them to obtain and remain in suitable employment is also stressed. Good links with careers advisers, youth training schemes, job centres and employment agencies are important. Children need support in adapting to a new lifestyle and in coping with the challenges and responsibilities of working life. <Vol. 4 (1.115-1.120)>*

Religious observance

The responsible authority shall ensure that each child accommodated is enabled, so far as practicable, to attend the services or (to receive instruction in) and to observe any requirement (whether as to dress, diet or otherwise) of the religious persuasion to which he belongs. <Regulation 11>

> *Special efforts must be made to ensure that important parts of a child's cultural and religious heritage are not lost. The results of enquiries and plans made should be recorded in the child's case record. Great sensitivity may be needed in supporting the child in practising his religion in a manner appropriate to his age; the child's family should be asked to assist. <Vol. 4 (1.121-1.124)>*

Food provided for children and cooking facilities

The responsible authority shall ensure that:

children accommodated are provided with food in adequate quantities for their needs which is properly prepared, wholesome and nutritious;

so far as practicable at each meal there is a choice for each course;

any special dietary needs (whether attributable to health, religious persuasion, racial origin or cultural background) are met.

They shall provide within the home:

suitable and sufficient catering equipment, crockery and cutlery to meet the needs of the children;

proper facilities for the refrigeration and storage of food;

and so far as practicable, adequate facilities for children to prepare their own food if they so wish. <Regulation 12>

> *Guidance indicates that diets should contain a mixture of many different foods, account needs to be made of individual preferences whilst it is important that children are encouraged to try a wide variety of foods including the unfamiliar. Children should be involved in the planning of menus and account taken of their*

wishes and preferences. The kitchen should, as far as possible, be like an ordinary domestic kitchen. Mealtimes as a point of social contact should be recognised. Children should be involved in shopping as an important life skill. <Vol. 4 (1.125-1.142)>

Purchase of clothes

So far as is practicable the responsible authority shall enable each child to purchase clothes according to his needs; where a child does not wish to (or is not able to) purchase his own clothes, the responsible authority shall purchase clothes for him to meet his needs. (Does not apply to qualifying schools.) <Regulation 13 as amended by The Children (Homes, Arrangements for Placement, Reviews and Representations) (Miscellaneous Amendments) Regulations, 1993>

Attention is particularly drawn by the Department of Health to the importance of codes of dress in religious observance of minority groups. <Vol. 4 (1.146)>

Fire precautions

The responsible authority shall ensure that:

- before any child is accommodated in the home and at all times they are accommodated, that the fire authority are notified of:
  - the location of the home;
  - the numbers of children accommodated or to be accommodated and their minimum and maximum age;
  - and whether any children suffering from any impairment of movement or intellect are accommodated or are to be accommodated, and if so the nature of the impairment;
- in respect of the home:
  - precautions are taken against the risk of fire;
  - means of escape in the event of fire are provided;
  - arrangements are made for detecting, containing and extinguishing fire;
  - arrangements are made for warning of an outbreak of fire and for evacuation in the event of fire;
  - and means for fighting fire are provided;
- which are such as may be reasonably required;
- arrangements are made so that:
  - the staff and (so far as practicable) the children are aware of the procedure to be followed in the event of fire at the home including practices of the evacuation procedure and the techniques of resuscitation and the saving of life;
  - any outbreak of fire requiring an evacuation of children accommodated from the home or part of it is notified to them immediately. <Regulation 14 as amended by The Children's Homes Amendment Regulations, 1994>

Guidance on smoking and alcohol consumption

As part of the establishment's health education role, staff should take an active role in discouraging children from smoking. Programmes of health education and health care should be included in the establishment's aims and objectives. Policies (affecting staff, residents and visitors) are required in each establishment limiting smoking. Staff should not smoke in front of children, visitors may smoke only in specially designated areas No child under 16 years may smoke in the establishment, habitual smokers should be engaged in programmes designed to remove the habit. Smoking by over 16 year olds is to be actively discouraged. Smoking should be restricted to designated room(s) these should be separate from living and other common areas. Staff must not supply children under 16 years of age with cigarettes. Staff may not smoke on duty, smoking in break periods should only occur in a designated smoking room. Policies on smoking are to be evaluated and monitored. <Circular LAC(94)4>

Staff should not consume alcohol while on duty or arrive on duty suffering from the effects of alcohol. The policy of the establishment should discourage the use of alcohol by staff and children and promote non-alcoholic drinks. It is recommended that children under 16 should be dissuaded from drinking alcohol. Habitual drinkers should be cared for with an approved programme of treatment designed to achieve a sensible use of alcohol by adulthood. Young people between the ages of 16 and 18 should be allowed to consume alcohol (under supervision of a responsible adult) only where it has been purchased for them. Limits on weekly consumption are recommended.

Exceptions may be made at the discretion of the local authority in the case of special celebrations. Policies on sensible drinking should be made clear on such occasions, and alcohol should not be consumed by staff or children to the extent of intoxication or impaired response. No more that one third of staff on duty should consume alcohol, at least two members of staff on duty should abstain. Alcohol should not be stored in residential establishments. <Circular LAC(94)4>

Part III Administration of Children's Homes

Confidential records concerning children

The responsible authority shall arrange to be maintained in each children's home (except in qualifying schools) a record in permanent form relating to each child who is accommodated there, which shall as far as practicable include:

the child's name (and any name the child has previously been known by other than a name used by the child prior to adoption);
the child's sex and date of birth;
the child's religious persuasion (if any);
a description of the child's racial origin, cultural and linguistic background;
where the child came from before he was accommodated in the home;
the person by whose authority the child is provided with care and accommodation and the statutory provision involved;
the name, address and telephone number and the religious persuasion (if any) of the child's parents, and any person with parental responsibility;
the name and address and telephone number of any social worker assigned to the child;
the date and circumstance of any absence of the child from the home including whether the absence was authorised and where the child went during the period of absence;
the date and circumstances of any visit to the child whilst in the home by any parent, person with parental responsibility, relative or friend, independent visitor, social worker, guardian ad litem or solicitor;
a copy of any statement of special educational needs (with details of any such needs) maintained in relation to the child under the 1993 Education Act;
the name and address of any school or college attended by the child, and of any employer of the child;
every school report received by the child while accommodated in the home;
the date and circumstances of any disciplinary measures imposed on the child;
any special dietary or health needs of the child;
arrangements including any restrictions with respect to contact between the child and his parents, a person with parental responsibility, or any other person;
the date and result of any review of the child;
the name and address of the medical practitioner with whom the child is registered;
details of any accident involving the child;
details of any immunisations, illness, allergy, or medical examination, any medical or dental need of the child;
details of any health examination or developmental test conducted with respect to the child at or in connection with his school;
details of all the medicinal products taken by the child while in the home and by whom they were administered, including those which the child was permitted to administer to himself;

the date on which any money or valuables are deposited by or on behalf of the child for safe-keeping, and the date on which such money is withdrawn/ valuables returned;

and where the child goes to when he ceases to be accommodated in the home. <Regulation 15/ Schedule 2 as amended by The Children (Homes, Arrangements for Placement, Reviews and Representations) (Miscellaneous Amendments) Regulations, 1993>>

Department of Health guidance indicates that the case record should be seen as a significant and positive feature of the child's life. Written entries should be signed and dated and the name of the signatory clearly identified. Information should be factual and clear. Value judgments should be avoided. Colloquialisms where used should be in reported speech or indicated by inverted commas. Fact should be separated from opinion. Descriptive and stigmatising terms avoided. <Vol. 4 (1.155 / 1.160)>

The record shall be kept securely and treated as confidential subject only to any provision by statute or court order covering access. They shall be retained for at least 75 years from the date of birth of the child or, if the child dies before attaining the age of 18, for a period of 15 years from the date of his death. <Regulation 15 (2/3)>

Department of Health guidance indicates that the papers constituting the case record should be held in a good quality file capable of holding different categories of information (including certificates, photographs, school reports etc. accumulated during the child's life). The case file should be stowed away in a steel lockable cabinet and access controlled to ensure confidentiality and security. A child of sufficient understanding should be allowed regular access consistent with its safekeeping and the best interests of the child. He should read or be told what has been recorded unless knowledge of the material will cause harm to the child or to a third party. A child should be encouraged to record his own observations including disagreement about entries. If information is required to which the child cannot have access this should be held in a separate part of the file and clearly marked confidential. Consideration should be given as to whether highly sensitive information should be held on the children's home file at all. <Vol. 4 (1.153 / 1.161)>

Boarding schools are also required to maintain individual records for all pupils concerning admissions and attendance. <The Pupils Registration Regulations 1956/ Pupils Registration (Amendment) Regulations 1988>

Access by guardians ad litem to records and register

Each voluntary organisation (where they are not acting as an authorised person) and every person carrying on a registered children's home shall provide a guardian ad litem of a child such access as may be required to records (in any form) maintained in accordance with these regulations (including records maintained on a computer) and any copies of records as he may require. <Regulation 16>

Records relating to running a children's home

The responsible authority shall maintain in each children's home (except in qualifying schools) the following records (and ensure that the details are kept up to date):

the date on which each child was first accommodated, the date on which any child ceased to be accommodated, where each child came from before being accommodated, where each child went on ceasing to be accommodated, the identity of the person (authority or organisation) responsible for placement, which (if any) child accommodated was being looked after or in the care of any authority or organisation and under what legal authority;

details of every person employed, working (or it is intended will work) at the home; showing whether they work full time, or part time (whether paid or not) showing full names, sex, date of birth, relevant qualifications and experience of work with children, average number of hours worked and whether they reside at the home;

other persons resident at the home;

accidents occurring in the home;

details of any medicinal product administered to any child including the date and circumstances of its administration and by whom it was administered, including medicinal products which the child is permitted to administer himself;

every fire drill or firm alarm test, with details of any deficiency in procedure or equipment together with the steps taken to remedy that deficiency;

all money deposited by a child for safekeeping together with the date on which the money was withdrawn or the date of its return;

all valuables deposited by a child and the date of their return;

all accounts kept in the home;

menus;

every disciplinary measure imposed, giving full particulars of the circumstances and reasons as required by regulation 8 (see above);

duty rosters;

a daily log of events occurring in the home, including the names of visitors to any child accommodated.

The Department of Health indicate that entries should be signed and dated and the name of the signatory clearly stated. The actions of staff in the events should be described as well as children. <Vol. 4 (1.164)>

All records shall be retained for at least 15 years, except for records of menus which shall only be kept for one year. <Regulation 17/ Schedule 3 as amended by The Children (Homes, Arrangements for Placement, Reviews and Representations) (Miscellaneous Amendments) Regulations, 1993>>

Regulations and guidance

A copy of the Children's Homes Regulations 1991 and of any relevant Department of Health guidance shall be kept in the home and made available to:

all staff;
every child accommodated;
their parents or guardians;
and any person with parental responsibility of/for any child accommodated. <Regulation 18>

The Department of Health indicate that in the case of poor readers the main features of the regulations may be explained in language appropriate to their age and understanding. <Vol. 4 (1.65)>

Notification of significant events

The responsible authority shall forthwith notify: the parents of the child concerned, any person with parental responsibility for him, any person who has undertaken to meet any fees or expenses incurred in accommodating the child at the home, the district health authority, the local authority in whose area the home is situated and the registration authority (where they are not the responsible authority) of:

the death of a child accommodated (giving such detail to the circumstances as is known to the responsible authority). This should also be notified to the Secretary of State;
the suffering of serious harm by a child resident at the home. This should also be notified to the Secretary of State;

Attention is drawn by the Department of Health to the need for clear policies and written procedures for responding to abuse (if it occurs) which are integrated with the procedures agreed by the Area Child Protection Committee. <Vol. 4 (1.179-1.192)>

any serious accident involving a child accommodated. This should also be notified to the Secretary of State and a constable;
any serious illness of a child accommodated;
any outbreak in the home of any notifiable infectious disease;
and any conduct on the part of a member of staff which is, or may be (in the opinion of the responsible authority) that which would make them not to be a suitable person to be employed in work involving children. This item does not need notifying to the district health authority. (Does not apply to qualifying schools.) <Regulation 19 as amended by The Children (Homes, Arrangements for Placement,

Reviews and Representations) (Miscellaneous Amendments) Regulations, 1993>>

Absence of a child without authority

The responsible authority shall draw up in writing the procedure to be followed when a child accommodated is absent without permission. They will ensure that it is drawn to the attention of the children accommodated, and the staff and others working in the home. (Does not apply to qualifying schools.) <Regulation 20 as amended by The Children (Homes, Arrangements for Placement, Reviews and Representations) (Miscellaneous Amendments) Regulations, 1993>>

Absence of person in charge

Where a person in charge of a voluntary home or registered children's home proposes to be absent from the home for a continuous period of four weeks or more, he shall give written notice to that effect to the registration authority at least four weeks before the absence is due to commence.

Where it would be impracticable to give four weeks notice the registration authority may accept such shorter period as appears reasonable.

Notification is not required if no child is accommodated during the absence. <Regulation 21 (1/2/4)>

The person for the time being in charge shall inform the registration authority at least seven days before the commencement of the absence of:

- its occurrence and anticipated duration;
- the reason for it;
- the number of the children accommodated when the information is given;
- the arrangements which have been made for the running of the home;
- the name, address and qualifications of the person who will for the time being be in charge. <Regulation 21 (3)>

This also applies within seven days of a child being provided with accommodation when previously no child was to be accommodated during the period of absence. <Regulation 21 (5)>

Within seven days of the return of the person in charge or the appointment of some other person in his place the responsible authority shall notify the registration authority of that fact. <Regulation 21 (6)>

If in the case of a registered children's home the person in charge is also the responsible authority the temporary person in charge shall take over these functions for the time being. <Regulation 21 (7)>

Accountability and visiting on behalf of the responsible authority

The person carrying on a children's home, if not also the person in charge, shall visit the home once a month, or cause some other person to do so on his behalf and report to him in writing on the conduct of the home. <Regulation 22 (1)>

Where the person carrying on a voluntary home or registered children's home is a body (whether incorporated or not) the directors, or other persons responsible for the conduct of the body, shall cause one of their number, or an employee of that body who is not directly concerned with the conduct of the home, to visit the home once a month and report to them in writing on the conduct of the home. <Regulation 22 (2) as amended by The Children (Homes, Arrangements for Placement, Reviews and Representations) (Miscellaneous Amendments) Regulations, 1993>

The managers of a controlled or assisted community home shall cause one of their number to visit the home once a month and a report to them be made in writing on the conduct of the home. <Regulation 22 (3)>

The local authority who maintain a maintained community home shall cause the home to be visited once a month and a report to them be made in writing on the conduct of the home. <Regulation 22 (4)>

> *The Department of Health indicate that an important purpose of these visits is to ensure that the day to day conduct of the home is seen by someone not involved in its operation. The visits should be unannounced and reports seen by the responsible authority without amendment or deletion. <Vol. 4 (1.170)>*

Part IV Community Homes

Secretary of State's directions

The Secretary of State may give (and revoke) directions requiring the local authority (in respect of a controlled community home) or the voluntary organisation (in respect of an assisted community home) to accommodate in the home a child looked after by a local authority (for whom no places are made available) or to take such action in relation of a child accommodated in the home as may be so specified. <Regulation 23>

> *The Department of Health indicates that the local authority shall cause the home to be inspected in a similar manner to registered children's homes (see below). The inspection unit shall visit twice a year (at least one visit should be unannounced). Short visits may also examine particular aspects of care that could not be*

included in the main inspection. Inspectors should plan visits through examination of objectives and standards, and deciding on information sources / devise questionnaires, interview and observation schedules etc. After the visit material will be analysed systematically establishing to what extent criteria have been met. Judgments should be made on this evidence regarding standards, and findings communicated so that changes may be implemented. There will be a continuing evaluation of the inspection process. <Circular LAC(93)1>

Part V Application for Registration of a Voluntary Home

An application in writing shall be made to the Secretary of State, by the person carrying on (or intending to carry on) the home. The following particulars shall be furnished:

- the name of the voluntary organisation and the address and telephone number of the registered or principal office;
- the names and addresses of the chairman and secretary or any other person responsible for the management of the organisation, their dates of birth and (if the Secretary of State requests) their qualifications and experience (if any) in running a home;
- the name, address and telephone number of the premises of which registration is sought;
- the name and address of any other community, voluntary or registered home under the Act or care or nursing home under the Registered Homes Act 1984, in respect of which the voluntary organisation has at any time had a financial interest, and details of the interest;
- a description of the premises and the area in which they are situated and details of any comments made by the health officer or environmental health officer for the area;
- particulars of the accommodation provided for residents in the home and for the employees and volunteers at the home;
- the date on which the home was established or is to be established;
- particulars of any other business which is or will be carried on in or from the same premises as the home;
- the name sex and date of birth of the person in charge or intended to be in charge of the home and whether or not he resides or is to reside in the home together with:
  - the names and address of each person by whom he is or has been employed in the past ten years,
  - the name and addresses of two additional persons (in addition to these employers) who are willing and able to give a reference as to his suitability to be in charge of a home,
  - and particulars of his health and undertaking to provide a report by a registered medical practitioner where the Secretary of State considers it necessary;

the number and sex of every person employed or proposed to be employed in the home (as an employee or otherwise) with particulars of:
whether or not they are or will be resident,
whether they are full or part time (and if part time the number of hours for which they are or will be employed),
the positions they hold,
and any relevant qualifications;
particulars of the equipment, facilities and services provided or to be provided in the home, and any special arrangements or services for any particular category of children;
the arrangements for the storage and administration of medicines;
the arrangements for medical and dental examinations and treatment;
details of the scale of charges payable in respect of residents;
the arrangements for the education of the children and what contact there is with the local education authority;
particulars of any children in residence, including their name, sex, date of birth and details of who was responsible for placement in the home;
particulars of any prospectus or advertisement relating to the home;
and the particulars specified to the responsible authority as to the purpose and function of the home (under regulation 4 and schedule 1, see above). <Regulation 24/ Schedule 4>

Part VI Registered Children's Homes

Application for registration

An application in writing shall be made by or on behalf of the body or organisation to the registration authority. <Regulation 25/ Schedule 6>.

Where the applicant is a natural person his application shall be accompanied by the following particulars:
his name, date of birth, address and telephone number;
the qualifications and experience (if any) held by the person intending to carry on the children's home which are relevant to his suitability to carry on the children's home;
the names and addresses of any person by whom the applicant is, or has at any time in the preceding ten years been, employed;
the name and addresses of two persons, in addition to those employers, who are willing and able to give a reference as to the suitability of the applicant to carry on a children's home;
and a report (where the registration authority deem it necessary) by a registered medical practitioner as to the physical and mental health of the applicant. <Regulation 25/ Schedule 5>

These particulars are also additionally required in all cases where the person carrying on, or intending to carry on the home is not the person in charge. <Schedule 5>

Where the applicant is a body corporate the application shall be accompanied by the following particulars:

the address of the registered office or principal place of business of the applicant;

the names, dates of birth and addresses of the chairman and secretary of the applicant;

the qualifications and experience (if any) held by the person whom the applicant intends to be in charge of the home which are relevant to his suitability to be in charge;

and the names and addresses of two persons who are willing and able to give a reference as to the suitability of the person intending to be in charge of the home. <Regulation 25/ Schedule 5>

In addition all applicants shall furnish the following particulars:

the name, address and telephone number of the premises in respect of which registration is sought;

a description of the premises and the area in which they are situated, any comments made by the local fire or environmental health authorities;

the name and addresses of any other community, voluntary or registered children's home or registered care or nursing home in respect of which the applicant has at any time had a financial interest, or in the case of a natural person at which he was employed, and details of the interest or employment;

the date on which the home was established or is to be established;

any children in residence, including their name, sex, date of birth and the local authority in whose care they are;

the name sex, date of birth and other particulars including date of employment or proposed employment of every person employed or proposed to be employed in the children's home as a manager (i.e. a person entrusted with the day to day responsibility for the business of the home or any part of it) together with details of:

his qualifications (in so far as they are relevant to his employment);

his previous experience in work involving or related to the care of children;

and whether he is intended to live on the premises, or resident in the home;

their proposed hours of work;

the name, sex, date of birth and the responsibilities of every person working in the home (whether as an employee or otherwise) or whom it is proposed should work in the home (other than the manager or a person working at the home only as a teacher) their proposed hours of work; and which of these persons will be resident in the home;

the scale of charges payable for residents;
the equipment, facilities and services to be provided in the home, if any, and particular needs of children which are intended to be met by means thereof;
arrangements made or proposed for the education of resident children, and, if education is to be provided on the premises, information on the home's status as a school under the Education Act 1944;
the accommodation provided for resident children and for other resident at the home;
a copy of the statement of purpose and function required under Regulation 4/ Schedule 1 (see above);
a copy of any prospectus or advertisements relating to the home;
any other business which is, or is proposed to be carried on or from the premises.

Additional requirements relating to registered children's homes

The registration authority may limit the number of children to be accommodated (by means of a condition based upon the qualifications and experience held by the proposed person in charge which are relevant to his suitability to carry on the home). <Regulation 26>

In connection with the annual review of registration the person carrying on the home shall notify the registration authority of any changes in any particulars furnished in the application which there may have been since the previous review (or the original application). <Regulation 27>

The registration authority shall cause the home to be inspected where an application has been made for it to be registered before reaching a decision on registration. Within the period of one month ending upon the anniversary of the registration, the registration authority shall cause the home to be inspected (after notifying the person in charge of their intention). On at least one other occasion in any year the registration authority shall cause the home to be inspected unannounced. The registration authority shall consider the report of any inspection of the home conducted in accordance with this regulation when determining whether or not the registration of the home should be reviewed or cancelled. <Regulation 28>

If the person carrying on a home desires the cancellation of registration he shall apply to the registration authority in writing stating: the date on which he wishes the cancellation of registration to take effect (giving at least one month's notice); and the action he intends should be taken with regard to the placement in alternative accommodation of any child then accommodated in the home. <Regulation 29>

The responsible authority shall give at least one month's prior notice in writing to the registration authority of any proposed change in the identity of the person in charge of a home giving the same particulars required about the person at the time of registration. <Regulation 30/ Schedule 5/6>

Part VII Notification of Particulars with Respect to Voluntary Homes

The person in charge of a voluntary home shall send to the Secretary of State annually on the 3rd of April (and within three months from the establishment of the home) the following particulars:

the name, address and telephone number of the home;

the name and date of birth of the person in charge;

the name, address and telephone number of the organisation or person carrying on the home;

the name and address of the chairman and secretary;

the maximum number of children who can be accommodated at any one time in the home;

the criteria for admission to the home (if any);

the religious persuasion(s) (if any) in which the home undertakes to bring up the children;

the weekly charge made in respect of each child accommodated;

the name of any Government Department(s) inspecting the home (other than the Department of Health) and the date of the last inspection by each of them;

the details and number of staff employed by the organisation broken down into care staff, ancillary staff, full and part time, and including volunteers who work in the home;

and the number of children accommodated at the time of notification (giving the total number, the number in local authority care, the number receiving full time education or vocational training at the home, the number receiving full time education or vocational training outside the home, the number who are in full time employment within the home, and the number who are in full time employment outside the home (in each case stating how many are boys and how many girls and dividing them into age groups of 1-4, 5-9, 10-15, and 16+)) <Regulation 31/ Schedule 7>

Part VIII Local Authority Visits

Circumstances necessitating visits

Every local authority shall arrange for one of their officers to visit every child who is accommodated in their area in a voluntary or registered children's home (except in qualifying schools) in any of the following circumstances (and time periods):

where the local authority are informed that a child not in the care of, nor looked after by, any local authority has been placed in such

accommodation (within 28 days of being informed);
where the voluntary organisation or the person carrying on a registered children's home providing such accommodation makes representations to the local authority that there are circumstances relating to the child which require a visit (within 14 days of the receipt of those representations);
and when the local authority are informed that the welfare of a child may not be being safeguarded or promoted (within 7 days of being so informed). <Regulation 32 as amended by The Children (Homes, Arrangements for Placement, Reviews and Representations) (Miscellaneous Amendments) Regulations, 1993>>

Every local authority shall arrange for further visits to the child by one of their officers as appears to them to be necessary, (whether in the light of a change of circumstances or not) and shall in any event arrange for further visits where:
they are informed that the child is not in the care of, nor looked after by, any local authority and they are satisfied following the first visit that the child's welfare is being safeguarded and promoted (visiting again within 6 months);
they are not satisfied following the first visit that the child's welfare is being safeguarded and promoted but have decided that the child should continue to reside in the same accommodation (visiting again within 28 days). (Does not apply to qualifying schools.) <Regulation 33 as amended by The Children (Homes, Arrangements for Placement, Reviews and Representations) (Miscellaneous Amendments) Regulations, 1993>>

The local authority shall ensure that in the course of these visits an officer of the authority will:
see the child alone (unless exceptionally he considers it unnecessary);
read all the relevant case papers and records concerning the child kept by the voluntary organisation or the registered children's home, and sign and date them to indicate he has seen them;
and make a written report of his visit which shall be copied to the voluntary organisation or person carrying on the registered children's home. <Regulation 34 (1)>

The voluntary organisation or the person carrying on the home shall provide suitable accommodation for the visit. <Regulation 34 (2)>

SECTION 25: SECURE ACCOMMODATION

Definition

Accommodation provided for the purpose of restricting liberty. <S25(1)>

Department of Health guidance indicates that although interpretation is a matter for the courts, any measure or practice which prevents a child from leaving a room or building of his own free will may be deemed to constitute "restriction of liberty". In cases of doubt (where the issues may not be clear cut) the advice of the authority's legal department should be sought. <Vol. 4 (8.10)>

Placement outside the community homes system will in general be covered by this definition. The exception here may be where an order exists under other legislation (e.g. the Mental Health Act 1983). In cases of doubt the Department of Health advise application to the court to determine whether section 25 applies. <Vol. 4 (8.12)>

Criteria for Restriction of Liberty

A child who is being looked after by a local authority, or who is being provided with accommodation by a health authority, a health service trust or a local education authority may not be placed or kept in secure accommodation unless it appears:

that he has a history of absconding and is likely to abscond from any other description of accommodation, and if he absconds, he is likely to suffer significant harm (i.e. ill treatment or the impairment of health and development, the significance of which is determined by comparison with other similar children);

or that if he is kept in any other description of accommodation he is likely to injure himself or other persons. <S25(1)/S31(9/10)/S105(1)/ The Children (Secure Accommodation) Regulations 1991 (Regulation 7)>

Restricting the liberty of children is a serious step which must be taken only when there is no genuine alternative. It is the "last resort" in that all else must first have been considered, explored and then rejected. If the criteria are not met and the accommodation is not designated, restriction of liberty is unlawful. Restriction of liberty includes any short-term placement of a child in a locked room for "time out" or seclusion purposes.

Regulations may specify description of a child to whom the provision of secure accommodation shall or shall not apply, and the particular circumstances involved. <S25(7)>

In the case of the following children, grounds to be met before placement are modified:

children detained under section 38 of the Police and Criminal Evidence Act;

and children remanded to local authority accommodation under section 23 of the Children and Young Persons Act 1969 (when the child has a history of absconding while remanded to local authority accommodation, and is charged with or convicted of an imprisonable offence alleged or found to have been committed whilst so remanded; or when charged with, convicted or previously convicted of a violent offence punishable in the case of an adult with imprisonment for a term of 14 years or more).

The modified grounds are:

unless it appears that any accommodation other than that provided for the purpose of restricting liberty is inappropriate because:

he is likely to abscond from such accommodation, or he is likely to injure himself or other persons if he is kept in any such accommodation. <The Children (Secure Accommodation) Regulations 1991 (Regulation 6) as amended by The Children (Secure Accommodation) Amendment Regulations 1992>

Exceptions and Restrictions

Provisions also apply to children accommodated by Health Authorities, National Health Service Trusts, Local Education Authorities and children accommodated in residential care homes, nursing homes or mental nursing homes. <The Children (Secure Accommodation) Regulations 1991 (Regulation 7)>

Applications to court in respect of a child provided with accommodation by a local education authority, health authority or a National Health Service trust shall be made only by that authority or trust (unless the child is looked after by a local authority).

Applications to court in respect of a child provided with accommodation in a residential care home, nursing home or mental nursing home shall be made only by the person carrying on the home (unless the child is looked after by a local authority). <The Children (Secure Accommodation) (No. 2) Regulations 1991>

Provisions do not apply to a child detained as follows:

under the Mental Health Act 1983;

under section 53 Children and Young Persons Act 1933 (punishment of certain grave crimes);

Children over 16 but under 21 accommodated under section 20(5) of the Act (see chapter 3);

children kept away from home under section 43 of the Act (Child Assessment Order) (see chapter 5). <The Children (Secure Accommodation) Regulations 1991 (Regulation 5)>

The use of accommodation for the purpose of restricting the liberty of children in voluntary homes and registered children's homes is prohibited.

The contravention or failure to comply without reasonable excuse, shall be an offence. <The Children (Secure Accommodation) Regulations 1991 (Regulation 18)>

Local Authorities are required to take reasonable steps to avoid the need for children within their area to be placed in secure accommodation. <Schedule 2 (7)>

Department of Health guidance indicates that careful consideration needs to be given to the existing range of alternative facilities and services. Any gaps or inadequacies in such provision need to be identified and steps taken to remedy situations. All decisions to seek a placement for a child in secure accommodation need to be taken at a senior level. <Vol. 4 (8.6)>

Maximum Periods in Secure Accommodation

The regulations may specify: a maximum period beyond which a child may not be kept in secure accommodation without the authority of the court; and the period (or further period) for which the court may authorise a child to be kept in secure accommodation. <S25(2)>

The maximum period beyond which a child may not be kept in secure accommodation without the authority of the court is an aggregate of 72 hours (whether or not consecutive) in any period of 28 consecutive days.

Where the authority of a court has been given, any period during which the child has been kept in secure accommodation before the giving of that authority shall be disregarded for the purposes of calculating the minimum period in relation to any placement after the period authorised by the court has expired.

Special arrangements apply for placements during public holidays and Sundays. <The Children (Secure Accommodation) Regulations 1991 (Regulation 10)>

The maximum period for which a court may authorise a child to be kept in secure accommodation is three months.

Further authorisations can be given by the court for periods not exceeding six months in total at any one time. <The Children (Secure Accommodation) Regulations 1991 (Regulation 11/12)>

In the case of children remanded under section 23 of the Children and Young Persons Act 1969 the total maximum period is the duration of the remand.

Individual periods of authorisation shall also not exceed 28 days. <The Children (Secure Accommodation) Regulations 1991 (Regulation 13)>

(Children on remand to local authority accommodation and placed in secure accommodation will have the time so spent deducted from an eventual custodial sentence. These arrangements are described in local authority circular LAC(88)23. <S130 Criminal Justice Act 1988>)

In practice the 28 day maximum period of authorisation when a child on remand needs to have his liberty restricted applies only to Crown court proceedings.

Secure Accommodation in Community Homes

Accommodation in a community home shall not be used as secure accommodation unless it has been approved by the Secretary of State for such use.

Approval shall be subject to such terms and conditions as he sees fit. <The Children (Secure Accommodation) Regulations 1991 (Regulation 3)>

A child under the age of 13 years shall not be placed in secure accommodation in a community home without the prior approval of the Secretary of State and such approval shall be subject to such terms and conditions as he sees fit. <The Children (Secure Accommodation) Regulations 1991 (Regulation 4) as amended by The Children (Secure Accommodation) Amendment Regulations 1992>

Where a child is placed in secure accommodation in a community home which is managed by an authority other than that which are looking after him, the local authority which manages that accommodation shall inform the authority which are looking after him that he has been placed there, within 12 hours of his being placed there, with a view to obtaining their authority to continue to keep him there if necessary. <The Children (Secure Accommodation) Regulations 1991 (Regulation 9)>

Where a child is kept in secure accommodation in a community home and it is intended that an application will be made to a court to keep the child in that accommodation, the local authority looking after the child shall if practicable inform: his parent, any person with parental responsibility, the child's independent visitor (if one has been appointed), and any other appropriate person, of the intention as soon as possible. <The Children (Secure Accommodation) Regulations 1991 (Regulation 14)/ The Magistrates' Court (Children Act) Rules 1991>

Each local authority looking after a child in secure accommodation in a community home shall appoint at least three persons (at least one of whom shall not be a member nor an officer of the local authority by or on behalf of which the child is being looked after). These persons shall:

- review the keeping of the child in such accommodation for the purpose of securing his welfare within one month of the inception of the placement and then at intervals not exceeding three months where the child continues to be kept in such accommodation;
- satisfy themselves as to whether or not the criteria for keeping the child in secure accommodation continue to apply; the placement in such accommodation continues to be necessary and that no other description of accommodation is appropriate for him; and in doing so shall have regard to the welfare of the child;
- if practicable, in undertaking the review, ascertain and take into account the wishes and feelings of:
  - the child,

any parent,
any person with parental responsibility,
any other person who has had the care of the child whose views the persons appointed consider should be taken into account,
the child's independent visitor if one has been appointed,
and the local authority managing the accommodation.

The local authority shall also, if practicable inform all these persons of what action, if any, the local authority propose to take in relation to the child in the light of the review, and their reasons for taking or not taking such action. <The Children (Secure Accommodation) Regulations 1991 (Regulations 15/16) as amended by The Children (Secure Accommodation) Amendment Regulations 1992>

Department of Health guidance indicates that the responsibility for undertaking the reviews rests solely with the local authority looking after the child, and not with the local authority managing the secure unit. If the conclusion of the review panel is that the criteria for restricting liberty no longer apply, the authority looking after the child must immediately review the child's placement. <Vol. 4 (8.53 / 8.56)>

Records must be kept (by the local authority which manages the accommodation) of:

the name, date of birth and sex of the child;
the care order or other statutory provision and the local authority involved with the placement of the child;
the date and time of placement in secure accommodation, the reason for placement, the name of the officer authorising the placement and where the child was living before the placement;
all those informed by virtue of regulations concerning placement by other authorities, applications to court and review;
court orders made in respect of secure accommodation;
reviews undertaken under the regulations concerning secure accommodation;
the date and time of any occasion on which the child is locked on his own in any room in the secure accommodation other than his bedroom during usual bedtime hours, the name of the person authorising this action, the reason for it and the date and time the child ceases to be locked in that room;
and the date and time of his discharge and his address following discharge from secure accommodation. The Secretary of State may require copies of these records to be sent to him at any time. <The Children (Secure Accommodation) Regulations 1991 (Regulation 17)>

Before a remanded child is escorted outside a secure accommodation unit there should be an explicit and witnessed understanding between the child and the escort about how close a *child should stay to the escort, and how they should indicate their wishes. The escort(s) should carry official identification, and be trained in methods of control and restraint The number of escorts used should take fully into account the nature and seriousness of any offence and the need to protect the public, or likelihood of serious self injury. Managers and staff should be prepared to stop escape by the use of physical restraint. Where that fails and the child successfully absconds, the escort must inform the unit and the police immediately. <Circular LAC(93)13, Guidance on Permissible Forms of Control in Children's Homes, 1993 (3.4/5)>*

The guidance details aspects of training which are essential for staff working in secure accommodation:

creating a positive child care setting;

pre-emptive discussions regarding the issues of acceptable behaviour;

dealing with hostility constructively to avoid spiralling tension;

defusing aggression; and

managing violence.

Self defence, if taught, should be in relation to training in positive means of control. <Circular LAC(93)13, Guidance on Permissible Forms of Control in Children's Homes, 1993 (11.1-4)>

Removal by Persons with Parental Responsibility

Any person who has parental responsibility for the child (if the service of accommodation is provided at their behest) may at any time remove him from secure accommodation provided by or on behalf of the local authority. <S25(9)/S20(8)>

Court Proceedings

The court, on hearing an application shall (so as to make an order authorising the child to be kept in secure accommodation and to specify the maximum period involved) determine whether any relevant criteria for keeping a child in secure accommodation are satisfied. Such applications may only be made by the local authority which are looking after the child.

An interim order may be made permitting the child to be kept in secure accommodation for the period of an adjournment.

All children must be legally represented unless having been informed of their right to apply for legal aid, they refuse or fail to apply. <S25(3-6)/ The Children (Secure Accommodation) Regulations 1991 (Regulation 8)>

The Department of Health indicate that social workers and other staff need to prepare children adequately for hearings; particular regard should be paid to the age and understanding of the child.

The entitlement to legal aid should be carefully explained. Reports should be prepared with careful attention to requirements for evidence concerning the statutory criteria. <Vol. 4 (8.39)>

Courts may still give directions to the child to whom the authorisation relates. <S25(8)>

Appeals

May be made to the high court. <S94>

SECTION 51: REFUGES FOR CHILDREN AT RISK

The Department of Health indicate that refuges provide a breathing space for runaways, where project workers can help them to return to parents or local authority care, or to sort out some other solution (if a return home is not appropriate). Section 51 provides a clear legal framework in which those running such facilities may work. <Vol. 4 (9.1/9.2)>

Department of Health guidance indicates that social services departments should aim to work with refuges in their area to establish a satisfactory basis for operation. <Vol. 4 (9.16)>

Where it is proposed to use a voluntary home or registered children's home to provide a refuge for children who appear to be at risk of harm, the Secretary of State may issue a certificate with respect to that home. <S51(1)>

Where a local authority or voluntary organisation arrange for an existing foster parent to provide a refuge, the Secretary of State may also issue a certificate. <S51(2/3)>

Regulations may be made by the Secretary of State making provision as to the manner in which certificates are issued; impose requirements which must be complied with while any certificate is in force; and provide for the withdrawal of certificates in prescribed circumstances. <S51(4)>

Department of Health guidance indicates that the views of social services department and the police will be sought: "Certificates will not be issued lightly". <Vol. 4 (9.13)>

Effect

When a certificate is in force with respect to a home the provisions relating to abduction of children in care (see chapter 5) do not apply; nor do those relating to harbouring children who have absconded from residential establishments (section 71 of the Social Work Scotland Act 1968); compelling, persuading, inciting or assisting any person to be absent from detention (section 32(3) of the Children and Young Persons

Act 1969; and also section 2 of the Child Abduction Act 1984). <S51(5-7)>

THE REFUGES (CHILDREN'S HOMES AND FOSTER PLACEMENTS) REGULATIONS 1991

Requirements

The following provisions shall apply whilst a certificate issued under section 51 is in force with respect to a home or foster parent.

A child may not be provided with a refuge unless it appears to the person providing it that the child is at risk of harm unless the child is or continues to be provided with a refuge.

As soon as is reasonably practicable after admitting a child to a home for the purpose of providing a refuge or after a foster parent provides a refuge for the child, the person providing the refuge shall notify to the officer designated by the police ("designated officer"):

that a child has been admitted to the home, or provided with a refuge by a foster parent, together with the telephone number by which the person providing the refuge for the child may be contacted (within 24 hrs of admission) ;

the child's name and last permanent address (if they are known, within 24 hrs of admission or by giving them as soon as they are known);

the name and address of the "responsible person" for the child (i.e. parent, person with parental responsibility, and any person who has care of the child other than in the refuge). This is to be done within 24 hours of becoming aware of their identity.

The designated officer shall inform the responsible person that the child is being provided with a refuge, by whom the refuge is provided, and a contact phone number (without disclosing the address of the refuge).

When the child ceases to be accommodated the designated officer shall be notified by the person providing the refuge.

No child can be provided with a refuge in any one place for a continuous period of more than 14 days or for more than 21 days in any period of three months. <Regulation 3>

Withdrawal of Certificate

The Secretary of State may withdraw a certificate at any time where:

a person providing a refuge fails to comply with the requirements;

where the person providing a refuge fails to comply with any of the regulations concerning conduct of homes contained in the Children's Homes Regulations (see above);

a foster parent providing a refuge fails to comply with any provision contained in the agreement relating to him concerning obligations in foster care or placement (or regulations concerning emergency placement) under the Foster Placement Regulations (see chapter 7) the person providing a refuge or any person assisting him in that respect has had proceedings instituted against him, or has been convicted of, any criminal offence.

Where a certificate has been withdrawn it shall be returned immediately to the Secretary of State. <Regulation 4>

The Department of Health indicate that there is no formal right of appeal against refusal or withdrawal of a certificate although any representations may be considered. <Vol. 4 (9.14)>

SECTION 87: CHILDREN ACCOMMODATED IN INDEPENDENT SCHOOLS

Welfare of Children

It shall be the duty of any proprietor of, or person conducting an independent school, which provides accommodation for any child; to safeguard and promote the child's welfare. <S87(1/10)>

Department of Health guidance indicates that S87 concerns the welfare of boarding pupils, not education (which is covered by other provision). Safeguarding and promoting a child's welfare concerns the health, happiness and proper physical, intellectual, emotional, social, and behavioural development of the child as well as protecting him against the risk of suffering significant harm. Sound practice indicates that there may be differences in measures taken to safeguard a child's welfare, depending upon (for example) the age of the child, boarding arrangements and distance from home. <Vol. 5 (2.4.1 / 2.4.2) / Circular LAC(95)1>

Guidance also indicates that there should be an appropriately experienced senior member of the school staff nominated specifically for liaison with the social services department over welfare matters. <Vol. 5 (2.6) / Circular LAC(95)1>

The guidance illustrates how standards should be managed:

there should be a statement of principles, on which the life of the school is based, dealing with such matters as the delivery of care and discipline. This should be available to parents, pupils, staff and where relevant, placing authorities;

good management and professional skills covering employment ratios, training and deployment of staff, should be dealt with;

care principles and procedures should be stated so that pupils are aware of expectations and staff can respond to the child in confidence;

staff induction, training and supervision should be considered and requirements pursued;

accountability via systems of record keeping, giving clarity and detail concerning how a child's welfare has been met, should be enabled. <Vol. 5 (3.1.1-3.1.8) / Circular LAC(95)1>

Additionally proprietors will need to carry out thorough checks on the suitability of staff prior to appointment, including checks with the Department of Education and Science and with the police (via SSDs). <Vol. 5 (3.3.1-3.3.6) / Circular LAC(95)1>

Standards of accommodation in all premises used by pupils should be such as to enable them to live a full life in the school community. Guidance details how personal space should be utilised for social well being. The Education (School Premises) Regulations 1981 contain standards for the suitability of school accommodation. <Vol. 5 (3.4.1-3.4.4)>

Health and safety needs are detailed in the guidance <Vol. 5 (3.5.1-3.6.3) / Circular LAC(95)1>

Contact with parents, relations and visitors in privacy should be facilitated <Vol. 5 (3.7) / Circular LAC(95)1>

The guidance elaborates how a broad view of discipline should be taken in relation to good personal and professional relationships and how this is important for the growth, welfare and development of pupils. Clear policies should be made on standards of behaviour expected of pupils and how these standards are to be maintained and unacceptable behaviour tackled. Particular guidance is given as to when corporal punishment or restriction of liberty are not appropriate. SSDs will wish to have regard to the principles and practice regarding control and discipline in the Children's Homes Regulations 1991 (see above) Circular LAC(93)13, Guidance on Permissible Forms of Control in Children's Homes, 1993 (see above) and in section 25 concerning Secure Accommodation (see above). <Vol. 5 (3.9.1-3.10.3) / Circular LAC(95)1>

The guidance also details requirements in respect of complaints procedures so that there are clear and accessible avenues for children to alert an appropriate adult to situations which are causing them distress. <Vol. 5 (3.11.1-3.11.7) / Circular LAC(95)1>

Scope

Section 87 does not apply in relation to non-maintained special schools (under the Education Acts) and any school which is a children's home (i.e. schools not approved by the local education authority for special needs provision, with 50 or fewer accommodated pupils; and independent schools that provide accommodation for more than 3 children for more than 295 days in a year and are not approved by the Secretary of State under the Education Act 1993, S189) or a residential care home (providing personal care and accommodation for 50 or fewer children who are disabled or mentally disordered). <S87(2)/S63(5) Education Act 1993 S292>

Other (more detailed) provision takes precedence over section 87 of the Act for these children. Non-maintained special schools are not independent schools and are provided by voluntary organisations and approved by the Secretary of State. They are thus covered by section 61 of the Act (see above). Children's homes are covered by part VIII (see above). The Children's Homes Regulations 1991 (see above) apply to both voluntary homes and registered children's homes. The Registered Homes Act 1984 applies in the case of residential care homes.

In addition, Department of Health guidance indicates that proprietors and SSDs need to be clear whether the residential accommodation provided for a pupil is the responsibility of the residential school or another agency (e.g. a landlady). If the school arranges accommodation section 87 applies, otherwise Part IX private fostering (see chapter 7) or Part VIII registered homes (see above) may apply. The SSD is under a duty to satisfy itself as to the welfare of such children. <Vol. 5 (2.7)Circular LAC(95)1>

Although section 87 does not apply in respect of any children accommodated in schools that are children's homes the standards expected by the guidance on section 87 schools are considered appropriate and should be used in inspections. <Circular LAC(93)24>

Powers of Inspection

The local authority shall take such steps as are reasonably practicable to enable them to determine whether the child's welfare is adequately safeguarded and promoted while he is accommodated by the school. <S87(3)>

The Secretary of State, rather than the social services authority is responsible for any enforcement action that may become necessary on welfare grounds. The social services department is responsible for determining whether the school is adequately safeguarding and promoting the welfare of children accommodated in independent schools and for notifying the Secretary of State for Education if it is of the opinion that the school has failed in its duty to safeguard and promote welfare. <<Circular LAC(95)1>

The Secretary of State may appoint a person <an authorised inspector> to undertake welfare inspection functions in relation to independent boarding schools, where the person already acts as an inspector in relation to independent boarding schools, and the Secretary of State is satisfied that the person is an appropriate person to determine whether the welfare of children provided with accommodation is adequately safeguarded and promoted while they are accommodated by them.

Where the proprietor of an independent school enters into an agreement with the authorised inspector, and the agreement provides for the person to have the function of determining whether the welfare of children is adequately safeguarded and promoted (and the local authority receive notice in writing) the authority's duty in relation to the school shall be suspended.

This suspension will apply until:

notice to the contrary is given by Secretary of State following the request of the authorised inspector, or

the Secretary of State terminates the appointment of the authorised inspector (being no longer satisfied that the person is an appropriate person to determine whether the welfare of children is adequately safeguarded and promoted), or

the relevant agreement expires (in which case the authorised inspector will notify the local authority in writing). <S87A, inserted by Deregulation and Contracting Out Act 1994 (S38)>

The Secretary of State may impose on an authorised inspector such requirements relating to, or in connection with carrying out a substitution agreement, as he thinks fit.

The authorised inspector shall notify the Secretary of State where it appears that there has been a failure to safeguard or promote the welfare of children accommodated by the school.

If it appears to the authorised inspector that a child provided with accommodation by the school is suffering, or is likely to suffer significant harm, the inspector shall notify the local authority and supply them with a copy of the latest inspection report. <S87B, inserted by Deregulation and Contracting Out Act 1994 (S38)>

Department of Health guidance states that nothing in the Act or guidance replaces or diminishes the other duties placed upon social services departments and local education authorities towards children they have placed in independent schools.

Where the local authority is of the opinion that the child's welfare is not being safeguarded and promoted, they shall notify the Secretary of State. <S87(4)>

Department of Health guidance indicates that a child protection investigation is separate from an inspection under S87. Social services departments would be expected to use any available means to satisfy themselves about welfare matters. This could include developing working arrangements to integrate school *practice into established child protection procedures. In all contacts the aim should be to establish and develop sound working arrangements based upon mutual respect. <Vol. 5 (2.2) / Circular LAC(95)1>*

The document "Working Together for the Protection of Children from Abuse: Procedures in the Education Service" frames guidance in this area. Schools should have recognised procedures for dealing with allegations of abuse: good practice should provide for a senior member of staff to have responsibility for child protection and welfare issues within the school and for liaison with the SSD; a detailed note is to be made when abuse is alleged and the SSD is to be informed at once (it is for that department and the police to conduct the investigation); appropriate arrangements are to be made with the SSD for counselling the child and for the parents and/or the placing authority to be informed; and the complaint to be reported by the school to the Secretary of State without delay. <Vol. 5 (3.2.1-3.2.4)>

Any person authorised by the local authority, or the Secretary of State <an "authorised person"> may enter at any reasonable time any independent school within their area which provides accommodation for any child, to enable them to discharge their duty.

They may carry out an inspection of premises, children and records as prescribed by regulations made by the Secretary of State. <S87(5/6)>

Any person exercising the power of inspection shall, if asked to do so, produce some duly authorised document showing his authority. <S87(7)>

An authorised person may carry out an inspection of the children who are accommodated in a relevant independent school either individually or together with other such children in the school.

The inspection may include a physical examination of the child, subject to the consent of the child being given or withheld (where the child is of sufficient understanding to give or withhold that consent).

These regulations do not apply in respect of a child of a member of staff or a child living with a member of staff as a member of his household, unless the child is also attending the school as a pupil. <Inspection of Premises, children and records (Independent Schools) Regulations 1991, Regulation 3>

Department of Health guidance indicates that such examinations will be limited visual examinations only: e.g. removal of a shirt to see whether bruising was visible. This power should not be used as a substitute for Part V of the Act (see chapter 5 on child protection). Vol. 5 (Annex B)>

If a social service department suspect that a child is suffering significant harm or is likely to suffer significant harm, they should consider taking such action as asking a court to issue a child assessment order or an order for emergency protection (see chapter 5).

Department of Health guidance indicates that inspections should be less frequent, less formal, more focused and targeted than previously under the act. Schools need not be formally inspected more than once in four years where:

the school is accredited member of an association that is a constituent of the Independent Schools Joint Council (ISJC) and subject to regular inspections by that association, reports being provided to the social services department;

the school has a regularly meeting governing body (or equivalent);

most children return home at weekends, or are regularly visited by their families;

the school does not cater mainly for children with statements of special needs;

the social services department has made no significant recommendations in letters and reports on previous inspections and has no significant welfare concerns about the school;

visits / inspections by OFSTED and or ISJC association have not given rise to any significant recommendations regarding children's welfare;

and the Registrar of Independent Schools has not asked the social services department to visit the school.

Visits to schools that do not meet these criteria will continue to take place at least every two years. In the case of schools accommodating children with special needs particular attention should be paid to individual care and support requirements on inspection and reporting. Regular informal contact in writing should be maintained in the intervening years to ensure that there have been no significant changes in welfare or practice. The Registrar of Independent Schools will also indicate whether there has been a significant change to a school's boarding provision. <Circular LAC (95)1>

The SSD, OFSTED and the ISJC association will need to keep in close touch and phase their inspection programmes.

Visits should be notified in advance. Inspectors should agree the nature and purpose of their work with the head teacher of the school. SSDs should be expected to inspect all aspects of the school's practices that impinge on the children's welfare but should not concern themselves with matters that are primarily educational. During the course of inspections SSDs should meet individual children and observe them during the normal course of the school's activities.

Inspection and reporting should relate to current and future welfare of pupils, not to past issues and event unless these have a clear relevance to current or future welfare.

Questionnaires can be used with pupils to obtain views, and focus an inspection. Before use, consultations with the head teacher are required.Further guidance is given in circular LAC (95)i.

Social service departments are free to visit any school at any time, announced or unannounced if they have any good grounds for welfare concerns. They should also aim to visit a school if requested by the school and schools should not hesitate to contact them for advice and information. Unannounced visits should be neither excessive nor insensitive. Care should be taken to avoid disrupting school activities and inspectors should identify themselves to a responsible member of staff on arrival.

Inspectors should not normally interview pupils alone, any discussions should be carried out in groups or informal settings. Interviews with pupils alone should only be carried out if it is felt to be essential in order to gain necessary information about a serious welfare concern or if a pupil requests it. The reasons for this should be recorded by the inspector and records monitored by the Head of the Inspection Unit. A parent, second inspector or other responsible person should if practicable be present at an interview.

Inspectors must differentiate between legitimate differences in standards of accommodation and provision which is so inadequate or inappropriate as to constitute a failure to safeguard and promote welfare. Such general advice and recommendations should be distinguished in reports.

The age of pupils should be taken into account in considering welfare arrangements.

It is reasonable that teaching and support staff rather than those with care qualifications look after children unless it is clear that the welfare of pupils is being adversely affected.

Inspections should be confined to welfare issues and not cover more general educational, religious or cultural matters within the curriculum. <Circular LAC (95)1>

An authorised person may carry out an inspection of the records containing information concerning the health, emotional or developmental well-being or welfare of the children in a relevant independent school, held by the proprietor or person who is responsible for conducting the school. <Inspection of Premises, children and records (Independent Schools) Regulations 1991, Regulation 4 (1/2)>

These records may include the following:

the name and address of the person (if any) with parental

responsibility for a child;
details of medical and dental treatment undergone by a child while he is at the school, whether or not administered by a member of staff of the school;
details of any accidents to any child in the school, the death of any child in the school, serious illness or infectious disease suffered by any child at the school, and other significant harm sustained by a child while at the school;
the names and qualifications of the staff responsible for the welfare of children in the school (including non-teaching, part time staff and volunteers, inside and outside teaching hours);
details of any cases of a child absconding from the school;
details of fire practice drills and fire alarm tests;
details of any complaints made by any person in respect of the state of health, emotional or developmental well-being or welfare of a child in the school;
and details of punishments administered to any child in the school. <Inspection of Premises, children and records (Independent Schools) Regulations 1991, Regulation 4 (2)>

Department of Health guidance indicates however that the regulations do not place any duty upon a school to maintain specific records. The Secretary of State is not empowered to make such regulations. The authorised person is empowered only to inspect such records as the school keeps. However failure by a school to maintain adequate records could indicate failure to adequately safeguard and promote the child's welfare. Documents to indicate that schools have properly checked out staff recruited should be available. <Vol. 5 (Annex B)>

Any person authorised by the regulations to inspect the records; shall at any reasonable time have access to, and inspect and check the operation of, any computer and any associated apparatus or material which is or has been in use in connection with the records in question; and may require such assistance as may reasonably be required. <S87(8/9)>

Visits should be recorded and reports shown to the proprietors of the school in draft form for factual correction. Head teachers should be invited to sign final reports that they regard them as factually correct and add any comments. The final copy should in all cases go to the Registrar of Independent Schools at the Department of Education. All reports should distinguish between general welfare advice and recommendations concerning a failure to safeguard and promote the welfare of boarders. Such recommendations should be cross referenced to the requirements of volume 5 of the guidance (see above) Reports should clarify that schools are not required to comply with general welfare advice but that non-implementation of recommendations concerning current or potential safeguarding and promotion of welfare could lead to a notification to the Secretary of State for Education.

Reports should be concise covering: boarding accommodation, staffing, welfare policies and procedures, organisation and management, welfare support and other provision for boarders.

Notifications to the Secretary of State that a school has failed to safeguard and promote the welfare of a child should be separate and be in writing to the Registrar of Independent Schools: identifying the school; the contact person in the authority; the specific grounds for an opinion that the school has failed to comply with duties under section 87, giving the grounds for each contravention; and state and steps taken in response to the failure and any relevant recommendations made. The Secretary of State is empowered to serve a notice of complaint on the school stating required remedies and the deadlines involved.Vol. 5 (4.1.1.-4.3.1) / Circular LAC (95)1>

Warrants on Refusal of Entry

If, on application to the court it appears that a person attempting to apply these powers has been prevented from doing so by being refused entry to the premises concerned, or access to the child concerned; or that they are likely to be prevented from exercising such powers, a warrant authorising any constable to assist that person, using reasonable force if necessary, may be issued.

The court may direct that the constable be accompanied by a registered medical practitioner, registered nurse or registered health visitor if the person so chooses. <S102>

7
FOSTERING, CHILD MINDING AND DAY CARE

This chapter begins by detailing the parts of the act that concern fostering provision by local authorities and voluntary organisations, including the detailed regulations that govern the practice of approvals, placements and supervision.

Then the registration and inspection of private fostering is outlined as in Part IX of the Act. Here the role of the local authority in relation to the child's welfare is detailed. Similarly registration and inspection of private day care and childminding is contained in Part X.

Local authority day care provision (section 18) has, however, been placed in this book in chapter 3 as part of a statutory child care service. Voluntary organisations accommodating children in foster homes are also governed by the provisions common to voluntary homes in Part VII of the Act. This is discussed in this text in chapter 6. The local authority are required in certain circumstances and within specified periods to visit foster homes administered by voluntary organisations. This is governed by regulations 15/16 of the Foster Placement (Children) Regulations 1991 which are discussed in this chapter.

FOSTER PARENTS: APPROVAL BY LOCAL AUTHORITIES AND VOLUNTARY ORGANISATIONS

Foster placements fall within the range of services for families of children in need which local authorities are required to provide under section 17 (see chapter 3). All foster placements of children also fall within the scope of the Arrangements for Placement of Children (General) Regulations 1991 (see chapter 8).

Planning will elaborate the aims of foster placement, the skills involved, specific tasks associated and the expected duration of the placement.

Duty to Consider Racial Groups

Every local authority shall in making any arrangements designed to encourage persons to act as foster parents, have regard to the different racial groups to which children within their area who are in need belong. <Schedule 2 (11)>

Guidance from the Department of Health indicates that social services departments must address and seek to meet the needs of children and families from all groups in the community. Particular needs will require efforts in recruitment so that all children who need substitute families have the opportunity of placements that share their ethnic origin and religion. <Vol. 3 (3.8)>

Limits on the Number of Foster Children

Except where the children are all siblings, a person may not foster more than three children unless he is exempted from "the usual fostering limit" by the local authority.

In granting any exemptions, the local authority shall have particular regard to:

the number of persons it is proposed to foster;
the arrangements for care and accommodation;
the intended and likely relationship between the person and the fostered children;
the period of time proposed for fostering;
and whether the welfare of the fostered children (and any other children who are or will be living in the accommodation) will be safeguarded and promoted.

Exemptions shall be informed by notice in writing giving the children's names and any conditions involved.

At any time by giving notice in writing there may be variations or cancellation of exemptions and conditions, or the imposing of new conditions.

If a person exceeds the usual fostering limit, or where exempted he fosters a child not mentioned in the exemption, he shall be treated as carrying on a children's home.

Every local authority is required to establish a procedure for considering representations (including complaints) by persons exempted or seeking to be exempted under these provisions (see chapter 3). <Schedule 7>

Department of Health guidance indicates that the limit does not mean that placement of three children in a foster home should be taken as the norm. In many cases the welfare of a child needing placement will be best served by being the only foster child in a family. Where more than one child is to be placed, the interests of *both must be carefully considered and weighed. The needs of foster parent's own children must also be considered. <Vol. 3 (4.6)>*

In making a judgment whether an establishment is a foster home or a children's home, guidance indicates that small scale, family atmosphere and an excellent standard of care are to be seen as common factors. Reception of children on a different basis from the extension of a family circle will affect the determination of status. Dimensions supporting children's home registration are:

a fixed number of places offered;
all places ideally to be filled to ensure viability;
investment in the fabric of the premises to accommodate a larger number of children;
and whether a voluntary organisation has arranged for a couple to run an establishment providing care for a fixed number of children.

The issue is that appropriate safeguards and support should be applied in each case. <Vol. 3 (4.9/4.10)>

Regulations as to Placing of Children

May make provision:

with regard to the welfare of the child;
for the arrangements to be made for health and education;
for the records to be kept;
for securing that a child is not placed with a local authority foster parent unless approved;
for securing that where possible a foster parent with whom a child is to be placed is of the same religious persuasion as the child, or gives an undertaking that the child will be brought up in that religious persuasion;
for securing that children and premises in which they are accommodated will be supervised and inspected by a local authority and that children will be removed from those premises if their welfare appears to require it;
and as to the circumstances in which local authorities may make arrangements for duties imposed upon them by the regulations to be discharged on their behalf. <Schedule 2 (12)>

Regulations may also provide for:

the persons to be notified of any proposed arrangements;
the opportunities such persons have to make representations in relation to the proposed arrangements;
the persons to be notified of any proposed changes in arrangements;
the records to be kept by local authorities;
and the supervision by local authorities of any arrangements made. <Schedule 2 (13)>

THE FOSTER PLACEMENT (CHILDREN) REGULATIONS 1991

Scope

The regulations apply to any placement of a child by a local authority looking after a child who is accommodated and maintained by them; or by a voluntary organisation providing accommodation for a child with a family, relative or other suitable person. <Regulation 2(1) /S23(2) & S59(1)>

They do not apply in relation to a child in care living with a parent, a person who has parental responsibility or a residence order (see chapter 2). (In these cases the Placement of Children with Parents etc. Regulations 1991 apply: see under care orders, chapter 4.)

They do not apply if any child is not in the care of the local authority and is living with a parent or person with parental responsibility, or where a placement has been made pursuant to an adoption. <Regulation 2(2)>

Where a care order is in force directions given by the court may alter the application of these regulations.

Where a child is already living with a prospective foster parent before placement, temporary removal is not required by the regulations. <Regulation 2 (3/4)>

Approvals and Placements

Except in the case of an immediate emergency no placement may be made unless the foster parents are approved under these regulations.

Any local authority and any voluntary organisation (responsible for the placement of the child) may approve a foster parent unless approval has already been given by another local authority or voluntary organisation.

"Approving authorities" are required to consult with and take into account the views of the local authority in whose area the child is to be placed (the "area authority") before approving a foster parent. <Regulations 1/3(1-3)>

A local authority or voluntary organisation are not to give approval unless they have required the prospective foster parents to supply the names and addresses of two personal referees and have arranged for them to be interviewed.

The following information relating to the prospective foster parent is also required to assess suitability:

age, health (supported by a medical report), personality and marital status (including any previous marriage);

particulars of other members of their household;

the children in their family (whether or not members of their

household) and any other children in their household;
their accommodation;
their religious persuasion and the degree of their religious observance and capacity to care for a child from any particular religious persuasion;
their racial origin and cultural and linguistic background and their capacity to care for a child from any particular origin or cultural or linguistic background;
their past and present employment or occupation, standard of living and leisure activities and interests;
their previous experience of caring for their own and other children and their capacity in this respect;
their previous criminal convictions, if any, and those of other adult members of his household (subject to the Rehabilitation of Offenders Act 1974);
the outcome of any request or application made by them or any member of their household to foster or adopt children or to register as a child minder or provide day care of children; and any previous approval, refusal or termination of approval as a foster parent relating to them or any other member of their household.

The local authority or voluntary organisation must be satisfied that the person is suitable to act as a foster parent and that his household is suitable for any child in respect of whom approval is given. <Regulation 3(4)/ Schedule 1>

Department of Health guidance is clear that where an applicant is married both partners should be assessed and approved. <Vol. 3 (3.13)>

An approval may be in respect of a particular named child, or number and age range of children, or of placements of any particular kind or in any particular circumstances. <Regulation 3 (5)>

Where an approving authority approve a foster parent they shall give him notice which specifies whether the approval is in respect of a particular named child or children or number and age range of children, or of placements of any particular kind or in any particular circumstances.

They will enter into a written agreement with him covering the following matters and obligations:
the amount of support and training to be given;
the procedure for review of approval;
the procedure in connection with the placement of foster children and in particular:
the matters to be covered in foster placement agreements and the respective obligations under any such agreement, of the responsible authority and the foster parent;

the authority's arrangements for meeting and legal liabilities of the foster parent arising by reason of a placement;

and the procedure available to foster parents for making representations to the local authority in whose area the child is placed;

to give written notice to the authority forthwith, giving full particulars of:

any intended change of address,

any change in the composition of his household,

any change in his personal circumstances and any other event affecting either his capacity to care for any child placed or the suitability of his household,

and any further request or application concerning fostering, adoption, child minding or day care;

not to administer corporal punishment to any child placed with him;

to ensure that any information relating to a child placed with him or to the child's family or to any other person which has been given to him in connection with a placement is kept confidential and is not disclosed to any person without the consent of the responsible authority;

to comply with the terms of any foster placement agreement, to care for the child placed as if he were a member of the foster parent's family and to promote his welfare having regard to the responsible authority's long and short term arrangements for the child;

to notify the responsible authority immediately of any serious illness of the child or of any other serious occurrence affecting the child;

and, where required by the responsible authority or the area authority, under regulation seven to allow the child to be removed from the foster home. <Regulation 3(5)/ Schedule 2>

Department of Health guidance indicates that these matters and obligations to be covered in the foster care agreement are minimum requirements. Authorities should ensure that foster parents have a full understanding of expectations and enter into specific agreement when an individual child is placed. <Vol. 3 (3.53)>

Where an approving authority decide not to approve a person as a foster parent they are to give him notice of the decision. <Regulation 3(7)>

Reviews and Terminations of Approvals

Where a foster parent has been approved, the approving authority are to review, at intervals of not more than a year, whether the foster parent and his household continue to be suitable.

The approving authority are to seek, and take into account, the views of the foster parent and of any responsible authority who have placed the child with the foster parent within the preceding year or who have an earlier placement with the foster parent which has not yet terminated.

At the conclusion of the review the approving authority are to prepare a report and give notice to the foster parent of their decision (including any revision of the terms of approval). (A copy of this notice is to be sent to any other local authority or voluntary organisation who have a child placed with the foster parent.) <Regulation 4(1-3/6)>

> *Department of Health guidance indicates that reviews should be carried out by a social worker with a responsibility to the fostering service rather than the social worker of a child in placement, although consultation will be necessary.*
>
> *The guidance also states that a review should include a visit to the foster home, discussion with the foster parent and generally meeting members of the household. It should be the opportunity for airing and discussion of the foster parent's view of the service offered by the authority and of their own experience and difficulties.*
>
> *The terms of approval should also be included in a review. Non-use or under use of a foster home are also factors to investigate. The process should lead to an understanding of the strengths and weaknesses of the fostering service as a whole. Opportunities for training and support should be provided. <Vol. 3 (3.45)>*

Where on a review the approving authority are no longer satisfied that:

the terms of the approval are appropriate they shall revise the terms;

the foster parent and his household are suitable they are to terminate the approval from a date specified in the required notice.

Where a foster parent notifies the approving authority that he no longer wishes to act as a foster parent, or where the authority are otherwise satisfied that this is the case, the authority are to terminate the approval from a date to be specified by notice. (A copy of this notice is to be sent to any other local authority or voluntary organisation who have a child placed with the foster parent.) <Regulation 4(3-6)>

Placements

This part of these regulations should be read in conjunction with The Arrangements for Placement of Children (General) Regulations 1991 (see chapter 8). The placement regulations cover the making of arrangement for placement, notification of health requirements, educational needs and agreements with parents and children.

A responsible authority are not to place a child with a foster parent unless they are satisfied that:

this is the most suitable way of performing their general duty to promote the child's welfare and to make use of services available for children cared for by their own parents (as appears reasonable in the case);

and the placement with the particular foster parent is the most suitable having regard to all the circumstances.

In the case of voluntary organisations the general duty also applies to advise, assist and befriend the child with a view to promoting his welfare when he ceases to be so accommodated. <Regulation 5(1)/ S22(3) & S61(1)>

In making arrangements for a placement the responsible authority are to satisfy themselves that where possible the foster parent:

is of the same religious persuasion as the child;

or gives an undertaking that the child will be brought up in that religious persuasion. <Regulation 5(2)>

So long as it is consistent with the details of approval (e.g. those specifying named children or the number and age range of children) the responsible authority may place a child with a foster parent whom they have themselves approved or with a foster parent approved by another local authority or voluntary organisation.

In these cases, the following conditions would also have to be satisfied:

the approving authority consent to the placement;

any other local authority or voluntary organisation who already have a child placed with the foster parent also consent to the placement;

and the area authority (if they are not also the approving authority) are consulted, and their views taken into account, and are given notice of the placement.

A responsible authority which places a child after consulting an area authority shall given notice on the placement to the area authority. <Regulation 5(3-5)>

Except in the case of an emergency or immediate placement, a responsible authority are not to place a child unless the authority and the foster parent have entered into a written agreement covering the following matters and obligations:

the provision by the responsible authority of a statement (provided at the time of signing the agreement, or if this is not practicable within the following 14 days) containing all the information which the authority consider necessary to enable the foster parent to care for the child. In particular:

the authority's arrangements for the child and the objectives of the placement,

the child's personal history, religious persuasion, cultural and linguistic background and racial origin,

the child's state of health and need for health care and surveillance, and

the child's educational needs;

the responsible authority's arrangements for the financial support of the child during the placement;
any arrangements for delegation of responsibility for consent to medical or dental examination or treatment of the child;
the circumstances in which it is necessary to obtain in advance the approval of the responsible authority for the child to live, even temporarily, away from the foster parent's home;
the arrangements for visits to the child, in connection with the supervision of the placement, by the person authorised by or on behalf of the responsible authority or area authority and the frequency of visits and reviews under the Review of Children's Cases Regulations 1991 (see chapter 8);
the arrangements for the child to have contact with his parents and other persons, including: in relation to a child in care, any arrangements made for contact by a parent, guardian or person with a residence order under section 34 of the Act (see chapter 2); or any contact order under section 8 of the Act (see chapter 2);
compliance by the foster parent with the terms of the foster care agreement <see Regulation 3, above>;
co-operation by the foster parent with any arrangements made by the responsible authority for the child. <Regulation 5(5) /Schedule 3 Part I>

Department of Health guidance indicates that the purpose of the information is to enable the foster parent to care for the child. In some circumstances less information, about the child's history for example, may be needed in connection with a very short term placement. Authorities should ensure that foster parents are given the information they need to help a child during a placement. <Vol. 3 (4.14)>

Supervision of Placements

A responsible authority are to satisfy themselves that the welfare of each child placed by them continues to be suitably provided for by the placement. The authority are to make arrangements for a person authorised by them to visit the child, in the home in which he is placed, from time to time as the circumstances may require and when reasonably requested by the child or the foster parent.

In the first year of the arrangement visits will be within one week from its beginning and then at intervals of not more than six weeks, and subsequently at intervals of not more than three months.

The authority are to give such advice to the foster parent as appears to be needed.

If appropriate it should be arranged to see the child alone. A written report is to be prepared by the person who made the visit <Regulation 6(1/3/4)>.

Department of Health guidance indicates that visits during the first weeks of placement can be particularly important to check that the arrangements made at the time of placement for schooling and access are working smoothly, or to give any help needed during the settling in period.

Guidance also indicates that overall the role of visits is to safeguard and reassure a child who is vulnerable and isolated away from family and other familiar people. The standard of care should be observed and the child's bedroom sometimes seen. Some visits should be unannounced. Visits should occasionally take place when all the members of the household are at home.

Both the child and the foster parent should feel free to get in touch with the social worker at any time. Visits should be used to evaluate and monitor the achievement of goals and to keep the plan under review; to monitor, with the foster parents, the child's educational progress and to identify where help is needed. Contact arrangements should be monitored. Support should be given to the foster parent.

The Department of Health state that the regulations prescribe minimums: there may be some circumstances (when a foster parent or placement is under particular stress) where visits in excess of the minimum frequency will be necessary. <Vol. 3 (4.19-4.23)>

In the case of an emergency or immediate placement (see regulation 11 below) the responsible authority are to arrange for the child to be visited at least once each week during the placement. <Regulation 6(2)>

Series of short term placements may be treated as a single placement. A visit is to be made during the first in the series of placements, and again if not more that six months pass from the beginning of that first placement.

(Short term placements are defined as situations where all the placements take place (with the same foster parent) within a period which does not exceed a maximum of one year; no single placement lasts for more than four weeks; and the total duration of the placement does not exceed 90 days.) <Regulation 6(1)/ 9>

Respite care schemes are thus subject to a unified view in relation to planning and supervision.

Termination of Placements

A responsible authority are not to allow the placement of a child with a particular foster parent to continue if it appears to them that the placement is no longer the most suitable way of performing their general duty to promote the child's welfare and to make use of services available for children cared for by their own parents (as appears reasonable in the case). <Regulation 7(1) /S22(3) & S61(1)>

Where a child has been placed by some other local authority, or by a voluntary organisation, in the area of the area authority and it appears to the authority that continuation of the placement would be detrimental to the welfare of the child, the area authority are to remove the child forthwith at the same time notifying the responsible authority. <Regulation 7(2/3)>

Arrangements Between Local Authorities and Voluntary Organisations as to Placements

Where a local authority looking after a child are satisfied that the child should be placed with a foster parent they may make arrangements for the other duties imposed upon them to be discharged on their behalf by a voluntary organisation.

They should be satisfied as to the capacity of the voluntary organisation to discharge duties on their behalf, and that these arrangements are the most suitable way of arranging for the discharge of their duties. Written agreements with the voluntary organisation, providing for exchange of information and reports will be entered into. <Regulation 8>

The Department of Health indicate that such delegation of duties can only relate to a particular child, after the local authority is satisfied that the child should be placed with a foster parent. Areas of delegation may only include approval of foster parents, review and terminations of approval of foster parents, placements, supervision of placements and termination of placements. Arrangements will need to be worked out in advance so that they may be applied to a particular child. As foster parents approved under delegated arrangements will be deemed to be on the list of the local authority it is essential that the criteria and procedures are fully agreed between the agencies. The local authority should only use a voluntary organisation if they are satisfied with the organisation's structure, including its financial arrangements, management accountability and complaints procedures. A placement agreement will need drawing up as part of the individual care plan of the child. A contract will also need drawing up delegating the various duties. <Circular LAC(94)20>

Placements Outside England and Wales

A voluntary organisation are not to place a child outside the British Islands (the United Kingdom, the Channel Islands and the Isle of Man).

Where a responsible authority make arrangements to place a child outside England and Wales they are to ensure that, so far as practicable, requirements are complied with in relation to the child which would have applied under these regulations if the child had been placed in England and Wales.

Local authorities may only assist in arranging for any child in their care to live outside England and Wales with the approval of the court; in the case of other children looked after by them, the local authority may, with the approval of every person who has parental responsibility for the child arrange for, or assist in arranging for, the child to live outside England and Wales. <Regulation 10 /1989 Act, Schedule 2 (19)>

Emergency and Immediate Placements by Local Authorities

Where arrangements have been made for the placement of a child in an emergency, a local authority may, for a period not exceeding 24 hours, place a child with a person who has not been approved (under regulation 3, see above) provided that:

they are satisfied that it is the most suitable way of performing their general duty to promote the child's welfare and to make use of services available for children cared for by their own parents (as appears reasonable in the case);

and they obtain a written agreement from the person with whom the child is to be placed that that person will carry out the following duties:

to care for the child as if he were a member of that person's family;

to permit any person authorised by the local authority, or (if different) the area authority, to visit the child at any time;

if the requirements for the local authority, or the area authority, to remove the child apply (see regulation 7 "Termination of Placements", above) to allow that removal;

to ensure that any information which the foster parent may acquire relating to the child, or to his family or any other person, which has been given to him in confidence in connection with the placement is kept confidential and is not disclosed except to, or with the agreement of, the local authority;

and to allow contact with parents etc. of a child in care, in accordance with the section 34 of the Act (see chapter 4) and with any person holding a contact order under section 8(1) (see chapter 2) and with any arrangements made or agreed by the local authority. <Regulation 11 (1/2>

Where a local authority are satisfied that an immediate placement of a child is necessary they may for a period not exceeding six weeks place a child with a person who has been approved under regulation 3 (see above) provided, after interviewing the person, inspecting the accommodation and obtaining information about other persons living in his household the authority are also satisfied that:

the person is a relative or friend of the child;

it is the most suitable way of performing their general duty to promote the child's welfare and to make use of services available for children cared for by their own parents (as appears reasonable in the case);

and the person has made a written agreement with the local authority to carry out the following duties:

to care for the child as if he were a member of that person's family;

to permit any person authorised by the local authority, or (if different) the area authority, to visit the child at any time;

if the requirements for the local authority, or the area authority, to remove the child apply (see regulation 7 "Termination of Placements", above) to allow that removal;

to ensure that any information which the foster parent may acquire relating to the child, or to his family or any other person, which has been given to him in confidence in connection with the placement is kept confidential and is not disclosed except to, or with the agreement of, the local authority;

and to allow contact with parents etc. of a child in care, in accordance with the section 34 of the Act (see chapter 4) and with any person holding a contact order under section 8(1) (see chapter 2) and with any arrangements made or agreed by the local authority. <Regulation 11 (3/4)>

Where a local authority make an emergency or immediate placement outside their area they shall notify the area authority. <Regulation 11 (5)>

Department of Health guidance indicates that the term emergency is intended to imply some exceptional and unforeseen circumstance and not, for example, circumstances for which contingency plans could be made. Where such planning has not been possible the powers may be used when it would clearly be advantageous to the child to be placed with, or remain in the care of a familiar figure in reassuring surroundings. In guarding against inappropriate use of the powers, local procedures should provide for authorisation at a senior level. <Vol. 3 (4.26)>

Register of Foster Parents

A local authority are to enter, in a register kept for the purpose, the name and address of each approved foster parent (or for joint approvals, both foster parents) or the person with whom an emergency and immediate placement has been made, the date of approval and the terms of the approval or of the agreement as for the time being in force. <Regulation 12>

The register should serve as an index to the local authorities' own fostering resources and enable the authority to respond to enquiries from other authorities who are considering approval or placement.

Case Records for Foster Parents

An approving authority are required to compile and maintain a record for each foster parent whom they have approved and each person with whom an emergency and immediate placement has been made. Each record should include:

the notice of approval;

the written agreement between the authority and the foster parent;

the report of review of approval;

any notice of termination of approval;

any notice of agreement to carry out duties of an immediate placement;

a record of each placement with the foster parent (including the name, age and sex of each child placed, the dates on which each placement began and terminated and the circumstances of the termination);

the information obtained by the approving authority in relation to the approval of the foster parent and any review or termination of the approval;

the record of any enquiries and the agreement relating to an immediate placement. <Regulation 13 (1-4)>

An approving authority is required to compile a record for each prospective foster parent to whom notice has been served not giving approval.

This record is to include a copy of the notice and the information as to the foster parent and his household and family, obtained in connection with the question of approval. <Regulation 13 (5)>

Retention and Confidentiality of Records

The case records for a foster parent compiled under regulation 13 and any entry on him in the register compiled under regulation 12, is to be retained for at least 10 years from the date of his approval or from the date of termination of approval, or until his death if earlier.

The original written record may be kept (or a copy of it) or it may be kept in some other accessible form (e.g. on a computer). <Regulation 14 (1/2)>

The authority or organisation responsible for the maintenance of any register or record are to secure its safekeeping and to take all necessary steps to ensure that the information which it contains is treated as confidential subject only to any court order, or provision in or under a statute under which access may be obtained. <Regulation 14 (3)>

Local Authority Visits to Children Placed by Voluntary Organisations

Every local authority shall arrange for one of their officers to visit every child who is accommodated with a foster parent within their area by or on behalf of a voluntary organisation (except where they have made arrangements for their duties to be discharged by that voluntary organisation under regulation 8 <see above) in any of the following circumstances (and within the periods specified):

within 28 days of the placement;

where the voluntary organisation which made the placement make representations to the local authority that there are circumstances relating to the child which require a visit (within 14 days);

where the local authority are informed that the welfare of the child may not be being safeguarded or promoted (as soon as reasonably practicable but in any event within seven days);

where the local authority are satisfied, following a visit that the child's welfare is being safeguarded and promoted (at intervals of not more than six months). <Regulation 15>

Every local authority shall ensure during the course of these visits an officer sees the child, unless he considers it unnecessary to do so or the child is not in fact with the foster parents at the time of the visit. If the child is not there he should make arrangements to see the child as soon as reasonably practicable.

The officer will take steps to discover whether the voluntary organisation which placed the child have made suitable arrangements to perform their duties under the regulations and under section 61 of the Act (see chapter 6). <Regulation 16>

PART IX PRIVATELY FOSTERED CHILDREN

Definition

A child under 16 (18 if disabled) who is cared for and provided with accommodation by (or living in premises with) someone other than:

a parent of his;

a person holding parental responsibility;

or a relative. <S66(1)/Schedule 8(2)>

The arrangement constitutes a private arrangement between the two parents and the private foster parents. Private fostering is to be distinguished from placement with local authority foster parents (see above).

In the case of a child under 16 who is a pupil in a non-maintained residential school, after two weeks of the school holidays he shall be classed as a privately fostered child although the local authority may not impose requirements. <Schedule 8 (9)>

Exceptions to Definition

A child being looked after by a local authority. <Schedule 8 (1)>

Where the child is cared for in a personal capacity in:

children's homes;
accommodation provided by voluntary organisations;
schools;
health service hospitals;
any residential home, nursing home or mental nursing home;
any home or institution managed by a government department or provided by a local authority. <Schedule 8 (2)>

Children cared for in compliance with: a supervision order under the 1969 Children and Young Persons Act; or a supervision requirement under the 1968 Social Work (Scotland) Act. <Schedule 8 (3)>

Children liable to be detained or subject to guardianship under the 1983 Mental Health Act. <Schedule 8 (4)>

Protected children within the meaning of the 1976 Adoption Act or under the care of a prospective adoptor. <Schedule 8 (5)>

Periods of less than 28 days. <S66(2)>

Cases of more than three children will normally be treated as registered children's homes (see chapter 6). <S63(12) /Schedule 7>

The parameters of private fostering are clearly set so that it is understood which requirements placements are subject to.

Notification

The Secretary of State may make regulations concerning and requiring the notification to the local authority of children who are actually or proposed to be privately fostered.

The regulations may detail the circumstances involved, and the manner and form a notification is to take.

Under the regulations any person who is the parent or has parental responsibility and who knows that it is proposed that the child should be privately fostered is required to give notice including any change of address of the child.

Private foster parents are required to notify the authority of their proposals, any change in their address, any offence of which they have been convicted and any disqualification or requirements previously imposed under this legislation.

When a child has ceased to be privately fostered the private foster parent is required to notify the local authority (if the child has died they must also give the reason). <Schedule 8(7)>

Any person who proposes to foster a child for whom he is already caring and providing accommodation shall notify the appropriate local authority not less than six, nor more than 13 weeks before he receives the child unless he receives him in an emergency.

In cases of emergency private fostering (or where a child is already being cared for and provided with accommodation when he became a private foster child) the foster parent shall notify the appropriate local authority not more than 48 hours after the fostering arrangements began.

All notices shall specify:

the name, sex, date and place of birth, religious persuasion, racial origin and cultural and linguistic background of the child;

the name and address of the person giving the notice and any previous address within the last five years;

the purpose and intended duration of the fostering arrangements;

the name and address of any parent of the child or of any other person who has parental responsibility and (if different) of any person from whom the child was, or is to be received, plus the name and address of any other person who is involved directly or indirectly in making the fostering arrangement;

the intended date of the beginning of the fostering arrangement (or the date upon which the arrangement actually began);

particulars of any offence of which the person giving notice (or any other person living in, or employed at, the same household) has been convicted, plus any disqualification or prohibition imposed on him/them as a private foster parent. This is subject to the Rehabilitation of Offenders Act 1974. <The Children (Private Arrangements for Fostering) Regulations 1991 (Regulation 4 (1-4/7)>

Any person who is fostering a child privately shall notify the appropriate local authority (in advance if practicable, and in any other case, within not more than 48 hours) of:

any change in his address;

any person who begins, or ceases to be part of his household;

and any further conviction, disqualification or prohibition imposed on him as a private foster parent (or on any other person living in, or employed at, the same household). This is subject to the Rehabilitation of Offenders Act 1974. <The Children (Private Arrangements for Fostering) Regulations 1991 (Regulation 4 (5-7)>

Any person who has been fostering a child privately, but has ceased to do so, shall notify the appropriate local authority within 48 hours and shall include in the notice the name and address of the person into whose care the child has been received. (This does not apply if the foster parent intends to resume the fostering arrangement after 27 days; unless this intention is subsequently abandoned or the interval expires without resumption of private fostering. In such cases notice shall be given within 48 hours of the change in intention or of the expiry of the interval.)

Where death of a private foster child is involved, the foster parent shall notify forthwith the local authority and also the person from whom the foster parent received the child. <The Children (Private Arrangements for Fostering) Regulations 1991 (Regulation 5)>.

Any person who is, or proposes to be, involved (whether directly or not) in arranging for a child to be fostered privately, shall notify the appropriate authority not less than six, and not more than 13, weeks before the fostering arrangement begins (except in an emergency arrangement when 48 hours notification applies).

A parent of a child, and any other person who has parental responsibility, who knows that it is proposed that the child should be fostered privately shall notify the appropriate authority not less than six, nor more than 13 weeks before the fostering arrangement begins unless the arrangement is an emergency in which case the notification shall be not more than 48 hours thereafter.

All notices shall specify:

the name, sex, date and place of birth, religious persuasion, racial origin and cultural and linguistic background of the child;

the name and address of the person giving the notice and any previous address within the last five years;

the purpose and intended duration of the fostering arrangement;

the arrangements for the care of any brother or sister not included in the fostering arrangement;

the name and address of any other person involved (whether directly or indirectly) in the fostering arrangement;

where a notice is given by any person who is, or proposes to be, involved (whether directly or not) in arranging for a child to be fostered privately, their relationship to the child and their name and address; plus the name and address of any parent of the child or of any other person who has parental responsibility and (if different) of any person from whom the child was, or is to be received. <The Children (Private Arrangements for Fostering) Regulations 1991 (Regulation 6 (1-3)>

Any parent of a privately fostered child, and any person who has parental responsibility shall notify the appropriate local authority of the ending of the fostering arrangements; and any change in his own address. <The Children (Private Arrangements for Fostering) Regulations 1991 (Regulation 6(4)>

Any notification shall be given in writing and may be sent by post. "Address" includes a temporary address. <The Children (Private Arrangements for Fostering) Regulations 1991 (Regulations 1/7)>

The Department of Health indicate that whilst the day to day care of the child can be delegated to the private foster parent, parental responsibility is retained by the natural parent. <Vol. 8 (1.4.6)>

If the natural parents are falling short of their responsibilities action may need to be taken by the social worker. <Vol. 8 (1.4.7)>.

Duties of Local Authorities

The Department of Health state that the role of local authorities is *to satisfy themselves that the arrangements are satisfactory and that the foster parents are suitable. A proper balance needs to be maintained between parental private responsibilities and statutory duties towards private foster children. <Vol. 8 (1.1.5)>*

The purpose and intended duration of a fostering arrangement needs to be clearly established by the local authority prior to the placement and reviewed on every visit. If the child has special needs or is "in need" under the Act (see chapter 3) he should receive the appropriate services. <Vol. 8 (1.4.8/1.4.14)>

To satisfy themselves that the child's welfare is satisfactorily safeguarded and promoted and to secure that such advice is given to those caring for him as appears to be needed. <S67(1)>

Volume 8 of the Department of Health's guidance gives extensive notes on how the welfare of the child may be promoted. This particularly applies to areas such as health; race, culture, religion and linguistic needs; siblings; equal opportunities; continuity and change; and recording the child's development. <Vol. 8 (1.7.1-1.7.33)>

Where a person authorised by the local authority has reasonable cause to believe that any privately fostered child is being accommodated in premises in the authority's area; or it is proposed to accommodate the child, he may at any reasonable time inspect those premises and any children there.

If required some duly authenticated document must be produced. <S67(3/4)>

The Department of Health state that the purpose of visits include:

child protection: the standard of care should be observed, the child's bedroom occasionally seen, some visits may be appropriate unannounced or when all members of the household are at home;

providing a link and encouragement to improve standards of child care;

a check that requirements are met and whether they need to be changed or cancelled;

ensuring that the foster parent receives appropriate advice;

enquiring how the arrangements with the natural parents are working and whether it would be appropriate for the local authority to intervene;

satisfying the local authority that the welfare of the child is satisfactory. <Vol. 8 (1.8.8)>

If, on application to the court it appears that a person attempting to apply these powers has been prevented from doing so by being refused entry to the premises concerned, or access to the child concerned; or that they are likely to be prevented from exercising such powers, a warrant authorising any constable to assist that person, using reasonable force if necessary, may be issued.

The court may direct that the constable be accompanied by a registered medical practitioner, registered nurse or registered health visitor if the person so chooses. <S102>

The Secretary of State may make regulations requiring the circumstances and frequency of visiting and imposing requirements. <S67(2)>

A local authority shall make arrangements for each child who is privately fostered within their area to be visited by an officer of the local authority from time to time as considered necessary in order to safeguard and promote the welfare of the child (and when reasonably requested by the child and foster parent). In particular:

- in the first year of the fostering arrangement, within one week from its beginning and then at intervals of not more than six weeks;
- in any second or subsequent year, at intervals of not more than three months.

If appropriate, the child shall be arranged to be seen alone. A written report shall be made by the officer to the local authority after each visit. <The Children (Private Arrangements for Fostering) Regulations 1991 (Regulation 3)>

The local authority and the officer visiting shall satisfy themselves as to the following (where relevant in the particular circumstances):

- the purpose and intended duration of the fostering arrangement;
- the child's physical, intellectual, emotional, social and behavioural development;
- whether the child's needs arising from his religious persuasion, racial origin and cultural and linguistic background are being met;
- the financial arrangements for the care and maintenance of the child;
- the suitability of the accommodation;
- the arrangements for the child's medical and dental care and treatment and, in particular, that the child is registered with a GP;
- the arrangements for the child's education and, in particular, that the local education authority have been informed of the fostering arrangement;
- the standard of care which the child is being given;
- the suitability of the foster parent to look after the child and the suitability of the foster parent's household;
- whether the foster parent is being given any necessary advice;
- whether the contact between the child and his parents, or any other person which whom contact has been arranged, is satisfactory;
- whether the child's parents, or any other person, are exercising

parental responsibility for the child;
and the ascertainable wishes and feelings of the child regarding the fostering arrangements. <The Children (Private Arrangements for Fostering) Regulations 1991 (Regulation 2)>

Details of Department of Health guidance concerning records to be kept by local authorities are contained in Vol. 8 (1.10.1-1.10.5)>

Where the local authority are not satisfied that the welfare of the child is being satisfactorily safeguarded or promoted they shall (unless it is not in the best interests of the child) take such steps as are reasonably practicable to secure that the care and accommodation of the child is undertaken by: a parent; a person with parental responsibility; or a relative and consider the possibility of any other action under the act. <S67(5)>

Limits on the Number of Foster Children

Except where the children are all siblings, a person may not foster more than three children unless he is exempted from "the usual fostering limit" by the local authority.

In granting any exemptions, the local authority shall have particular regard to:
the number of persons it is proposed to foster;
the arrangements for care and accommodation;
the intended and likely relationship between the person and the fostered children;
the period of time proposed for fostering;
and whether the welfare of the fostered children (and any other children who are or will be living in the accommodation) will be safeguarded and promoted.

Exemptions shall be informed by notice in writing giving the children's names and any conditions involved.

At any time by giving notice in writing there may be variations or cancellation of exemptions and conditions, or the imposing of new conditions.

If a person exceeds the usual fostering limit, or where exempted he fosters a child not mentioned in the exemption, he shall be treated as carrying on a children's home (see chapter 6).

Every local authority is required to establish a procedure for considering representations (including complaints) by persons exempted or seeking to be exempted under these provisions (see chapter 3). <Schedule 7>

Power to Impose Requirements

The local authority can impose requirements by notice in writing informing the person concerned of the reason for imposing the requirement and his rights of appeal including time limits. Requirements can include:

the number age and sex of the children;
standard of the accommodation and equipment;
the health and safety arrangements;
the provision of care.

It shall be the duty of the private foster parent to comply with any such requirement.

Requirements can be varied or removed at any time or additional requirements imposed.

A requirement may be limited to a particular child or class of child. <Schedule 8 (6)>

A private foster parent is deemed to have no interest in the life of the foster child for insurance purposes. <Schedule 8 (11)>

Disqualification and Prohibition

Regulations will provide for persons to be disqualified from being private foster parents unless they have disclosed their circumstances to the local authority and obtained their written consent.

The authority can refuse to give such consent to private fostering. The regulations may in particular provide for disqualification of a person where:

a specified order has been made at any time in respect to him or the child who has been in his care;
a specified requirement has been imposed at any time with respect to a child who has been in his care;
he has been convicted, placed on probation, discharged absolutely or conditionally for any specified offence with respect to a child;
a prohibition has been imposed at any time with regard to private fostering;
or his rights or powers with respect to a child have been vested in a specified authority under a specified enactment. <S68(1/2)>

A person is disqualified from being a private foster parent and from registering as a private foster parent if:

he is a parent of a child who at any time has been the subject of a care order, a supervision order with a residence requirement, an approved school order, or (in Northern Ireland) a fit person order or a training school order;
a supervision requirement has been imposed at any time (in Scotland) with respect to any child for the purpose of removing that child from his care, or his rights and powers with respect to the child has at any time been vested in a local authority;
an order has been made at any time for the purpose of removing a protected child under the adoption acts, who was being kept by him, or about to be received by him, in unsuitable surroundings;

an order has been made previously for the removal of a foster child;
he is a person who carried on, or was otherwise concerned with the management of, or had a financial interest in a voluntary home which was removed from the register (or registration had been refused);
he is person who carried on or was otherwise concerned with the management of, or had a financial interest in a registered children's home which was removed from the register (or an application for registration was refused and he was the applicant);
he is a person in respect of whom a prohibition has been imposed under powers to prohibit private fostering (or in Northern Ireland, consent to the care and maintenance of a child being undertaken by them was withheld);
he has at any time been refused registration in respect of nurseries, day care or child minding or had such registration cancelled (in Scotland, the registration of an establishment);
he has been convicted of any of the following offences:

any offence against a child or young person specified in schedule 1 of the Children and Young Persons Act and corresponding legislation in Scotland or Northern Ireland;
any offence involving injury or threat of injury to another person;
any offence under the Adoption Acts involving refusing to allow the visiting of a protected child, or inspection of the premises, or refusing to comply with or obstructing the removal of the child;
any offence of intentional obstruction of a person executing an emergency protection order (or in Scotland or Northern Ireland a place of safety order, or abduction or obstruction of lawful recovery of an abducted child);
providing day care or acting as a child minder in unregistered premises or contravening such an enforcement order (relates to offences in Northern Ireland);
caring for and accommodating a child in a children's home which is not registered or breaching conditions attaching to registration;
offences in respect of private fostering;
carrying on a voluntary home without it being registered or in contravention of a condition attached to registration;
under Scottish law, refusal of registration and offences in respect of day care or residential care, the theft of a child below the age of puberty or offences relating to indecent photography of children.

<The Disqualification for Caring for Children Regulations 1991 (Regulations 1/2/Schedule)>

A person shall not foster a child privately if he lives in the same household as a person who is himself prevented from fostering a child or he lives in a household at which such a person is employed; unless he has disclosed the fact to the appropriate local authority and obtained their written consent.

If consent is refused the applicant shall be informed by written notice stating the reason for the refusal and the applicant's right of appeal including the timescale involved. <S68(4/5)>

The authority can prohibit fostering when in their opinion:
the parent is not a suitable person to foster;
the premises are unsuitable;
or it would be prejudicial to the welfare of the child.

The Department of Health indicate that these duties can be best accomplished by consulting with the person who proposes to foster and the parent (or person with parental responsibility) about the reasons to privately foster the child and by making advice available. Discussions should be frank and make clear that the welfare of the child is paramount and the enquiry process involved. <Vol. 8 (1.4.20 / 1.5.1 / 1.5.2)>

Assessment as to suitability of the foster parent should include police records, household relationships, parenting capacity, religion, ethnicity, expectations and attitude towards parental visits, life style, and attitudes to the child's education and discipline. <Vol. 8 (1.5.3-1.5.14)>

In deciding the suitability of accommodation local authorities should pay attention to:
access to garden and safety within it, access to the road (children should be unable to leave the premises unsupervised);
outside playspace;
safety of fires, electrical sockets, windows, floor coverings and glass doors;
cooking facilities; and safety in the kitchen or cooking area;
use of stairgates;
arrangements for keeping the premises clean;
facilities for rest and sleep;
washing and toilet facilities and hygiene;
fire safety;
equipment such as cots should be British Standards approved;
safe storage of medicines and dangerous household substances;
presence of pets and arrangements for their control;
quality of transport - car seats, safety belts, etc. <Vol. 2 (7.33) & Vol. 8 (1.4.19)>

In inspections the local authority should take into account condition such as dampness and extremes of temperature which will have a direct effect on the health of a child who has a condition such as sickle cell anaemia or thalassaemia.

Assessment should also include living and sleeping facilities and the effect of overcrowding. <Vol. 8 (1.4.22)>

The prohibition may specify the premises involved, any child in any premises within the area of the local authority, or an identified child in specified premises.

A prohibition may be cancelled at any time if the local authority think fit or an application is made by the person involved. The local authority should be satisfied that the prohibition is no longer justified. <S69(1-4)>

The Department of Health state that where lifting a disqualification is an issue the case should be scrutinised at a senior level with legal advisors. The decision should turn on whether the facts or circumstances which prevailed at the time of the offence or order no longer apply (given the date, type of offence or order, the degree of culpability and the person's activity and involvement with children since). Reasons given for refusing to exercise discretion will need to be of sufficient force to stand up in court. <Vol. 8 (2.7/2.8)>

Where a local authority impose a requirement that has not been complied with and the time specified for compliance with the requirement has expired they may then impose a prohibition by written notice stating the reason for prohibition and the person's right of appeal including the timescale involved. <S69(5-7)>

Appeals

A person aggrieved by the local authority's action in:

imposing a requirement;

refusing consent to privately foster;

imposing or refusing to cancel a prohibition;

refusing to make an exemption, variation, or cancellation to exceed the usual fostering limit,

or imposing conditions;

may appeal to the court within fourteen days of notification.

In the case of appeals against requirements, variation, cancellation or imposition of conditions of exemption to the usual fostering limit, these shall not have effect while the appeal is pending.

The court may vary requirements or prohibitions to allow for more time for compliance.

An absolute prohibition may be substituted for a prohibition on using premises after a specified time.

In the case of appeals against refusals to make an exemption, the court may vary the exemption, impose a condition or make an exemption. <Schedule 8(8)>

Offences

These are listed in section 70 and include:

failure to give required notice or information without reasonable excuse within the timescale specified or reasonable time;

causing or procuring another person to make a statement in the notice or information which is known to be false or misleading;

refusing to allow a privately fostered child to be visited by a duly authorised officer of a local authority;

intentional obstruction of another in the exercise of their powers relating to the welfare of privately fostered children;

intentional contravention of disqualification imposed;

failure without reasonable excuse to comply with requirements imposed by a local authority in relation to private fostering;

accommodation of a privately fostered child in any premises in contravention of a prohibition imposed by a local authority;

publishing or causing to be published an advertisement indicating that a person will undertake or arrange for a person to be privately fostered which knowingly contravenes the requirement to indicate the foster parent's name and address. <Schedule 8 (10)>

PART X CHILD MINDING AND DAY CARE FOR YOUNG CHILDREN

Definitions

Child Minding: One or more children under eight looked after for reward for total periods of more than two hours in any day in domestic premises. <S71(1/2)>

Day Care is provided where children under the age of eight are looked after on premises other than domestic premises in any day for periods in excess of two hours. <S71(1/2)>

The regulations concerning registration and the requirements for the two are slightly different although there are many common elements.

Thus for child minding persons are registered (in relation to their domestic premises) whilst in respect of day care the premises are registered (although the persons carrying out the activity have to be fit persons).

Exceptions to Definitions

Day care provided in particular premises on less than six days per year (providing notification is made on the first occasion that the premises are used in that year). <Schedule 9 (5)>

A person is not a child minder if: a parent, relative, foster parent or nanny of the child, or they have parental responsibility. <S71(4-5)>

A person is a nanny when they look after the child wholly or mainly in the home of a parent of the child, a person with parental responsibility or a relative who has assumed responsibility for his care and for employing her. When employed by two different employers a nanny is not a child minder where any of the children concerned are looked after wholly or mainly in the home of either of her employers. <S71(6/13)>

This section of the act does not apply to any child looked after in:

a school maintained or assisted by the local authority, under the management of the local authority, or a school in respect of which payments are made by the Secretary of State;

an independent, grant-maintained or self governing school;

or a play centre maintained or assisted by a local education authority;

so long as the person involved is employed by that establishment and is carrying out activities authorised as part of that establishment's provision. <Schedule 9 (3)>

Day care in:

a registered children's home;
a voluntary home;
a community home;
a residential care home, nursing home or mental nursing home;
a health service hospital;
a home equipped, and maintained by the Secretary of State is exempt;

so long as the person involved is employed by that establishment and is carrying out activities authorised as part of that establishment's provision. <Schedule 9 (4)>

Applications for Registration

The local authority shall keep a register of child minders and persons who provide day care.

The local authority must accept valid applications for registration. To be valid an application should comply with regulations made by the Secretary of State and be accompanied by a prescribed annual fee.

Certificates of registration will be issued. The register shall be open to inspection by members of the public at all reasonable times and may be kept by means of a computer.

Where day care is provided on different premises situated in the same area of the local authority the person involved shall separately apply and be separately registered with respect to each of those premises. <S71(1/3/15) Schedule 9 (1/6/7)>

Department of Health guidance gives details of how the register is to be kept and publicised so that it may fulfil the purpose of *providing information about day care services and child minders in the area to parents and other interested parties such as employers. <Vol. 2 (7.47/7.48)>*

Department of Health guidance indicates that the purpose of registration is to protect children, provide reassurance to persons using independent services, ensure that services meet acceptable standards and to ensure that people wishing to provide services for children do so within an agreed framework. <Vol. 2 (4.9)>

Information to be supplied to the local authority is as follows:

- the full name of the applicant, including (if different) name at birth and any former names (or where day care is to be provided by a partnership, committee or corporate or unincorporate body, the full names of the partners, members of the committee, Board of Directors or the Board, identifying the Chairman, Secretary and Treasurer, and the person in charge (i.e. the person providing the actual day care);
- the address at which the children are to be looked after, and the applicant's and person in charge's address if different;
- whether the premises at which the children are to be looked after are domestic premises;
- in the case of day care, a description of the facilities available to the applicant for day care, including the number of rooms, their functions, the numbers of lavatories and washbasins, any separate facilities for adult workers and access to the premises for cars;
- whether the applicant wishes to register as:
  - a child minder,
  - a provider of full day care (i.e. day care provided for children under the age of eight for a continuous period of four hours or more in any day in premises other than domestic premises) or,
  - as a provider of sessional day care (i.e. day care provided for children under the age of eight for less than a continuous period of four hours in any day in premises other than domestic premises);
- in the case of day care, the proposed hours of provision;
- relevant experience of the applicant and any person in charge, including any previous work with children or with elderly or disabled people, whether paid or not;
- in respect of the applicant or the person in charge:
  - the number and ages of any of their children or any children for whom they are to be responsible;
  - any relevant qualifications (with dates) giving details of the organisation running the course, the subjects studied, the length of the course and the name of the qualification;
  - the names of two referees who may be contacted;
  - the name and address of their general medical practitioner and whether he may be approached for details concerning their state of

health, together with details of anything for which he is currently being treated and details of any hospital admissions during the last two years and serious illnesses in the last five years;
details of any criminal convictions including;
the date and nature of the offence,
the place where it occurred,
the name of the court which gave the conviction,
and the penalty imposed;

in respect of day care, details of how many staff will be employed in looking after the children and in what capacity; and the name, address, date of birth and details of any criminal convictions (as above) of:

any person living (or likely to live) on the premises;
any person in charge,
and any person assisting (or likely to be assisting) in looking after the children;

in respect of any child minders, the name, address, date of birth and details of any criminal convictions (as above) of;

any person living (or likely to live) on the premises in which they intend to look after children including members of the family and lodgers;
and any other person assisting (or likely to be assisting) in looking after the children. <Child Minding and Day Care (Applications for Registration) Regulations 1991/The Child Minding and Day Care (Applications for Registration and Registration and Inspection Fees) (Amendment) Regulations 1991>

The standard fees payable for registration, annual inspection and copy certificates are detailed in: The Child Minding and Day Care (Registration and Inspection Fees) Regulations 1991, as amended by The Child Minding and Day Care (Applications for Registration and Registration and Inspection Fees) (Amendment) Regulations 1991.

The premises shall be inspected by an officer of the local authority at least once per year. <S76>

Co-operation between Social Services Authorities and Local Education Authorities is required to help carry out functions under this part of the Act. <Schedule 9 (8)>

The Department of Health indicate that the provision of a coherent and efficient service to children in need by both departments will involve for example identifying gaps in services using information obtained in the exercise of statutory functions such as registration of day care. <Vol. 2 (4.7)>

Power to Impose Requirements

In respect of child minding <S72>

The local authority shall impose reasonable requirements on child minders as to:

the maximum number and age of the children (taking into account the number of other children who may at any time be on the premises);

the security, maintenance and safety of the premises and equipment;

and the records to be kept.

Where the local authority impose additional requirements these must not be incompatible with those listed in this part of the Act.

Requirements may be varied, or removed and additional requirements imposed at any time.

It shall be the duty of the child minder to comply with any such requirement.

In respect of day care <S73>

The local authority shall impose reasonable requirements on persons seeking registration to provide day care:

specifying the maximum numbers, or the maximum number of children within specified age groups, who may be looked after on the premises (taking into account the number of other children who may at any time be on the premises);

requiring the security, maintenance and safety of the premises and equipment;

requiring notice of any change in facilities provided or in the period in which they are provided;

specifying the number of persons required to assist in looking after children on the premises;

requiring records of the name and address of any child looked after on the premises;

requiring records to be kept of and notification of any changes in respect of persons who assist in looking after children and any person who lives or is likely at any time to be living at the premises.

The Secretary of State may make regulations to make provision as to requirements which must be applied under prescribed circumstances and requirements that must not be imposed by local authorities.

The local authority may impose additional requirements these must not be incompatible with those listed in this part of the Act.

Requirements may be varied, or removed and additional requirements imposed at any time.

Power to Refuse or Cancel Registration

Child minding

The local authority may refuse registration as a child minder if:

the applicant, or other persons looking after, or likely to be looking after any children on the premises are not fit to look after children or be in the proximity of children under the age of eight;

or the premises are not fit to be used (because of condition, situation, size or the condition of equipment). <S71(7/8/11)/S74(1)>

Where the care provided by a child minder is seriously inadequate (having regard to the child's needs; particularly religious persuasion, racial origin and cultural and linguistic background) or requirements imposed are ignored; or where the annual fee for inspection of premises is not paid within the prescribed time, cancellation of registration may be made. <S74(1/6)>

Cancellation of registration will normally be through a hearing involving all parties to the case <R v At Alban's Magistrates' court, ex parte Read; Queens Bench Division, judgement 11-1-94, see also Family Court Reporter Jan 1994 no 2, p 50-52>

Day care

The local authority may refuse registration for day care if they are satisfied that:

any persons looking after, or likely to be looking after any children on the premises to which the application relates, or any person employed or likely to be employed on those premises, is not fit to look after children under the age of eight;

the premises concerned are not fit to be used (because of condition, situation, size or the condition of equipment). <S71(9-11)>

In respect of premises for day care, where it appears that:

the circumstances are such that the local authority would be justified in refusing to register that person;

or where the day care provided by that person is seriously inadequate (having regard to the children's needs; particularly religious persuasion, racial origin and cultural and linguistic background);

or requirements imposed are contravened or not complied with;

or where the annual fee for inspection of premises is not paid within the prescribed time;

cancellation of registration may be made.

All registrations of a person may be so cancelled if it appears justified.

In respect of requirements to carry out repairs or make alterations, cancellation will not apply if the time set has not yet expired or it is shown that the condition of the premises is due to repairs not being carried out or additions not having been made. <S74(2-4/6)>

The Department of Health states that guidance issued in respect of registration requirements for Day Care (see below) does not prescribe legally required standards, rather it draws attention to factors that should be considered and points of reference. There is a presumption under the legislation that registration should be granted unless there is some good reason why not to. Local needs should also be respected . <Circular LAC(93)1>

Guidance on fit persons

Department of Health guidance indicates a number of points which should be considered in deciding whether someone is a fit person to look after children aged under eight:

- *previous experience of looking after or working with young children or people with disabilities or the elderly;*
- *qualification and / or training in a relevant field such as child care, early years education, health visiting, nursing or other caring activities;*
- *ability to provide warm and consistent care;*
- *commitment and knowledge to treat all children as individuals and with equal concern;*
- *knowledge of and attitude to multi-cultural issues and people of different racial origins;*
- *physical health;*
- *mental stability, integrity and flexibility;*
- *known involvement in criminal cases involving abuse to children.*

With persons living or working on the premises the points are:

- *previous records;*
- *known involvement in criminal cases involving abuse to children.*

People applying for registration should know what factors are being considered when their fitness is being assessed. <Vol. 2 (7.32)>

A Department of Health circular states that general overall fitness is pertinent rather than each individual factor being used to render a person unfit. The issue here is the overall quality of care that will be available to the children. <Circular LAC(93)1>

Guidance: suitable domestic premises

The Department of Health indicate that in registering child minders local authorities should pay attention to:

- *access to garden and safety within it, access to the road (children should be unable to leave the premises*

unsupervised);
outside playspace;
safety of fires, electrical sockets, windows, floor coverings and glass doors;
cooking facilities; and safety in the kitchen or cooking area;
use of stairgates;
arrangements for keeping the premises clean;
facilities for rest and sleep;
washing and toilet facilities and hygiene;
and fire safety. <Vol. 2 (7.33)>

The Department of Health states that safety standards would be those normally expected in a private home. Regulations under the Food safety Act 1990 must be complied with however. <Circular LAC(93)1>

Guidance: suitable non-domestic premises

The Department of Health State that with regard to day care providers, attention will be given by the local authority to:
standards and organisation of rooms <details are given in Vol. 2 (6.3-6.51)>;
access to the road (children should be unable to leave the premises unsupervised) and outside playspace;
safety in the outside play area;
glass doors (safety glass or protective plastic film should be used);
arrangements for arrival and departure;
washing, toilet facilities and hygiene;
safety of fires, electrical sockets, windows, floor coverings;
cooking facilities and safety in the kitchen area;
use of stairgates;
arrangements for keeping the premises clean;
facilities for rest and sleep;

The local authority should consult the Fire Authority before granting registration. <Vol. 2 (7.33)>

The Department of Health states that general overall fitness is pertinent rather than each individual factor being used to render premises unfit. The issue here is the overall quality of care that will be available to the children. Regulations under the Food safety Act 1990 must be complied with however. <Circular LAC(93)1>

Guidance: equipment

The Department of Health suggest that the local authority should take account of:
that which might be appropriate to the ages of the children;
the conformity to "British Standards";

the amount of equipment and furniture and their quality and type in relation to the number of children and to the adults working there;

the organisation of kitchen equipment in non-domestic premises which should accord with the environmental health regulations. <*Vol. 2 (7.34)*>

Guidance: numbers of children

Restrictions may be placed on the number of children. The Department of Health advises the following childminder/child ratios:

0 to 2 years = 1:3
2 to 3 years = 1:4
3 to 5 years = 1:5

The Department of Health states however that for "home playgroups" run on domestic premises a sessional ratio of 1:8 for 3 to 5 year olds is relevant. <*Circular LAC(93)1*>

General

In all cases cancellation must be in writing, notice of intent will also be given with reasons and a statement of the person's rights of appeal made. <*S74(5)/S77*>

Department of Health indicate that local authorities should ensure that the evidence produced to justify cancellation would stand up in court. They should always obtain the advice of their legal department. The guidance indicates some of the factors that may be taken into account. <*Vol. 2 (7.52)*>

It is permissible for each local authority to adopt an inflexible interpretation of the guidance, in relation to registration. Such a decision may however be appealed against. The court would then decide for themselves, on the evidence, and in the light of official guidance, the question of that person's fitness to be a childminder. <Sutton London Borough Council v Davis (Times 17/3/94; Independent 17/3/94)>

Emergency protection

If an application is made by the local authority to court for cancellation of registration, varying, removing or imposing an additional requirement and the child is suffering, or is likely to suffer, significant harm (as a result of child minding or day care made by that person), an order (see chapter 5) may be made with immediate effect.

Application can be made ex-parte and supported by a written statement of reasons for making it. <*S75(1-3)*>

Section 75 only applies to really urgent cases such as where a child is found to have a non-accidental injury. An ex-parte hearing is seen as a provisional hearing. <Bowden v Lancashire County Council>

Where an order is made, as soon as reasonably practicable the local authority shall serve upon the registered person the notice of the order and a copy of the authority's reasons which supported their application to the court. <S75(4)>

Disqualification from registration

Regulations made by the Secretary of State provide for disqualification of applications for day care or child minding where:

- certain prescribed orders have been made against the applicant or against a child who has been in their care;
- a prescribed requirement has been made in respect of a child in their care;
- they have previously been refused registration (or registration has been cancelled) as a child minder or provider of day care;
- they have been convicted of a prescribed offence, placed on probation, discharged absolutely or conditionally;
- they have been disqualified from privately fostering a child or a prohibition made under the Foster Children 1984 (Scotland) Act or other prescribed enactment;
- his rights and powers with respect to a child have been vested in a prescribed authority under a prescribed enactment.

Disqualification will apply unless the applicant has disclosed the fact to the appropriate local authority and has obtained their written consent. <Schedule 9 (2) / Courts and Legal Services Act 1990, Schedule 16(30)>

A person is disqualified from registering as a child minder on domestic premises or from providing day care on non-domestic premises if they are in the same category as a person who is disqualified from registering as a private foster parent (see above). <The Disqualification for Caring for Children Regulations 1991 (Regulations 1/2/Schedule)>

A person who lives in the same household as a person disqualified or in the same household as such a person who is employed shall be disqualified unless he disclosed this to the appropriate local authority. <Schedule 9 (2)>

Any person who is disqualified shall not provide day care, be concerned in the management of day care, or have a financial interest in the provision of day care unless he has disclosed the *fact to the appropriate local authority and obtained their written consent. <Schedule 9 (2)>*

No person who is disqualified shall be employed in the provision of day care unless he has disclosed the fact to the appropriate local authority and obtained their written consent. <Schedule 9 (2)>

Registration should not be refused solely on the grounds that the minder is prepared, as a last resort, with the consent of the parents, to smack or slap a child they are looking after. Any type of punishment should be used in a way which assures the child of the childminder's continuing care and regard for him or her. Shaking should in no circumstances be used. <Circular LAC(94)23>

Inspection

Any person authorised by the local authority may at any reasonable time enter any domestic premises within the authority's area in which child minding is at any time carried on or any premises within their area in which day care for children under the age of eight is at any time provided. <S76(1)>

Where there is reasonable cause to believe that a child is being looked after on any premises in contravention of the Act, any authorised person may enter those premises at any reasonable time. <S76(2)>

Inspections may be made (on production of some duly authenticated document) at least once per year.
These include the premises, any children looked after on the premises, the arrangements made for their welfare, and any records relating to them that are kept as a result of the Act.
(Inspectors are entitled at any reasonable time to have access to and reasonable assistance to enable a check upon the operation of any computer and associated material or apparatus used in connection with records.) <S76(3-6)>

Department of Health guidance indicates that as well as yearly visits, it is also desirable to make occasional visits to provide support and advice to registered persons. In this way it will be possible to identify at a very early stage areas of concern and remedial action can be instituted more effectively. <Vol. 1 (7.50)>

Appeals

In the case of:

refusal, or cancellation of an application for registration;
refusal of consent under provisions for the cancellation of registration;

imposing, removing or varying any requirement or refusing to grant an application for the variation or removal of any such requirement;

14 days minimum notice of intention to take the step in question shall be sent to the applicant or the registered person.
The notice shall specify the authority's reasons for proposing to take the step and inform the person of his rights. <S77(1/2)>

Where the applicant or registered person informs the authority in writing of his objections to the step being taken an opportunity for them or their representative to make objections in person shall be given.

The authority may nevertheless decide to take the step and will send written notice of their decision to the applicant or registered person. Appeal then lies to the court. <S77(3-6)>

The court on hearing an appeal may impose or vary requirements as appropriate. <S77(7-9)>

Offences

Provision of day care in unregistered premises without reasonable excuse. <S78(1/2)><Vol.2.(6.41)>

In the case of unregistered child minding, an enforcement notice having effect for one year may be served; if unregistered provision continues without reasonable excuse an offence has then been committed (even when more than local authority area is involved). <S78(3-7)>

Contravention without reasonable excuse, or failure to comply with requirements imposed upon a child minder or upon day care premises. <S78(8)>

Acting as child minder on domestic premises or provider of day care premises at any time when disqualified; or in circumstances which dictate disqualification; or when a disqualified person is employed (except, in cases where a person who is disqualified is living or employed in the same location, this was not known by the applicant and he had no reasonable grounds to believe this). <S78(9-11)>

Intentional obstruction of a person exercising powers of inspection. <S76(7)>

8
CASE PLANNING

The Arrangements for Placement of Children (General) Regulations and the Review of Children's Cases Regulations should be read in conjunction with each other.

> *Department of Health guidance indicates that The Arrangements for Placement of Children Regulations place a duty on local authorities, voluntary organisations and registered children's homes in making arrangements to place a child and to draw up and record an individual plan for the child. The Review of Children's Cases Regulations require that the plan is reviewed and amended as necessary on a regular basis. <Vol. 3 & 4 (2.9)>*

> *The Department states that they reflect the emphasis upon partnership between parents, children and the responsible authority and between the responsible authority and other agencies, as being the most effective means of meeting the needs of the individual child. They provide a statutory framework within which responsible authorities should work with children and*

families and act as good parents. <Vol. 3 & 4 (2.1)>

In the regulations the expression "arrangements" is used as co-terminus with the social work term "plan". The primary purpose of planning and review is to safeguard and promote the welfare of the child living away from his family. Planning is required from the earliest possible time after recognition of need or referral where the provision of accommodation (whether voluntarily or under a compulsory basis). Thereafter the plan should be reviewed on an ongoing basis.

There is no statutory requirement to plan, review and monitor the case of the child who is provided with a service other than accommodation, however good practice requires this. <Vol. 3 & 4 (2.9)>

ARRANGEMENTS FOR PLACEMENT OF CHILDREN (GENERAL) REGULATIONS 1991

Definitions

A placement means:

the provision of accommodation and maintenance by a local authority for any child whom they are looking after (except where maintained in a home on the Secretary of State's terms);

the provision of accommodation by a voluntary organisation (except where maintained in a home on the Secretary of State's terms);

or the provision of accommodation for a child in a registered children's home.

This also includes short term placements at the same place (these may be treated as a single placement) where:

all occur within a period that does not exceed one year;

no single placement is of more than four weeks duration;

and the total duration does not exceed 90 days.

Responsible authority means:

the local authority which place the child (includes children accommodated and maintained in a voluntary home or a registered children's home);

the voluntary organisation which place the child (where the child is not looked after by the local authority); and

the person carrying on a registered children's home (where the child is neither looked after by a local authority nor accommodated by a voluntary organisation).

Area Authority means:

the local authority in whose area a child is or is to be placed who is looked after by a different authority. (Regulations 1/13)

Application and Planning of Arrangements

The regulations apply to placements:

by the local authority of any child;

by a voluntary organisation (of a child who is not looked after by a local authority);

in a registered children's home (of a child who is neither looked after by a local authority nor accommodated in such a home by a voluntary organisation).

These regulations shall not apply to placements of a child (except by a local authority or a voluntary organisation) in an independent school which is a children's home in the meaning of the Act, or a special school which is not maintained by a local education authority or otherwise out of public funds. <Regulation 2 as amended by The Children (Homes, Arrangements for Placement, Reviews and Representations) (Miscellaneous Amendments) Regulations, 1993>>

Although the regulations do not apply to children who are accommodated in independent schools for more than 295 days a year schools will be expected, in the special consideration they will wish to give to the arrangements for the care of these children, to have regard to the principles and practice recommended in the regulations and in volume 4 of the Children Act guidance. Local authority inspectors should look specially at the welfare provision made by schools for these children. <Circular LAC(93)24>.

Department of Health guidelines indicate that planning arrangements are required to safeguard and promote the child's welfare. It is essential to involve all those concerned with the child from the outset. The drawing up of an individual plan for each child will prevent "drift" and focus work by: assessing the child's needs; determining the objectives that have to be met; appraising the options; making decisions in full consultation with those involved; identifying tasks that individuals are to undertake; and setting a timescale in which tasks must be achieved or reassessed.

Planning is a responsibility of all agencies providing services for children and their families. Assessment must precede planning. Plans should be regularly reassessed informally and at reviews and case conferences with those concerned. Details of the content of the plan are given in the guidance. <Vol. 3 & 4 (2.10/ 2.11/2.20-2.22)>

Making of Arrangements

The responsible authority shall, so far as is reasonably practicable, make, before a placement, (or where not practicable as soon as reasonably practicable thereafter) immediate and long term arrangements for placing and promoting the welfare of a child who is to be placed. <Regulation 3 (1/2)>

In the case of a child aged over 16 agreeing to be provided with accommodation, the arrangements shall (so far as reasonably practicable) be agreed by the responsible authority with the child before a placement is made and if that is not practicable as soon as reasonably practicable thereafter. <Regulation 3 (3)>

In any other case where the child is looked after or accommodated but not in care, the accommodation shall (so far as is reasonably practicable) be agreed by the responsible authority with:
a person with parental responsibility for the child,
or if there is no such person, the person who is caring for the child;
before a placement is made (and if that is not practicable as soon as reasonably practicable thereafter). <Regulation 3 (4)>

Department of Health guidance indicates that under voluntary arrangements the local authority does not obtain parental responsibility for a child looked after, but is obliged to comply with the regulations. Although a care order (see chapter 4) gives the authority parental responsibility for the child, any person who is a parent of guardian retains their parental responsibility and may continue to exercise it to the extent that their actions are not incompatible with the care order. This reflects the intention underpinning the Act that parents should be encouraged to exercise their responsibility for the child's welfare in a constructive way and that where compulsory intervention in the family is used it should where possible enhance rather than undermine the parental role. <Vol. 3 & 4 (2.3)>

Planning and review of a child's case with the involvement of parents will provide the basis of partnership between the responsible authorities and parents and the child. The successful development of partnership with parents should in most cases avoid the need for care proceedings or emergency action. The same kind of approach should be taken in cases where a child is in the care of the local authority as a result of a court order. This will be achieved by:

consulting and notifying the parents about decisions affecting the child;

promoting contact between the child and his parents and family where it is reasonably practicable and consistent with the child's welfare;

and seeking to work with the parents to achieve a safe and stable environment for the child to return to (where this is judged feasible) or by finding a satisfactory alternative placement for the child. <Vol. 3 & 4 (2.11/12)>

Further guidance is given concerning the purpose, process and format of planning. <Vol. 3 & 4 (2.20/2.43-2.72)>

Any arrangements made by the responsible authority shall be recorded in writing. <Regulation 3 (5)>

Considerations on Making and Contents of Arrangements

In making arrangements, responsible authorities will consider (so far as reasonably practicable):

whether (in the case of a child in care) an application should be made to discharge the care order;

whether (where the responsible authority is a local authority) they should seek a change in the child's legal status;

arrangements for contact, and whether there is any need for changes in the arrangements in order to promote contact with the child's family and others consistent with his welfare;

their immediate and long term arrangements for the child, previous arrangements in respect of the child, and whether a change in those arrangements is needed and consideration of alternative courses of action;

whether (where the responsible authority is a local authority) an independent visitor should be appointed if one has not already been appointed;

whether arrangements need to be made for the time when the child will no longer be looked after by the responsible authority;

and whether plans need to be made to find a permanent substitute family for the child. <Regulation 4/ Schedule 1>

The responsible authority shall have regard to the following health considerations:

the child's state of health, and health history;

the effect of the child's health and health history on his development;

existing arrangements for the child's medical and dental care and treatment and health and dental surveillance;

the possible need for an appropriate course of action which should be identified to assist necessary change of such care, treatment or surveillance;

and the possible need for preventive measures, such as vaccination and immunisation, and screening for vision and hearing. <Regulation 4/Schedule 2>

The responsible authority shall have regard to the following educational considerations:

the child's educational history;

the need to achieve continuity in the child's education;

the need to identify any educational needs which the child may have and to take action to meet that need;

and the need to carry out any assessment in respect of any special educational need under the Education Act 1993 and the meeting of any such needs identified in a statement of special educational needs made under that Act. <Regulation 4/Schedule 3>

In making arrangements to accommodate children (except where the child is in the care of the local authority) the responsible authority shall have regard to:

- the details of any services to be provided for the child;
- the respective responsibilities of the responsible authority and:
  - the child,
  - any parent of his, and
  - any person who has parental responsibility;
- what delegation there has been by these persons, to the responsible authority of parental responsibility for the child's day to day care;
- the arrangements for involving these persons and the child in decision making having regard to the local authority's duties to involve children before the provision of accommodation and their general duties in relation to children looked after by them, the voluntary organisation's duties, and the duties of the person carrying on a registered children's home;
- the arrangements for contact between the child and:
  - his parents,
  - people with parental responsibility, and
  - any relative, friend or other person connected with him,

  and if appropriate the reasons why contact with any such person would not be reasonably practicable or would be inconsistent with the child's welfare;
- the provision made for notifying changes in arrangements for contact to any of these persons;
- in the case of a child aged 16 or over, whether accommodation of that child despite parental opposition applies;
- the expected duration of arrangements and the steps which should apply to bring the arrangements to an end, including arrangements for rehabilitation of the child with the person with whom he was living before the voluntary arrangements were made (or some other suitable person). Particular regard (in the case of a local authority looking after a child) should be given to their duty to place children where practicable with parents etc. and the maintenance of contact between child and family. <Regulation 4/Schedule 4>

Notifications of Arrangements

The responsible authority shall, so far as is practicable (before a placement is made) notify in writing the arrangements to place a child to:

- any person whose wishes and feelings have been sought under section 64(2) of the Act (i.e. the child, parents, persons with parental responsibility and any person whose wishes and feeling appears relevant);
- the district health authority in whose district the child is living;

the local education authority for the area;
the child's registered medical practitioner;
the area authority;
any person who is caring for the child immediately before the arrangements are made;
any person in whose favour a contact order is in force (except for a child in care); and
where a child is in care, any person who has contact with the child pursuant to section 34 (contact with a child in care by parents etc., see chapter 4) or who has an order under that section.

Where it is not practicable to give the notification before the placement, it shall be given as soon as reasonably practicable thereafter.

The responsible authority shall send with the notification a copy of the arrangements or such part of the arrangements as they consider will not prejudice the welfare of the child. <Regulation 5, as amended by The Children (Representations, Placements and Reviews) (Miscellaneous Amendments) Regulations 1991 (Regulation 3)>

Department of Health guidance indicates that notification should include:
a summary of the proposed arrangements and the objectives covering details of placement and its likely duration;
who is responsible for implementing the plan;
the role of the child's parent on a day to day basis;
arrangements for (or issues of) reunification;
and contingency plans if the placement is unsuccessful. <Vol. 3 & 4 (2.72)>

In the case of persons or authorities (other than the child, parents, persons with parental responsibility and other person whose wishes and feeling appears relevant) the responsible authority shall send details of only such part of the arrangements as they consider those persons need to know. <Regulation 5)

Arrangements for Contact

A voluntary organisation or a person carrying on a registered children's home shall (in relation to a child not in care), endeavour to promote contact between the child and his parents, people with parental responsibility and any relative, friend or other person connected with him (unless it is not reasonably practicable or consistent with the child's welfare). <Regulation 6>

Health Requirements

A responsible authority shall ensure so far as is practicable before a placement is made (and if that is not practicable as soon as practicable after the placement is made) that:

arrangements are made for child to be examined by a registered medical practitioner;

and that the practitioner who carried out the examination makes a written assessment of the state of health of the child and his need for health care;

unless the child has been examined and assessed within three months preceding the placement of or the child is of sufficient understanding and he refuses to submit to the examination.

Department of Health guidance indicates that in cases where the child is in care, the parents refuse consent and the local authority has not acted to restrict the parents' exercise of parental responsibility they may need to do so in order to comply with the regulations. Where the child is not in care and the parents refuse consent, the local authority may have to resort to obtaining an appropriate court order (e.g. a section 8 specific issue order, see chapter 2 or an emergency protection order or child assessment order, see chapter 5). <Vol. 3 & 4 (2.30)>

There is no restriction on placement if the child is over 16 and refuses to be examined or if he is under 16 and the doctor considers him to be of sufficient understanding to understand the consequences of consent or refusal. The responsible authority should draw a child's attention to his rights to give or refuse consent to examination or treatment. <Vol. 3 & 4 (2.32)>

They shall also ensure that, during the placement, arrangements are made for the child to be provided with heath care services, including medical and dental care and treatment. <Regulation 7>

The Department of Health indicate that health care needs of ethnic minority groups (such as sickle cell disease and thalassaemia) may require particular attention. <Vol. 3 & 4 (2.26)>

Establishment of Records and Registers

A responsible authority shall establish, if one is not already in existence, a written case record in respect of each child whom it places. The record shall include:

a copy of the agreed arrangements for placement;

any written report in its possession concerning the welfare of the child;

any document considered or record established during the course or as a result of a review;

details of the arrangements for contact, of contact or other court orders relating to the child;

details of any arrangements whereby another person acts on behalf of a local authority or organisation which placed the child. <Regulation 8>

Such records shall be kept safe. They shall be treated as confidential except there statute provides access to records or information or where a court order permits access. <Regulation 9 (3)>

Case records shall be retained (either in written record, or copy, on computer, or in other accessible form) by the responsible authority for at least 75 years from the date of birth of the child; or 15 years after the child's death (if aged under 18). <Regulation 9 (1/2)>

A local authority (in respect of every child placed in their area) a voluntary organisation and a person carrying on a registered children's home (in respect of every child placed by them or supervised on behalf of the local authority) shall enter into a register to be kept for the purpose:

the name, sex and date of birth of the child;
the name and address of the person with whom the child is placed and if different of those of the child's parent or person with parental responsibility;
the name of the authority (if placed by a voluntary organisation, or registered children's home);
whether the child is on the at risk register;
whether the child is entered on the register of disabled children;
the date on which each placement began and terminated and the reason for each termination;
in the case of a child in care, the name of the local authority;
and the legal provisions under which the child is being looked after.
<Regulation 10 (1/-3)>

A local authority, a voluntary organisation and any person carrying on a registered children's home shall also enter into the register, as may be appropriate:

a note of arrangements made between a responsible authority and area authority, including the name of the local authority with whom they were made;
and where arrangements have been made for the supervision of the placement is to be carried out on behalf of the responsible authority, the name of the person with whom the arrangements were made.
<Regulation 10 (1/2/4>

Registers shall be kept safe. They shall be treated as confidential except where statute provides access to records or information or where a court order permits access. <Regulation 10 (7)>

Voluntary organisations (where they are not acting as an authorised person for care or supervision proceedings) and every person carrying on a registered children's homes are required to provide access by a guardian ad litem of a child to:

case records and registers;
information from such records or registers held in whatever form

(such as by means of a computer);
and such copies of records or entries in registers as he may require. <Regulation 11>

Arrangements between Authorities

Where arrangements are made by a local authority which is looking after a child with an area authority to carry out functions in relation to placement, the local authority shall supply the area authority with all such information as is necessary to carry out these functions; the area authority shall keep the other authority informed of the progress of the child furnishing reports following each visit to the home in which the child is placed and following each review.

Both authorities shall consult each other as necessary, and as soon as practicable after each review of the child with regard to what action is required. <Regulation 12>

REVIEW OF CHILDREN'S CASES REGULATIONS 1991

Application

Like the Placement of Children (General) regulations, these regulations apply to local authorities which are looking after children and to voluntary organisations and registered children's homes which accommodate children not looked after by the local authority. The "responsible authority" thus means the local authority, voluntary organisation, or person carrying on the registered children's home as appropriate.

These regulations shall not apply in the case of a child who is being provided with accommodation (except by a local authority or a voluntary organisation) in an independent school which is a children's home in the meaning of the Act, or a special school which is not maintained by a local education authority or otherwise out of public funds. <Regulation 12 as inserted by The Children (Homes, Arrangements for Placement, Reviews and Representations) (Miscellaneous Amendments) Regulations, 1993>

Although the regulations do not apply to children who are accommodated in independent schools for more than 295 days a year schools will be expected, in the special consideration they will wish to give to the arrangements for the care of these children, to have regard to the principles and practice recommended in the regulations and in volume 4 of the Children Act guidance. Local authority inspectors should look specially at the welfare provision made by schools for these children. <Circular LAC(93)24>.

Duty to Review and Timescale of Reviews

Each case is to be reviewed within four weeks of the date upon which the child is looked after or provided with accommodation by the "responsible authority" (local authority looking after the child, voluntary organisation providing accommodation for the child on behalf of the local authority, or person carrying on a registered children's home accommodating a child <otherwise than on behalf of the local authority or voluntary organisation>).

The second review shall be carried out not more than three months after the first, and thereafter subsequent reviews shall be carried out at not more than six months after the date of the previous review. <Regulations 1-3>

Department of Health guidance indicate that reviews form part of an ongoing, continuous planning process, the purpose of which is to ensure that the child's welfare is safeguarded and promoted in the most effective way. The planning process is inseparable from the review process; for example, the collection of information is seen as a continuous process rather than as a separate one-off exercise for a review. <Vol. 3 (8.1-8.26) / Vol. 4 (4.1-4.26)>

Manner of Review

Each responsible authority shall set out in writing their arrangements governing the manner in which cases of each child shall be reviewed and shall draw these to the attention of:

the child;
his parents;
any person with parental responsibility;
and any other person whose views the authority consider to be relevant.

The responsible authority who are looking after or accommodating a child shall make arrangements to co-ordinate the carrying out of all aspects of the review and shall appoint one of their officers to assist in its co-ordination. <Regulations 4/7)

The manner of the review shall, so far as practicable, include the following elements:

keeping informed of arrangements for looking after the child and of any relevant change in the child's circumstances;
keeping informed of the name and address of any person whose views should be taken into account in the course of the review;
making necessary preparations and providing any relevant information to the participants in any meeting of the responsible authority which considers the child's case in connection with any aspect of the review;
initiating meetings of relevant personnel of the responsible authority and other relevant persons to consider the review of the child's case;

explaining to the child any steps which he may take under the act including, where appropriate:

his right to apply, with leave, for a section 8 order (residence, contact etc., see chapter 2);

where he is in care, his right to apply for the discharge of the care order;

and the availability of the procedure established under the Act to consider representations;

making decisions or taking steps following review decisions arising out of or resulting from the review. <Regulation 4 (4)/Schedule 1>

Any other review, assessment or consideration under any other provision can be carried out at the same time as a review under these regulations. <Regulation 4 (5)>

Considerations to Which Responsible Authorities Must Have Regard

The conditions to which the responsible authority are to have regard so far as practicable in reviewing each case are:

in the case of a child who is in care, whether an application should be made to discharge the care order;

where the responsible authority are a local authority whether they should seek a change in the child's legal status;

arrangements for contact, and whether there is a need for changes in the arrangements in order to promote contact with the child's family and others so far as is consistent with his welfare;

any special arrangements that have been made or need to be made for the child, including the carrying out of assessments either by a local authority or other persons, such as those in respect of special educational needs under the Education Act 1993;

the responsible authority's immediate and long term arrangements for looking after the child or providing the child with accommodation <made pursuant to the provisions of the Arrangements for Placement of Children (General) Regulations 1991 (see above)>, whether a change in those arrangements is needed and consideration of alternative courses of action;

where the responsible authority are a local authority, whether an independent visitor should be appointed if one has not already been appointed;

the child's educational needs, progress and development;

whether arrangements need to be made for the time when the child will no longer be looked after or provided with accommodation by the authority;

and whether plans need to be made to find a permanent substitute family. <Regulation 5/ Schedule 2>

The conditions concerning the health of the child to which the responsible authority are to have regard are:

the child's state of health, and health history;

the effect of the child's health and health history on his development;

existing arrangements for the child's medical and dental care and treatment and health and dental surveillance;

the possible need for an appropriate course of action which should be identified to assist necessary change of such care, treatment or surveillance;

and the possible need for preventive measures, such as vaccination and immunisation, and screening for vision and hearing. <Regulation 5/ Schedule 3>

Health Reviews

The responsible authority shall make arrangements for a child who continues to be looked after or provided with accommodation by them to be examined by a registered medical practitioner and for a written assessment of the state of health and his need for health care to be made:

at least once in every period of six months before the child's second birthday;

and at least once in every period of twelve months after the child's second birthday;

unless the child is of sufficient understanding and he refuses to submit to the examination. <Regulation 6>

Consultation, Participation, Notification and Implementation

Before conducting any review the authority shall unless it is not practicable to do so, seek and take into account the views of:

the child;

his parents;

any person with parental responsibility;

and any other relevant person;

including in particular the views of those persons in relation to any particular matter which is to be considered in the course of the review.

These persons shall also so far as practicable be involved including (where the responsible authority consider appropriate) attending any meeting concerned with the review.

The responsible authority shall, so far as is practicable, notify details of the review and of any decision taken by them in consequence of the review to:

the child;

his parents;

any person with parental responsibility;

and any other person whom they consider ought to be notified. <Regulation 7>

The responsible authority shall make arrangements themselves or with other persons to implement any decision which the authority propose to make in the course, or as a result of the review. <Regulation 8>

Monitoring and Recording

Each responsible authority shall monitor the arrangements which they have made with a view ensuring that they do comply with the regulations.

The responsible authority shall ensure that information obtained, details of proceedings at any meeting arranged by the authority in connection with any aspect of the review, and details of any decisions made in the course or as a result of the review are be recorded in writing. <Regulations 9/10>

Application of Regulations to Short Periods

A case where the child is looked after or provided with accommodation by a responsible authority for a series of short periods at the same place may be treated as a single case if:

the periods do not exceed one year in total;
no single period is more than four weeks;
and the total duration does not exceed 90 days. <Regulation 11>

9
OTHER PROVISIONS

This chapter sets out the vital provisions that maintain the systems set out in the act. The details of central government control of local authorities and through them control of the voluntary and statutory sectors are outlined.

The parts of the Act that deal with the definition and meaning of various references in the act are also given here. These general definitions are in addition to those given in other the parts of this book where references specific to a particular set of regulations or to a particular section of the Act may have already been detailed.

OTHER PROVISIONS: INCLUDING FUNCTIONS OF THE SECRETARY OF STATE

Inquiries

The Secretary of State may cause an enquiry to be held into any matter connected with:

the functions of a social services committee relating to children;
the functions of an adoption agency;
the functions (relating to children) of a voluntary organisation;
a children's home or voluntary home;
a residential care home, nursing home or mental nursing home so far as it provides accommodation for children;
a home provided in accordance with arrangements made by the Secretary of State for the detention of child under provisions relating to grave crimes.

The enquiry may be held in private. <S81/ Courts and Legal Services Act 1990>

Financial Support by the Secretary of State

The fees or expenses may be defrayed or contributions made relative to child care training approved by the Secretary of State. <S82(1/6)>

Grants may be made to local authorities for expenditure in providing secure accommodation in community homes other than assisted community homes. <S82(2/3)>

Grants may be made to voluntary organisations in connection with the establishment, maintenance or improvement of assisted community homes or expenses incurred in borrowing money to defray expenditure on voluntary homes. <S82(4)>

The Secretary of State may arrange for the provision, equipment and maintenance of homes for the accommodation of children who are in need of particular facilities and services which are unlikely to be readily available in community homes. <S82(5)>

Research and Returns of Information

The Secretary of State, may conduct, or assist other persons in conducting, research into any matter connected with:

his functions, or the functions of local authorities;

the adoption of children, or the accommodation of children in a residential care home, nursing home or mental nursing home.

The local authority, may conduct, or assist other persons in conducting, research into any matter connected with:

their functions;

the adoption of children, or the accommodation of children in a residential care home, nursing home or mental nursing home. <S83(1/2/7)>

Every local authority shall, as directed by the Secretary of State, transmit to him such particulars as he may require with respect to: their performance of all or any of their functions; and the children in relation to whom they have exercised those functions. <S83(3)

Every voluntary organisation shall, as directed by the Secretary of State, transmit to him such particulars as he may require with respect to children accommodated by them or on their behalf. <S83(4)>

The Secretary of State may direct the clerk of each magistrates' court to which the direction is expressed to transmit to him such particulars as he may require with respect to proceedings of the court which relate to children. <S83(5)>

The Secretary of State shall in each year lay before Parliament a consolidated and classified abstract of information transmitted to him under these provisions. <S83(6)>

The Secretary of State shall keep under review the adequacy of the provision of child care training and for this purpose shall receive and consider any information from or representation made by:

the Central Council for Education and Training in Social Work;
such representatives of local authorities as appear appropriate;
or such other persons or organisations as appear appropriate. <S83(8)>

Powers of Inspection

The Secretary of State may cause a range of services and facilities to be inspected by a person authorised by himself at any time.

The Secretary of State may require the furnishing to him of any information, or the inspection of any records (in whatever form they are held) relating to:

any premises to which the inspection applies;
any child who is living in the premises;
the discharge by the Secretary of State of any of his functions under the Act;
or the discharge of any of the functions of a local authority under the Act;
as he may at any time direct. <S80(1-4/11/12)>

The range of services and facilities are:

children's homes;
premises in which a child looked after by a local authority is living;
premises in which a child is being accommodated by or on behalf of a local education authority, voluntary organisation, health authority or National Health Service trust;
premises in which a child is living with a person with whom he has been placed by an adoption agency;
premises in which a protected child is or will be living;
premises in which certain school children are privately fostered during the school holidays;
premises in which any person is acting as a child minder;
premises in which day care is provided for children under eight (other than domestic premises);
a residential care, nursing or mental nursing home used to accommodate children;
any premises provided by the local authority in which any service is provided for children and their families;

and independent schools providing accommodation for any child. <S80(1) as amended by The National Health Service and Community Care Act 1990 (Schedule 9 paragraph 36)>

Any person conducting an inspection has the right of entry at any reasonable time and may:

inspect the children;

and make an examination of the state and management of the home or premises and the treatment of the children as he thinks fit.

When inspecting the records he shall be entitled the have access to and inspect and check the operation of, any computer and any associated apparatus or material which is or has been in use in connection with the records and may require the affording of reasonable assistance from the people involved. <S80(6-8)>

Any person conducting an inspection shall, if so required, produce some duly authenticated document showing his authority to do so. Any person who intentionally obstructs another in the exercise of the powers of inspection shall be guilty of an offence. <S80(9/10)>

Where a person attempting to exercise the powers of inspection has been prevented from doing so by being refused entry to the premises concerned or refused access to the child concerned (or is likely to be prevented from exercising such powers) the court may issue a warrant authorising a constable to assist that person in the exercise of those powers, using reasonable force if necessary.

The court may direct that the constable concerned be accompanied by a registered medical practitioner, registered nurse or registered health visitor if he so chooses. <S102>

Default Power of the Secretary of State

Where the Secretary of State is satisfied that any local authority has failed, without reasonable excuse, to comply with any of the duties imposed upon them by or under the Act he may make an order (giving reasons) declaring that authority to be in default with respect to that duty.

An order may contain such directions for the purpose of ensuring that the duty is complied with, within such period as may be specified, as appear to be necessary. Any such direction shall, on the application of the Secretary of State, be enforceable by the appropriate court by an order of mandamus. <S84>

The Secretary of State may apply to the court for an order directing the local authority to carry out its duties.

Notification of Children Accommodated in Certain Establishments

Where a child is provided with accommodation by any health authority, national health service trust, or local education authority, they shall notify the responsible local authority, if the child is accommodated for a consecutive period of at least three months (or it is the intention on the part of the authority to accommodating him for such a period). Notification shall also be given when he ceases to be accommodated.

The responsible local authority is the one in whose area the child was ordinarily resident. Where the child appears not to be ordinarily resident in the area of any local authority, the responsible authority is that authority located within the area the accommodation is situated.

Where a local authority is so notified they shall take such steps as are reasonably practicable to enable them to determine whether the child's welfare is adequately safeguarded and promoted while he is accommodated, and consider the extent to which (if at all) they should exercise any of their functions under the Act with respect to the child. <S85 as amended by The National Health Service and Community Care Act 1990 (Schedule 9 paragraph 36)>

Where a Child is accommodated in any residential care, nursing or mental nursing home (and when he ceases to be accommodated) the person carrying on the home shall notify the local authority within whose area the home is carried on if the child is accommodated for a consecutive period of at least three months (or it is the intention on the part of the person taking the decision to accommodate him for such a period).

Where a local authority have been notified they shall take such steps as are reasonably practicable to enable them to determine whether the child's welfare is adequately safeguarded and promoted while he is accommodated in the home, and consider the extent to which (if at all) they should exercise any of their functions under the Act with respect to the child.

If the person carrying on any home fails without reasonable excuse to comply with these provisions he shall be guilty of an offence.

A person authorised by the local authority may enter any residential, nursing, or mental nursing home within the authority's area for the purpose of establishing whether the requirements have been complied with.

Any person obstructing another in the exercise of powers of entry shall be guilty of an offence.

Any person exercising the power of entry shall, if so required produce some duly authenticated document showing his authority. <S86>

The Department of Health draws particular attention to the need to ensue that consent to any treatment by children, including the administration of drugs is given following agreement by, and with the full understanding of the child. The provisions of Part IV of The Mental Health Act 1983 are important here. <Vol. 4 (1.196)>

If, on application to the court it appears that a person attempting to apply these powers has been prevented from doing so by being refused entry to the premises concerned, or access to the child concerned (or that they are likely to be prevented from exercising such powers) a warrant authorising any constable to assist that person, using reasonable force if necessary, may be issued.

The court may direct that the constable be accompanied by a registered medical practitioner, registered nurse or registered health visitor if the person so chooses. <S102>

SECTION 105 INTERPRETATION

In the Act the following definitions apply. <S105(1)>
CHILD means a person under the age of eighteen.
CHILD OF THE FAMILY in relation to the parties to a marriage means: a child of both those parties; any other child, not being a child who is placed with those parties as foster parents by a local authority or voluntary organisation, who has been treated by both of those parties as a child of the family.
DOMESTIC PREMISES means any premises which are wholly or mainly used as a domestic dwelling. <S71(12)>
FUNCTIONS includes powers and duties.
PRESCRIBED means prescribed by regulations under the Act.
RELATIVE in relation to a child, means a grandparent, brother, sister, uncle or aunt (whether of the full blood or half blood or by affinity) or step parent.
SERVICE includes any facility.
SIGNED in relation to any person, includes the making by that person of his mark.
UPBRINGING in relation to any child includes the care of the child but not his maintenance.
VOLUNTARY ORGANISATION means a body (other than a public or local authority) whose activities are not carried on for profit.

References in the Act and Their Meaning

Those to: A PERSON WITH WHOM A CHILD LIVES, OR IS TO LIVE, AS THE RESULT OF A RESIDENCE ORDER; OR A PERSON IN WHOSE FAVOUR A RESIDENCE ORDER IS IN FORCE; shall be construed as references to the person named in the order as the person with whom the child is to live. <S105(3)>

Those to: A CHILD WHO IS LOOKED AFTER BY A LOCAL AUTHORITY is a reference to a child who is: in their care; or provided with accommodation by the authority in the exercise of any functions (in particular those under the Act) which stand referred under the local Authority Social Services Act 1970. <S105(4/5)>

Where a child is said to be IN LOCAL AUTHORITY CARE, they are under a care order. "Care" no longer indicates a child who is accommodated by the local authority on a voluntary basis. Where a person is described as having "care" of the child in the non-technical sense, the word "care" has its ordinary meaning.

In determining the ORDINARY RESIDENCE of a child, there shall be disregarded any period in which he lives in any place: which is a school or institution; in accordance with the requirements of a criminal supervision order; or while he is being provided with accommodation by or on behalf of a local authority. Any further question arising between local authorities shall be determined between them by agreement or, in default of agreement, by the Secretary of State. <S105(6)/S30(2)>

Any NOTICE or document required to be served upon any person may be served on him by being delivered personally to him, or being sent by post to him in a registered letter or by the recorded delivery service at his proper address. <S105(8-10)>

A PARENT (except in respect of Orders for Financial Relief and Local Authority maintenance) includes a step-parent who has treated a child as a child of the family but does not include a cohabitee. <Schedule 1(16) /Re J (Times 12/11/92)>

Definition of Independent Visitors (Children) Regulations 1991

A person appointed by a local authority as an independent visitor shall be regarded as independent if they are not connected with the local authority (i.e. not a member, or co-opted member; an officer; or the spouse of any such person) and where the child is to receive visits from the person appointed is accommodated by an organisation other than the local authority the person appointed is also not a member, patron, trustee, or employee (paid or unpaid) of that organisation; or a spouse of any such person. <Regulation 2>

> *Department of Health guidance indicates that the local authority will need to devise a strategy for the recruitment of appropriate persons. They may consult with community groups, voluntary bodies and other organisations. The religious, racial, cultural and linguistic needs of the child should be met. Particular requirements may also arise in the case of children with disabilities. <Vol. 3 (7.18) & Vol. 4 (6.18)>*

> *In exceptional situations where an overnight stay of a child with the family of their independent visitor is desirable, the local authority will need to make checks under the Arrangements for Placement of Children (General) Regulations 1991 (see chapter 8). These will be in addition to those that they will have already made in approving an independent visitor. <Vol. 3 (7.39) & Vol. 4 (6.39)>*

INDEX